The Teaching of Science in Primary Schools

Third Edition

Wynne Harlen

David Fulton Publishers

London

David Fulton Publishers Ltd
Ormond House, 26–27 Boswell Street, London WC1N 3JZ

www.fultonpublishers.co.uk

First edition published in Great Britain by David Fulton Publishers 1992
Second edition published in Great Britain by David Fulton Publishers 1996
Reprinted 1996, 1997, 1998 (twice), 1999
**This third edition published in Great Britain by David Fulton Publishers
2000**
Reprinted 2000, 2001

Note: The right of Wynne Harlen to be identified as the author of this work has
been asserted by her in accordance with the Copyright, Designs and Patents Act
1988.

Copyright © Wynne Harlen 2000

British Library Cataloguing in Publication Data

A catalogue record for this book is available from the British Library

ISBN 1–85346–564–X

Typeset by FiSH Books, London
Printed in Great Britain by The Cromwell Press Ltd, Trowbridge, Wilts.

Contents

Introduction

Once primary science became an acknowledged part of basic education from the start of schooling, it was inevitable that it would become a focus of development and change. This has continued throughout the 1990s so that, since the second edition of this book in 1996, there have been many changes. In England the introduction of new requirements for entrants to teacher training and the National Curriculum for ITT (TTA 1998) are designed to provide future primary teachers with a better background in scientific knowledge than most serving teachers, and the publication of programmes of study by the DfEE and QCA (1997) has provided a framework for planning aimed to ensure that children have opportunity to cover the National Curriculum. There has also been more serious attention to findings of research and the evaluation of various initiatives. These have shown that, despite help with long-term planning and background information, what learning happens in the classroom depends on teachers' understanding of the children's learning, of the goals of learning in science and how to work towards them. Indeed it is the whole purpose of this book to give teachers reasons for what they do and, in particular, reasons for teaching science in certain ways – which may not be the easiest but do lead to children learning with understanding.

Despite the existence of national curricula, guidelines and standards, it is always necessary to keep under review the purposes of science education and what we want young people to achieve through it. There has been a welcome fresh look by science educators at the goals of science education in general and some consensus that we should be aiming to ensure that all of our future citizens leave school scientifically literate (Millar and Osborne, 1998). Most attention, has, however, been given to secondary school science and less to the contribution of primary science to scientific literacy. My own contribution on this matter is in Chapter 2. Chapters 3, 4 and 5 take further the identification of the meaning of progression in the development of scientific ideas, process skills and attitudes.

Consideration of what we want children to learn has to be accompanied by constant review of how they learn. From about the mid-80s to the mid-90s we had a decade of revelations about children's own ideas in science. On the basis of all that is now known as a result of this – and in no way diminishing its value – thinking has moved on to issues about how to take action to ensure that children are not left with their unscientific ideas unchallenged. The key question here is: how is the teacher to help children to grasp ideas that are more in line with scientific understanding while still having control of their own learning? There is considerable tension in the teacher's role here. Views about what constructivism means have developed. Important distinctions are now recognised between personal constructivism, where learners develop their ideas through testing them against evidence, and social constructivism, where learners have access to alternative ideas than their own through communication and developing understanding shared with others. The latter emphasises access to alternative ideas in a two-way process in which learners share ideas and teachers 'scaffold' more scientific ones. Reference to the emerging understanding of scaffolding and various approaches to it occur in several places in this book. This adds a significant aspect to the teacher's role, equal, perhaps, to the provision of materials for first-hand enquiry and effective questioning.

Understanding of the role of assessment in learning is a further area of significant development. The importance of finding out where children have reached in developing ideas and skills has been advocated for many years (for example, in the Match and Mismatch materials, Harlen *et al.* 1977). More recently, however, the value of using assessment of progress to help learning has received massive backing from research evidence. The research shows that the benefits of assessment for this purpose – formative assessment – follow when it has certain characteristics. Among these are that: teachers have to build into activities opportunities for children to express their ideas and show their skills; there has to be feedback to children in a way that enables them to know how to improve their work; children have to be involved in self-assessment; and teachers have to use information about children's current ideas and skills to adapt learning activities. The considerable benefits to be had mean that these things require serious attention. For that reason Chapters 14 to 18 are concerned with these aspects of formative assessment and Chapters 19, 20 and 21 with using information about where children have reached to help them develop their scientific ideas, process skills and attitudes. It is important to distinguish assessment for this purpose from assessment for other purposes such as summarising achievement, record keeping and target-setting, discussed in Chapters 22 and 23. While these also have an important place, they cannot be substituted for formative assessment.

Another change that could hardly have been anticipated in 1996 is the rapid spread of the use of ICT in the primary classroom. While computers were already being used in some schools for word-processing and data-logging, few would have thought that within such a short time children would be looking up information on the Internet (or local Intranet) and using interactive CD-ROMs to test out ideas. All of this has meant that we have to review the meaning of practical work and ensure that children are deriving the most benefit from it. We have to look at the purposes of 'hands-on' and take care that children are thinking as well as doing (Chapter 9). The new technologies can give children more control of their learning, but the role of the teacher in ensuring that understanding is being developed remains a central one, as noted in Chapter 11.

At the same time as identifying the parts that new technologies can take in children's learning, the study of effective practice continues to emphasise the oldest technologies of all – talking, listening, discussing, using words to share meaning and understandings. Material from earlier editions of this book on these topics and on teacher's questioning and handling of children's questions has been preserved in Chapters 12 and 13.

In summary, the main changes in this edition have been made to reflect recent thinking about

- the importance of progression in ideas, process skills and attitudes;
- the teacher's role in giving children access to more scientific ideas and in 'scaffolding' development of ideas and skills;
- the value and meaning in practice of using assessment to help learning, including the role of children in self-assessment and in reflecting on their learning;
- making the best use of practical work;
- the opportunities that using ICT offers to both children and teachers for improving science education.

In conclusion, my hopes for this book are, as before, that readers will enjoy it and find it helpful as a springboard for their own ideas. The ultimate purpose is to make a contribution to teachers' own understanding of and pleasure in teaching science and, through this, to children's enjoyment and understanding of the world around them and care for their environment.

Wynne Harlen,
Edinburgh, May 2000

Chapter 1
Teaching, learning and science

Introduction

Learning science is important for the future lives of all citizens and because of this it is a required part of primary and secondary education in practically all countries. Science is a major area of human mental and practical activity which generates knowledge, knowledge that can be the basis of important technological applications as well as adding to understanding of the world around. It follows that teaching science is important. Since science plays such a vital part in our lives and in the lives of future generations, it is essential that the education of the whole population, not just of future scientists, provides them with a broad understanding of the status and nature of scientific knowledge, how it is created and how dependable it is.

In the primary school, covering the education of children from age 5 to 12, we are concerned with laying the foundation for this understanding. How we do this depends on our view of how children of this age learn best. The view that this is through first-hand engagement in scientific activity and thinking, which permeates this book, is illustrated in the first part of this chapter by an example. This glimpse of some primary science in action is followed by brief discussions of different views of learning and of the nature of science. The reason for this is the strong evidence that teachers' view of these things have a powerful influence on what and how they teach. The particular view of these things taken here influences much of what it written in this book and so it is appropriate to make it explicit in this opening chapter.

Primary science in action

Graham was introducing science activities within an overall topic about growing food, to his class of 9 and 10 year olds. He planned that the children should discuss and investigate the differences between types of soil. He had in mind that the children should undertake some investigations of sandy, loamy and clay soil, so he provided samples of each of these, to which some of the children contributed samples that they brought from gardens at home. He wanted the investigations to advance the children' ideas and therefore to start from their ideas and questions. It would have been easy to ask the children to find out, for example 'Which soil holds most water?' 'Does water drain through some soils more quickly than others?' etc. and to start the children's investigations from these questions. These are perfectly good questions for children to investigate and likely to be among those the children ended up investigating, but he wanted to hold back his questions to find out what the children would ask and what ideas they had.

The first part of the work was an exploratory phase of looking at the different soils. In groups, the children were given samples of the three main types, some hand-lenses, sieves, disposable gloves and some very open instructions:

- Separate the different parts that each of the soils contains.
- Find out what is contained in all the soils.
- Find out what is different in each soil.
- Think about how these difference might affect how well plants grow in the soils.

This task required children to use their ideas about soil in making their observations. It encouraged them to look closely at the soil and to think about the differences they found. During this activity the teacher visited each group to listen in to what the children were saying about the types of soil. Many of their statements at this stage contained hypotheses and predictions. The children were quick to say which they thought would be best for plants to grow in (the darkest coloured one) and to identify the ability to hold water as a property that was needed.

There was then a whole-class discussion, pooling findings and ideas from different groups. Graham said that they would test their ideas about which was best for growing plants when they had found out more about the soils and the differences that might make one better than another. What would the plants need to grow? Water was the most popular answer. Some mentioned 'fertiliser' and there was a discussion of what this meant in terms of the soils they had looked at and it was eventually identified with the bits of leaves and decayed plant material they had found, particularly in the loam. Graham introduced the word 'humus' to describe this part of the soil. No-one mentioned the presence of air in the soil until the teacher asked them to think about the difference between soil that was compressed and the same soil in a loose heap. He challenged them to think about whether there was the same amount of air between the particles in each soil and whether this was likely to make a difference to how well plants would grow in it.

The discussion identified four main differences to be investigated: the differences in the amount of water held in the soil; how quickly water drained through each one; the amount of humus in each and the amount of air. Each of the six groups in which the children were working chose one of these and set about planning how they would go about their investigation. Although having different foci, the investigations of all the groups were relevant to developing understanding of the nature and properties of soil so that, when they did the trial of which enabled plants to grow best, they would be able to explain and not just observe the result.

The investigations provided opportunities to help the children develop their process skills, in order to carry out systematic and 'fair' tests through which they would arrive at findings useful in developing their ideas. He asked them first to plan what they would do and identify what they would need in terms of equipment. He probed their thinking about what variables to control and what to observe or measure by asking questions such as 'How will you be sure that the difference is only caused by the type of soil? How will you be able to show the difference?' He had ideas, gathered from various sources, about useful approaches but kept these 'up his sleeve' to be introduced only if the children did not produce ideas of their own. Graham encouraged the children to make notes of what they found as they went along and then use these to prepare a report from each group to the whole class. He told them that they should report what they did and what they found, but also say whether it was what they had expected and to try to explain the differences they found.

At the end of the practical work and after a period for bringing their ideas together in their groups, each group in turn presented a report, while other children were given opportunity to question. Graham refrained from making comments at this stage and asked questions only for clarification. When all the reports had been given he listed the findings for each soil and asked the children to decide which might be best for growing some seedlings. The choice was not as obvious as some children had initially thought, so they were very keen to try this next investigation and find out what really would happen.

Graham then turned to the samples of soil that the children had brought from home. In order to compare them with the three soils they had investigated he suggested mixing some of each with enough water to loosen the parts from each other and allow the constituents to separate as they settled to the bottom. They then used these observations on what they had found about soil to predict which might by 'good growing' soils. These samples were then included in the seedling trials.

> Before going on to set up the next investigations, Graham asked the children to reflect on which parts of the work just completed they had enjoyed most, which would they do differently if they could start again and what they now felt they could do better than before.

Behind these events there was, of course, a great deal of planning – long-term, medium-term and short-term. This topic fitted in to the long-term plan of the school's programme, which was devised to ensure progression in development of conceptual understanding and skills and meet the requirement of the national guidelines. In his medium-term planning, Graham worked out how the work on soil fitted into the current term's work and built on what the children had done previously about what was needed for plant growth and how it would lead on to ideas about the formation of soil and how its fertility has to be preserved. In his short-term planning, he worked out what both he and the children would do, considered some the questions he would pose and prepared himself with information about the ideas children might have and with suggestions for activities from sources such as the *Rocks, Soil and Weather* Teachers' Guide of Nuffield Primary Science.

Underpinning all of this planning was a view of the learning that Graham wanted to promote and of the kinds of activities and interactions most likely to bring this about. This view would explain why Graham decided to start by making sure that the children looked closely at the soil samples and identified for themselves what kind of things they contained, instead of telling them what soil contains (which would certainly have been quicker and much less trouble to organise). Why did he not demonstrate, for example, how to find out how much air is in a certain amount of soil and then let the children do this, rather than asking them to work this out for themselves? Why did he want them to try to explain their findings rather than just know what happened? Answers to these questions lie in the understanding of the meaning of 'learning science', which in turn depends on a view of learning and a view of science. We take a brief look at these in the rest of this chapter; later chapters deal with the other factors that influence teaching decisions.

The significance of a view of learning

The following extracts from conversations with two teachers indicate how a view of learning implicitly lay behind their decisions about the way to organise their classrooms and to interact with the children. Both were teachers in junior schools in a large city; both schools were of similar, early 20th century, architecture; both teachers taught classes of about thirty-two 10-11 year olds. The interviews were originally part of the Match and Mismatch materials (Harlen *et al.*, 1977).

The first teacher arranged the desks in straight rows, all facing the front, where the teacher's desk and blackboard occupied prominent positions. She explained her reasons for this formality in arrangement, which echoed the formality of her teaching, as follows:

> Well, you see the main thing – I can't stand any noise. I don't allow them to talk in the classroom...I just can't stand noise and I can't stand children walking about...in the classroom I like them sitting in their places where I can see them all. And I mean I teach from lesson to lesson. There's no children all doing different things at different times...And of course I like it that way, I believe in it that way.

When asked why the desks were all facing the front, she replied:

> ...if they're all facing me, and I – well, I can see them and I can see that they're doing. Because quite honestly I don't think that – when they're in groups, I mean all right they might be discussing their work. But, I mean, how do you know?

As well as her own preference for quietness, she was convinced that it was from the blackboard and from herself that the children would learn. She worked hard to make her method work, setting work on the blackboard and marking books every evening. She did not think that children handling things or talking to each other had any role in learning.

The second teacher arranged the desks in blocks of four but in no particular pattern. There was no discernible 'front' or 'back' of the class. The children moved about freely and chatted during their work. She explained:

> I hate to see children in rows and I hate to see them regimented. At the same time, you know, often I get annoyed when people think that absolute chaos reigns, because it doesn't. Every child knows exactly what they have to do....And, it's much more – you could say informal – but it's a much more friendly, less pressing way of working and...it's nice for them to be able to chat with a friend about what they're doing.

Asked if she worried that the chat may not be about work she replied:

> Oh no. I mean, obviously adults do when they work. As long as I get the end result that's sort of suited to that particular child I don't mind...If a child's not achieving what he should do then I do go mad because at ten and eleven they should know they've got a certain amount of work to do and the standard one expects of them.

She actively encouraged independence and considered that the class organisation helped in this:

> I hate to think of children sitting – I'm not against formal education I'm not against informal, there are advantages to both methods – but I think the great danger of very formal teaching is that the teacher's seen as a tin god figure. And very often the children aren't given the opportunity to think for themselves.

The point here is not to suggest that either teacher is 'right' but that both have a clear rationale for the decisions they make about the organisation and methods they use in the classroom and that this is related to their views of how children learn. Both show consistency between what they do and what they want to achieve through it and so both are at ease in their classrooms.

It is worth noting in passing that to change the practice of either of these teachers would require far more than different teaching materials or insistence on rearranging the desks. There are masses of examples of teachers who have been asked to make organisational changes, which simply result in children sitting in groups but being taught as a class and having to twist their necks to see the blackboard. To make real changes requires a change in the teacher which is far more than adopting different ways of working; it means changing their views of how children learn and of their own role and the role of materials in fostering learning.

The significance of the view of science

Although few primary teachers would regard themselves as scientists, we all have a view of what science is and, like it or not, we convey this through our teaching. So it is necessary to have a 'feel' for the current understanding of science, which may well be different from that we received through our own science education. Perhaps just as important is to have a feel for what is *not* science so that its characteristics are identified in both positive and negative terms.

Teaching science as facts reflects a prevalent view of science and illustrates the impact this view has on the learning experiences provided in school. When scientific activity is regarded as being the application of principles and skills which first have to be learned, the aims of education in science are conceived as being primarily to teach these principles and skills. The dominant role of class activities is then seen as being to demonstrate the skills and to 'prove' the principles. Both explicitly and implicitly science is conveyed as:

- objective;
- capable of yielding ultimate truths;

- 'proving' things;
- having a defined and unique subject matter;
- having unique methods;
- being value-free.

If scientific activity is seen as developing understanding through testing ideas against evidence, with the ideas being accepted as being as good as the evidence which supports them, then the classroom or laboratory experiences will be rather different. Ideas will be explored rather than accepted and committed to memory and alternative views examined in terms of supporting evidence. These activities will portray science as:

- a human endeavour to understand the physical world;
- producing knowledge which is tentative, always subject to challenge by further evidence;
- building upon, but not accepting uncritically, previous knowledge and understanding;
- using a wide range of methods of enquiry;
- a social enterprise whose conclusions are often subject to social acceptability;
- constrained by values.

When science is seen in the first of these ways, it leads to teaching dominated by ensuring that the wisdom of the past is received by new generations. If it is the latter, the teaching will inevitably involve learners in the process of developing understanding from evidence and in considering accepted scientific principles in this spirit. So how we view the nature of scientific activity is an important question. At the same time we don't have to go deeply into the philosophy of science to have a sufficient 'feel' for it. What is attempted here is a brief dip into the question of what is science which is hopefully enough to lay foundations for building a framework for teaching science. Like the foundations of any building, they will not subsequently be obvious, for it is not suggested that any of this is conveyed directly in teaching. Rather, again like other foundations, they should support all that comes later; their presence being essential even though it is not seen.

Views of what science is and is not

The social context of science

It is very easy to find statements about what science is not. John Ziman, one of those who has made significant contributions to the debate, has said that 'science is distinguished from other intellectual activity neither by a particular style or argument nor by a definable subject matter' (Ziman 1968, p. 10). The truth of this is easy to argue. The subject matter of science is the biological and physical world around which can be equally the subject of history, art, geography or almost any discipline you care to mention. Similarly the methods of science, of observation, prediction, inference, investigation and so on, are used in the study and research of other subjects. From this simple argument it is apparent that science cannot be characterised as being either content or process alone.

Having said what it is not, Ziman goes on to give his idea of what science is, using the phrase 'public knowledge'. Less cryptically he means by this that science is a corporate activity. Scientists begin with the ideas of others, past and present. As Newton remarked, one can stand on the shoulders of giants and so see further. Each adds a contribution of his or her own ideas and passes the combined ideas to others, whose reactions determine their acceptability at that time. The history of science has many examples of ideas which have 'been before their time' and for which their proponents paid a price, although in a different social climate the ideas were later entertained more sympathetically

Science as falsifiable

The philosopher Karl Popper made a significant contribution to the debate about the nature of science by distinguishing the difference between a scientific and a non-scientific theory in terms of whether it can be falsified rather than whether is can be verified. His view can be simply stated: a theory is scientific if it can be shown to be false by testing. This idea is not complicated. Often the greatest ideas have a simplicity which makes them seem obvious, once stated, and this is one of them.

A common sense way of explaining the importance of trying to show that a theory is wrong rather than that it is right is through thinking how easy it is to find support for an idea if you are looking just for this. It is easy to select evidence which is in agreement, to reinterpret that which does not agree, while ignoring the existence, or the significance, of evidence which might challenge the idea. More important, however, is the situation where evidence is not being ignored, but where it is conceptually impossible to find evidence which contradicts the idea.

To illustrate the point a good example is one used by Popper himself of psychoanalytical theories. He found that proponents of these theories, whether they were Adler's or Freud's, could always give an explanation of any human behaviour in terms of their chosen theory. Popper commented: 'I could not think of any human behaviour which could not be interpreted in terms of either theory. It was this fact – that they always fitted, that they were always confirmed

– which in the eyes of their admirers constituted the strongest argument in favour of these theories. It began to dawn on me that this apparent strength was in fact their weakness' (Popper 1988).

Popper contrasted this with Einstein's theory of general relativity, which is capable of being disproved by evidence. Einstein's theory was used to predict small changes in the apparent position of stars when light from them passes close to the sun. If found, these changes would support the theory but, if not, the evidence would refute it. Thus it was possible that evidence could be found either way. It appeared to Popper that here was the essential character of a scientific theory, that it could be tested and could be refuted by evidence. The psychoanalytical theories which could be used to explain every kind of human behaviour lacked this quality since any proposed test could, by definition, end only in a positive result.

Popper's ideas about the essential character of a scientific theory have become part of a widely accepted view of science. Stephen Hawking, writing more recently, expressed it as follows:

> Any physical theory is always provisional, in the sense that it is only a hypothesis: you can never prove it. No matter how many times the results of experiments agree with some theory, you can never be sure that the next time the result will not contradict the theory. On the other hand, you can disprove theory by finding even a single observation that disagreed with the predictions of the theory.
>
> (Hawking 1988, p. 10)

Note that scientific activity is characterised by developing theories which fit the evidence available but which may be disproved when further evidence comes to light, not by devising theories so malleable that they always fit the evidence, or for which there can be no disproving evidence (as in astrology). Thus Newton's theory, which failed where Einstein's succeeded, remains scientific by the very fact that it was disproved.

So the ideas which children create can be scientific if they are testable and falsifiable and the fact that they are often disproved by the evidence makes them no less scientific. *Learning* science and doing science proceed in the same way. Indeed we will find many parallels between the development of ideas by the scientific community and the development of children's ideas. For example, both are influenced, and to some extent formed, by the reactions and alternative views of peers. The ideas of both are provisional at any time and may have to be changed to be consistent with new experience or evidence not previously available. Children also have non-scientific ideas, which they hold on to by ignoring contrary evidence or adjusting their ideas to accommodate it bit by bit.

Summary

- A view of learning and of the nature of science is implicit in all decisions that teachers make
- A teacher's view of how children learn influences the opportunities they are given for learning through interaction with materials and with each other in the way exemplified in the vignette.
- If learning is seen as essentially receiving and mastering information then teaching will be organised to ensure maximum attention to authority rather than children developing understanding for themselves.
- The teacher's understanding of the nature of science influences the extent to which children learn through enquiry or learn about science and its findings.

Chapter 2
The foundations of science education

Introduction

This chapter is concerned with the goals of learning science. What is it that we want our children to know and be able and willing to do as a result of their science education? And what is the contribution that primary science makes to this? Some answers to these questions can readily be found by referring to national and district curriculum documents, guidelines or standards. But there is a danger of turning too soon to lists of concepts and skills; we may lose sight of the whole. For it is the whole that really gives purpose to teaching. We teach the parts – about particular events or phenomena, such as what makes a simple circuit – not just because they are interesting in themselves, but in order for children to develop an overall understanding that helps them make sense of new phenomena and events.

Therefore in this chapter we begin by considering the notion of scientific literacy, which is a way of expressing the outcomes of science education for all children, and the foundation for this that primary science provides. We then look at how the 'whole' is broken down into constituents and identify the concept areas, process skills and attitudes that are the way in which the goals of primary science are expressed in this book.

Scientific literacy

It is now common to describe the outcomes of science education for all children as 'scientific literacy'. This phrase is used to signify the essential scientific understanding which should be part of everyone's education. Scientific literacy has for some time been an important concept in thinking about scientific education in the United States and the meaning it conveys is well summed up in *Benchmarks for Science Literacy* (AAAS 1993).

The aim is to promote literacy in science, mathematics, and technology in order to help people live interesting, responsible, and productive lives. In a culture increasingly pervaded by science, mathematics, and technology, science literacy requires understandings and habits of mind that enable citizens to grasp what those enterprises are up to, to make some sense of how the natural and designed worlds work, to think critically and independently, to recognise and weigh alternative explanations of events and design trade-offs, and to deal sensibly with problems that involve evidence, numbers, patterns, logical arguments, and uncertainties.

(AAAS 1993, p. xi)

In the UK the term has been used to describe the aim of the science curriculum for all pupils from age 5 to 16 in *Beyond 2000: Science Education for the Future* (Millar and Osborne 1998). This report was the result of a series of seminars and meetings involving science educators from all phases of education. It recommended that 'The science curriculum for 5 to 16 should be seen primarily as a course to enhance general scientific literacy' (p. 9). What this means was spelled out in terms of the following aims:

...the science curriculum should:

❖ sustain and develop the curiosity of young people about the natural world around them, and build up their confidence in their ability to enquire into its behaviour. It should seek to foster a sense of wonder, enthusiasm and interest in science so that young people feel confident and competent to engage with scientific and technical matters.

❖ help young people acquire a broad, general understanding of the important ideas and explanatory frameworks of science, and of the procedures of scientific enquiry, which have had a major impact on our material environment and on our culture in general, so that they can:
  • appreciate why these ideas are valued;
  • appreciate the underlying rationale for decisions (for example, about diet, or medical treatment, or energy use) which they may wish, or be advised, to take in everyday contexts, both now and in later life;
  • be able to understand, and respond critically to, media reports of issues with a science component;
  • feel empowered to hold and express a personal point of view on issues with a science component which enter the arena of public debate, and perhaps to become actively involved in some of these;
  • acquire further knowledge when required, either for interest or for vocational purposes.

(Millar and Osborne 1998, p. 12)

Further support for the pre-eminence of scientific literacy is found at the international level in the OECD Programme for International Student Assessment (PISA). This project comprises a series of international surveys that will assess reading literacy, mathematical literacy and scientific literacy. Scientific literacy is defined as 'the capacity to use scientific knowledge, to identify questions and to draw evidence-based conclusions in order to understand and help make decisions about the natural world and the changes made to it through human activity' (OECD 1999, p. 60).

These and the many other statements made about scientific literacy indicate that what it means in practice is:

- being able to function with confidence in relation to the scientific aspects of the world around;
- being able to look at something 'in a scientific way', seeing, for example, whether or not evidence has been taken into account in the explanation of an event or phenomenon, whether it makes sense in terms of related events or phenomena, and so on;
- being aware of the nature of (and limitations of) scientific knowledge and the role of values in its generation.

The foundation of scientific literacy: science at the primary level

There are two parts to the conception of scientific literacy evident in both the AAAS statement and the aims set out in *Beyond 2000*. These are 'understandings', and ability and confidence to enquire (habits of mind). Primary science has a contribution to both of these.

Development of understanding starts from making sense of particular events that we encounter. We might call the ideas found useful for this 'small' ideas, because they are specific to the events studied and have limited application beyond these. As experience extends it becomes possible to link events which are explained in similar ways and so form ideas which have wider application and so can be described as 'bigger' ideas.

The ultimate aim of developing scientific literacy is to develop the 'big', widely applicable, ideas that enable us to grasp what is going on in situations which are new to us. But clearly the 'big' ideas are too abstract and too remote from everyday experience to be a starting point for this learning. Learning has to start from the 'small' ideas and build upwards so that at each point the ideas are understood in terms of real experience. The role of primary science is, therefore, to build a foundation of small ideas that help children to understand things in their immediate environment but, most importantly, at the same time to begin to make links between different experience and ideas to build bigger ideas.

The overall aim of scientific literacy in relation to the development of skills and attitudes is for pupils to develop the ability and willingness to recognise and use evidence in making decisions as informed citizens. Again the starting point is to become familiar with the ways of identifying, collecting and interpreting evidence in relation to answering questions about things around. Being able to do this is an essential starting point to reflecting on the kinds of questions that science can, and cannot, answer and the kinds of conclusions that can, and cannot, be drawn from certain kinds of evidence.

The achievement of scientific literacy depends on, but is more than, the acquisition of scientific knowledge, skills, values and attitudes. It does not automatically result from learning science; it has to be a conscious goal even at the primary level, by giving attention to linking together ideas from a range of experiences of real phenomena, problems and events both within the classroom and outside it. Indeed, extending first-hand experience beyond what the school can supply, in the way that museums and science centres can do (see Chapter 10), is essential to the development of scientific literacy.

Components of scientific literacy

While it is important to keep in mind the overall aim of developing scientific literacy, this overall aim has to be broken down into component parts for the purposes of planning a curriculum and programmes that enable it to be achieved.

It is not only for the sake of convention and convenience that these components are expressed in terms of scientific concepts, scientific process skills and scientific attitudes. All scientific enquiry or debate is about some subject matter, that is, it has some content and requires some knowledge and understanding of that content. There is no meaning to 'content free' processes. Thus concepts and ideas are one essential component of scientific activity. Then there has to be some way of engaging with the content, using mental and physical skills (leaving aside rote memorisation of facts and figures). These ways are common to most, if not all, scientific content and form the second essential component of scientific activity. Then there is a third component, the willingness to use skills and to engage with content, which is expressed in terms of attitudes and dispositions. Both process skills and attitudes can be applied to content other than science content and then become scientific process skills and scientific attitudes when applied to the study of scientific aspects of the world. If we look again at the aims identified in *Beyond 2000,* or indeed at any comparable statement, we can readily pick out these three components:

- concepts or ideas, which help understanding of scientific aspects of the world around and which enable us to make sense of new experiences by linking them to what we already know;
- processes, which are mental and physical skills used in obtaining, interpreting and using evidence about the world around to gain knowledge and build understanding;
- attitudes or dispositions which indicate willingness and confidence to engage in enquiry, debate and in further learning.

What is appropriate to primary science within each of these components? This question begins to be addressed here and in the following three chapters.

Scientific concepts for primary level

The concepts identified in the curriculum lead to the selection of the content of science activities and experiences. Concepts are expressed at different levels of generality for different purposes. In order to indicate the range of subject matter, the concepts are grouped under broad headings, such as the three of the National Curriculum: Life processes and living things; Materials and their properties; Physical processes. These are broken down into sub-headings and more specific statements of ideas within these for each key stage (ages 5–7, 7–11, 11–14, 14–16). This leads to long lists of statements which can be used for selecting learning activities.

It is not the purpose in this book to duplicate – or compete with – statements of outcomes published in national curricula or standards. Instead the purpose is to consider how the understanding of the ideas they convey can be developed by children. However, keeping in mind the overall aim of scientific literacy, it is important to ensure that primary science lays the foundation of understanding across a range of ideas about:

- living things and the processes of life (characteristics of living things, how they are made up and the functions of their parts, human health, etc.);
- the interaction of living things and their environment (competition, adaptation, effects of pollution and other human activities, etc.);
- materials (their variety, properties, sources, uses, interactions, conservation, disposal of waste, etc.);
- air, atmosphere and weather (presence of air round the Earth, features of the weather, causes of clouds, rain, frost and snow and freak conditions, etc.);
- rocks, soil and materials from the Earth (nature and origin of soil, maintenance of fertility, fossil fuels, minerals and ores as limited resources);
- the Earth in space (sun, moon, stars and planets, causes of day and night and seasonal variations);

- forces and movement (starting and stopping movement, speed and acceleration, simple machines, transportation, etc.);
- energy sources and uses (sources of heat, light sound, electricity, etc.).

In Chapter 3 we will consider the meaning of 'laying a foundation' in terms of progress in ideas about these aspects of the world.

Process skills for primary science

Most curriculum statements separate skills from knowledge while insisting that the skills are developed and used in relation to all contexts and content; the separation is simply to avoid repetition. Looking across various national curricula and across different versions of the same curricula, there is much in common, although no exact agreement. The National Curriculum for England, implemented in 2000, lists the following investigative skills:

Planning
Obtaining and presenting evidence
Considering evidence and evaluating.

The expansion of each varies between key stage 1 and key stage 2 (DfEE 1999).
In addition, key skills and thinking skills intended for implementation across the curriculum are identified. The key skills are:

Communication
Application of number
Information technology
Working with others
Improving own learning and performance
Problem solving.

Science has a particularly strong contribution to make to the 'thinking skills' which are:

- *Information processing skills:* These enable pupils to locate and collect relevant information, to sort, classify, sequence, compare and contrast, and to analyse part/whole relationships
- *Reasoning skills:* These enable pupils to give reasons for opinions and actions, to draw inferences and made deductions, to use precise language to explain what they think and to make judgements and decisions informed by reasons and evidence
- *Enquiry skills:* These enable pupils to ask relevant questions, to pose and define problems, to plan what to do and how to research, to predict outcomes and anticipate consequences, test conclusions and improve ideas.

- *Creative thinking skills:* These enable pupils to generate and extend ideas, to suggest hypotheses, to apply imagination and to look for alternatives innovative outcomes.
- *Evaluative skills:* These enable pupils to evaluate information, to judge the value of what they see, hear and do, to develop criteria for judging the value of their own and others' work or ideas and to have confidence their judgements.

(DfEE 1999)

In the Scottish curriculum, the 5–14 programme, science is a component of the national guidelines for *Environmental Studies* (Scottish CCC 1999), the other components being social subjects and technology. For science the following skill and attitude strands are identified:

Planning
Collecting evidence
Recording and presenting
Interpreting and evaluating
Developing informed attitudes.

The AAAS *Project 2001* (see page 11), which deals with mathematics and technology as well as science, defines 'habits of mind' which fulfil the same role as process skills in relation to knowledge goals. That is, they are ways of thinking and acting which can be – and indeed should be – related to the study of any content. In Benchmarks they are grouped under these headings:

Values and attitudes
Computation and estimation
Communication skills
Critical-response skills.

Also in the United States, the National Science Education Standards (NRC 1996) states that:

Students at all grade levels and in every domain of science should have the opportunity to use scientific enquiry and develop the ability to think and act in ways associated with enquiry, including asking questions, planning and conducting investigations, using appropriate tools and techniques to gather data, thinking critically and logically about relationships between evidence and explanation, constructing and analyzing alternative explanations and communicating scientific arguments.

(NRC 1996, p. 105)

Are there real differences among these three documents or are they presenting the same thing in different words? It would be necessary to look beyond the headings at the statements of targets, which exist in all three documents quoted, to see to what extent there is consistency among them. But even at the broad level of the headings it is clear that there is agreement about the identification of:

- observing (collecting evidence, measuring);
- raising questions (recognising and defining investigable questions);
- hypothesising (giving possible explanations);
- predicting (using ideas or evidence to predict an outcome);
- planning (devising enquiries);
- interpreting (considering evidence, evaluating, drawing conclusions);
- communicating (presenting reports, using secondary sources).

Chapter 4 looks at the meaning of and progression in these process skills.

Scientific attitudes at the primary level

It is useful to make a distinction between two kinds of attitudes:

- attitudes towards science as an enterprise;
- attitudes towards the objects and events which are studied in science and the use of evidence in making sense of them.

To develop an informed attitude towards science it is necessary to have an idea of what 'science' is. Without this, attitudes will be formed on the basis of the many myths about science and about scientists which persist in popular belief and the caricatures which are perpetuated in the media and in some literature. Typically these portray scientists as male, bespectacled, absent minded and narrowly concerned with nothing but their work (see, for example, Jannikos 1995). Science as a subject may be portrayed as the villain, the origin of devastating weapons and technology which causes environmental damage or as the wonder of the modern world in providing medical advances, expanding human horizons beyond the Earth and being responsible for the discoveries which led to computers and information technology.

Young children do not have enough experience of scientific activity and its consequences to form opinions and attitudes towards science as such. If they seem to hold such attitudes it is a result of accepting adult prejudices and parroting views which are not their own. At the primary level the concern is to give children experience of scientific activity as a basis for a thorough understanding, which will only come much later, of what science is and is not and of the responsibility we all share for applying it humanely. Therefore attention is given here only to those attitudes which we might call the attitudes *of* science, those which support scientific activity and learning.

Although development of scientific attitudes is not explicitly identified in all national curricula it is widely acknowledged as an important outcome of science education. The reason for the exclusion from the National Curriculum dates back to the recommendation made in the Report of the Task Group on Assessment and Testing (DES 1989) that 'the assessment of attitudes should not form a prescribed part of the national assessment system' (paragraph 30). The close link of the curriculum and assessment meant that what was not assessed was not included. In the non-statutory guidance issued to accompany the National Curriculum in 1989, however, it was acknowledged that willingness to take part in certain activities is important to learning and that the following attitudes and personal qualities should be developed at all stages of science education:

- curiosity;
- respect for evidence;
- willingness to tolerate uncertainty;
- critical reflection;
- perseverance;
- creativity and inventiveness;
- open mindedness;
- sensitivity to the living and non-living environment;
- co-operation with other.

In the Scottish curriculum, which is non-statutory, the development of informed attitudes is an explicit strand of attainment. It states that children should be encouraged to:

- appreciate the need to develop informed and reasoned opinions on the impact of science in relation to social, environmental, moral and ethical issues;
- appreciate the need to take responsibility for their own health and safety;
- be committed to participating in the safe and responsible care of living things and the environment;
- think through the various consequences for living things and for the environment of different choices, decisions and courses of action;
- participate responsibly in the conservation of natural resources and the sustainable use of the Earth's resources and appreciate the need for conservation of natural resources and endangered species at local and global level;
- appreciate the need to develop responsible attitudes that take account of different beliefs and values.

(Scottish CCC 1999, p. 36)

In the AAAS Benchmarks, reference is made to curiosity, honesty, openness and scepticism. Honesty here is close to respect for evidence and is identified for young children with keeping records and not altering them (AAAS 1993, p. 286).

All of these fall into the category of attitudes *of* science. Many of them would also fall into the category of supporting learning in several subject areas. Perseverance is one of these; it is certainly needed in practising science but it is equally relevant to learning a foreign language or writing a poem. The generalised nature of attitudes is such that no clear line can be drawn between 'scientific' and other attitudes, but the ones chosen for discussion here are particularly relevant to developing ideas through exploration of the world around. They are: curiosity, respect for evidence, willingness to change ideas, critical reflection and sensitivity to living things in the environment. These are discussed further in Chapter 5.

Summary

•   Scientific literacy is the term used to express the understanding of important 'big' ideas in science and the understanding of scientific enquiry that is needed by all citizens to make informed decisions about the impact of human activity on the world around.

•   The development of scientific literacy begins in the primary school.

•   It is widely agreed that primary children should begin to develop ideas about living things, materials, forces and movement, energy sources, the Earth as an environment and the Earth in space.

•   All national statements of aims of science recognise the importance of the development of enquiry skills: observing, raising questions, hypothesising, predicting, planning and conducting investigations, interpreting, communciating.

•   Similarly, there is widespread recognition of the role of scientific attitudes in learning and the need to help children develop curiosity, respect for evidence, willingness to change ideas, critical reflection and sensitivity to living things in the environment.

Chapter 3

Building towards the 'big' ideas

Introduction

This chapter is concerned with some of the questions that are most worrying in primary science; about the meaning of progression and what can be expected of younger and older children. These are not matters that are easily conveyed in a few words, for there are always different ways in which scientific ideas can be understood, as noted briefly in the first part of this chapter. The second part attempts to describe some overall dimensions of progress, in order to map the territory and indicate the directions of change that we can call 'progress'. We then provide examples of how progression can be expressed. One way is in the form of 'explanatory stories' which set out how ideas are linked to each other. The second is in terms of key ideas that children not only know but can use.

Problems in describing progression in ideas

Science goes beyond description and is concerned with explanation. But there is no end to the layers of explanation that can be peeled back in the attempt to uncover 'what's going on'. We can, for example, explain the phenomenon of 'dissolving' in terms of what happens when some solids are added to some liquids. This is on the border between describing and explaining. We can also explain it in terms of particles of the solid which mix with the particles of the liquid. A more sophisticated explanation is in terms of molecules of one substance being distributed in those of another without chemically combining and applying to solutions of gas in liquids and liquids in liquids. There are still further layers of explanation that scientists would use that link the property of dissolving to other properties of substances. Each of these explanations represents a 'bigger' idea than the one before because it links together a wider range of phenomena.

Curriculum statements often do not answer the question 'How far do we go?' in relation to levels of explanation. How 'big' are the big ideas that we can reasonably aim to help primary school children develop? Just as important is the question: How are the bigger ideas built from the smaller ones? Statements of what children should learn at various stages are typically set out in terms of statements isolated from each other. This encourages an approach of 'ticking off' items in a list. It neglects the links that there may be between the items and leaves children understanding parts but not how these parts link into a larger whole. These statements set out a sequence of topics to study rather than a progression in the ideas that the studies can help children to develop. They are not unhelpful, but they are not enough on their own. We also need to have in mind an overall view of progress, of how ideas can be linked together to build bigger ones.

The dimensions of progress in developing ideas

Let's start from an example. Children of all ages study living things in their habitats. Younger children (aged 5–8) may observe the animals and plants in a particular location – a part of the school garden or field, or a hedgerow or park – to see what is there and how it changes from season to season. They might begin to question why some things are found in some places and not others and in some seasons only. Through pictures (big books, for example) and visits (perhaps to a zoo, botanic garden or farm) they could consider a broader range of living things and the varying conditions they require.

Older children (8–12) may investigate in the classroom the particular preferences of certain creatures to live in certain conditions, linking these to where the creatures are found. In seeking for an explanation as to why this is, they begin to match the form and features of the living things to the conditions in the habitat, such as worms living in soil, cacti living in deserts. They will study how animals are adapted to finding and eating certain foods and how they respond to changes in the habitat, such as birds migrating, snails retreating into their shells or some trees dropping their leaves.

So what are the ideas that younger and older children might develop from these activities and how do they differ?

The ideas the younger children might develop from these activities are:

You find living things wherever you look. There are different kinds in different places and each kind likes a certain kind of place. Some animals would not be able to live where other ones live because they could not find the food they can eat or would be too hot or too cold. Some plants grow better in some places than others, too, and some die down or drop their leaves when it is cold.

The ideas the older children might develop from their activities are:

> The places where you normally find a living thing is called its habitat. In a particular place some things will be able to live and some things will not. The reason for this is that each living thing needs food, water, air, shelter and protection for its offspring, but different ones obtain these in different ways. What suits one will not suit others because of differences in their bodies and structures. Other living things are part of the habitat and each depends on others for its needs, often for food, but also for protection and helping in such things as pollination and seed dispersal.

There are clear differences between these two sets of ideas, although those suggested for the older children grow out of those for the younger ones. They differ particularly in three ways:

- *From description to explanation*

The ideas of the younger children are closely related to gathering information, finding out what is there, what is happening, as opposed to explaining why. There is the beginning of explanation in terms of what the habitat provides for the living things in it. The ideas of the older children are clearly much more related to explanation.

This is an important dimension because, as Hubert Dyasi puts it 'An explanation is the result of combining intellectual activity with discrete facts gathered through enquiry. The development of explanations is an essential component of science enquiry activity' (Dyasi 1999, p. 10).

- *From 'small' to 'big' ideas*

Each experience leads to a small idea that helps to make sense of specific observations. 'Worms can live in soil because they can slither through small spaces and can eat things that are in the soil' is an idea that applies to worms only. It is transformed to a bigger idea when it is linked to other ideas, such as 'fish can live in water because they can breathe through their gills and find food there', to form an idea that can apply to all animals. Eventually this idea may be linked to ideas about the habitats of plants, to become an even bigger idea about living organisms in general.

This is an important dimension of progress since the formation of widely applicable ideas, or concepts, is essential if we are to make sense of new experience. It is important to remember, however, that how concepts are called into play when we need to solve problems or understand new phenomena depends on process skills as well. This is a point we shall return to later.

- *From personal to shared ideas*

It is characteristic of young children to look at things from one point of view, their own, and this is reflected in their ideas. These are based on their personal experience and their interpretation of it. As children become older and willing to share how they see and how they explain things, their ideas are influenced by those of others, including their teacher and other adults and other children. Thus ideas are constructed on the basis of social and educational interactions as well as their own thinking.

Through becoming aware of others' ideas and sharing their own, children negotiate meaning for their experiences and for the words that are used to communicate them (such as 'habitat'). In this way children derive assurance that their understanding is shared by others. It is central to learning in science that children have access to the views of others and to the scientific view, but at the same time retain ownership of their own developing understanding.

These overall dimensions of progress are the kind of changes that it is helpful to have in mind and to encourage in children whatever the content of their activities. Ways of encouraging development are the subject of Chapter 19. Here we turn to ways of expressing development in particular ideas, beginning with the notion, suggested by Millar and Osborne in *Beyond 2000*, of using 'explanatory stories'.

Describing progression using explanatory stories

Using a narrative form enables the understanding of 'big' ideas to be expressed as a conherent whole, rather than as a set of disconnected and separate parts. The purpose of these explanatory series is to indicate the level of understanding (since understanding can be at a variety of levels from simple to highly sophisticated) that is appropriate for children at certain points in development. The first thing to emphasise is that these 'stories' are for teachers; they are not to be 'told' to children. By bringing together, rather than separating, ideas that the children will develop, stories preserve in teachers' minds the wholeness of the learning that is intended. The stories combine ideas that will come out of a range of activities appropriate to the stage of the children. They hopefully encourage the creation of links between ideas and help to ensure that details do not obscure the central ideas.

Explanatory stories for younger children are more limited than those for older children. They differ in the extent to which basic information and experience are linked, beginning with closely related events and gradually extending to less obviously related one. As an example of this approach, the following 'stories' were created to convey ideas appropriate at early and later stages of development that children should develop from activities and enquiries relating to food and its production.

The explanatory story for early development

We eat because food provides our bodies with what they need to grow, move and keep going. When food goes inside our body it is broken down into pieces, or particles, that can be carried by our blood to all parts to enable them to grow and be healthy. Food is needed to keep our brain working, our heart beating and our arms and legs moving. Different kinds of food help our body in different ways and the foods that it is important to eat often are fruit, vegetables, fish or meat or eggs, rice or bread and milk or things made from milk. Too much of one kind of food, particularly sugary things, is not good because our body will not get all the help that it needs. Our body does not use, or digest, all of what we eat and what is left comes out at the end when we go to the toilet.

Most of our food comes from plants and animals grown or raised on farms. In order to grow, these plants and animals also need food. The animals are fed on plants or on other animals which feed on plants. The plants use light, water and air for making their food. We are like the farm plants and animals because we also need air, water, food, light and enough warmth to grow well.

The explanatory story for later development

For our food to be used in our bodies, it has to be broken down into very small particles in the process of digestion. This process starts in the mouth, so having good teeth and chewing well helps digestion. When the food is swallowed the digestion continues as it passes through the intestines and stomach, leaving what cannot be digested to be eliminated. The digested food, in the form of small particles, goes into the blood stream, where it is pumped by our heart to all parts of our body. The blood also carries oxygen from the air we breathe in to our lungs, which is picked up by the blood as it passes through the lungs. The oxygen and some kinds of food particles react together rather like fuel burning in a stove to give energy to keep us warm and active. If our body gets too cold the processes slow down and may eventually not work at all.

We need other kinds of particles if we are to grow. For growth, the particles needed are ones that can be turned into new cells, the kind of building blocks of which all living things are made. Even when we have stopped getting bigger, new cells are needed all the time to replace old or damaged ones. We see this with our hair, nails and skin, but it is the same with cells inside our body as well. So all the time we need the kinds of food that give energy and the kinds that enable us to grow new cells. This means food that contains proteins, carbohydrates, fats, minerals and vitamins.

Some things that we eat can make us ill. This mostly happens when food has gone bad. So food has to be preserved in some way during the time it takes to get to us from the farm, because not all of it can be grown nearby. Some foods only grow in certain places where there is the right amount of heat or water. These days we eat many foods that are grown in other countries and so there are many stages of processing, packaging and transporting food between when it is grown and when it is bought in a shop or market. It is important at all stages, and when it reaches the home, to keep food clean, cool, and away from flies and other animals that would spoil it. Food can also have harmful effects, without making us ill straight away, if it is from an animal which has eaten something infected or containing a slow acting poison that has become part of the cells of the animal that ate it. Some of these things can pass along the food chain that links together living things that depend on each other for food. Almost all food can be traced back to plants through food chains and so in the end we and all living things depend on the sunshine that helps plants grow.

These narratives are not unlike the guides supplied in the US *National Education Standards for Science* (NRC 1996). For example the guide to concepts underlying the standard relating to 'properties of materials' for K-4 (5–9 year olds) is as follows;

Earth materials are solid rocks and soils, liquid water and the gases of the atmosphere. These varied materials have different physical and chemical properties. These properties make them useful, for example, as building materials, as sources of fuel, or for growing the plants we use as food. Earth materials provide many of the resources humans use.

Soils have properties of color and texture, capacity to retain water and ability to support the growth of many kinds of plants, including those in our food supply. Other Earth materials are used to construct buildings, make plastics and provide fuel for generating electricity and operating cars and trucks.

The surface of the Earth changes. Some changes are due to slow processes, such as erosion and weathering, and some changes are due to rapid processes such as landslides, volcanoes and earthquakes.

Fossils provide evidence about plants and animals that lived long ago and the nature of the environment at that time.

(NRC 1996)

Describing progression in terms of key ideas

An alternative and more succinct way of expressing progression is in terms of key ideas that children should be able to use at early and later stages of development.

The key ideas for early development tend to be descriptive and restricted in range to particular objects or situations. The key ideas for later development depend on linking different experiences together and so are 'bigger' and have greater explanatory power. The following tables give some examples relating to aspects of the eight areas of understanding listed in Chapter 2.

EARLY DEVELOPMENT: CHILDREN SHOULD BE ABLE TO USE THESE IDEAS:	LATER DEVELOPMENT: CHILDREN SHOULD BE ABLE TO USE THESE IDEAS:
Living things and life processes	
• There are different kinds of living things called plants and different kinds called animals, which include human beings. • Animals need air, water and food and plants need air, water and light. • Living things produce more of the same kind of thing. • Human beings need certain conditions to promote good health.	• Animals and plants can be identified by their features as belonging to various groups. • Different parts of the bodies of plants and animals carry out the major life processes. • Organs within the bodies of mammals are connected in systems which carry out the major life processes. • Different kinds of plants and animals are able to live and find food in very different places.
Interaction of living things and their environment	
• Changes occur in living things in response to daily and seasonal changes. • Different kinds of plants and animals are able to live and find food in very different places. • Different living things are suited in various ways to the place where they live.	• Competition for life-supporting resources determines which living things survive where. • Human activities can produce changes to the Earth's surface and atmosphere that have long-term effects. • Some waste products from human activity are biodegradable, others are not, and some materials can be recycled. • Human activity can interfere in the balance between resources and the plants and animals that depend on them, resulting in extinction of some species.

Materials	
• Materials differ in properties and can be grouped according to simple properties. • Materials are used for different purposes according to their properties. • Materials can be changed by heating or cooling or interaction with water.	• Materials vary in strength, hardness, flexibility, electrical, thermal and magnetic properties. • The properties of materials, including whether they are solid, liquid or gaseous, can be explained by their composition and structure. • Some changes in materials can be reversed and others cause new materials to be formed.
Air, atmosphere and weather	
• The weather affects living things and the lives of human beings. • There are patterns in the weather related to seasonal changes • There is air all around; wind is moving air.	• Air contains invisible water vapour which becomes visible when the air is cooled and it condenses into drops of water. • Certain conditions promote evaporation and condensation of water. • Weather is a result of factors relating to temperature and the amount of water vapour in the air.
Rocks, soil and materials from the Earth	
• Soil is a mixture of materials derived from rocks and living things. • There is a wide variety of different kinds, shapes and sizes of rock. • Changes in rock can be caused by erosion and weathering.	• Fertility of soil can be changed by human activity. • Rocks are composed of different combinations of minerals, including some ores from which metals are extracted. • Rocks have been formed over very long periods of time in different ways involving sedimentation and the effects of heat and pressure. • Mining for ores and fossil fuels takes materials from the Earth that cannot be replaced. • There are constant changes to the Earth's surface dues to erosion, volcanoes and earthquakes.

The Earth in space	
• The sun, moon and Earth are three-dimensional bodies that move relative to one another. • There are regular changes to the appearance of the moon. • Day and night and the seasons are related to the light from the sun.	• The movement of the sun during the day and the stars at night can be explained by the Earth rotating every 24 hours. • Stars are like the sun but very far away. • The Earth is one of several planets circling round the sun that make up the solar system. • Changes in the appearance of the moon and seasonal changes on Earth can be explained by a model of the solar system.

Forces and movement	
• Forces acting on something can make it move, stop moving or change speed or shape. • Speed is a way of saying how far something moves in a certain time. • Friction, including air resistance, is a force that stops things moving.	• How quickly an object will start moving depends on the amount of force acting on it; the faster it is moving the more force needed to stop it. • It takes more force to stop a heavier object than a lighter one. • Things fall because of a force called gravity, acting to pull them towards the Earth.

Energy sources and use	
• We detect heat, sound and light through different senses. • Light, sound, heat and electricity can be produced in different ways.	• Energy enables things to work and the more energy the more can be done. • Energy comes in various forms and can be converted from one form to another. • Energy can be stored and transferred to and from moving things. • Some energy sources are renewable but fuels form the Earth are being used up.

Summary

- As children's scientific ideas develop, three main dimensions of change can be identified: from description to explanation; from small to big ideas; from personal to shared ideas.
- Various ways are used to set out goals for the development of ideas but some do not bring out these dimensions of progression as well as others.
- The idea of 'explanatory stories' to convey goals retains the wholeness of understanding about various phenomena in ways that relate to children's experience.
- The alternative of identifying goals at the end of certain phases in terms of key ideas can reflect the main dimensions of development.

Chapter 4
Building scientific process skills

Introduction

As we have noted in Chapter 2, various kinds of skills are seen as important outcomes of experience across the curriculum. Here we are concerned with the seven that were identified as specifically scientific. However, we should acknowledge straightaway that the boundaries between these skills are artificial and fragment what is, in practice, essentially a whole, i.e. scientific enquiry. However the whole is so complex that, while admitting that the skills are not separable in practice, it is useful to identify and describe certain aspects of scientific activity. In this way we can at least hope to arrive at a common and clear notion of the parts which are interwoven in the investigation of the world around and the development of understanding. It will soon become apparent that these aspects of practice, which we call process skills, are not single skills but conglomerates of coherent skills. It is for convenience only that we refer to each as individual skills.

The development of scientific process skills is an important aim of science education for several reasons. They are important as part of the core, key and thinking skills that are valued as outcomes of education. They are also essential in enabling children to develop understanding and the ability to identify and use relevant scientific evidence in solving problems and making decisions. As we will see in Chapter 6, learning with understanding starts from children's ideas and involves the children using evidence and ideas from others to change and develop their ideas so that they become 'bigger'. Children have to acquire these skills; they are not born with them. This chapter is about the nature of process skills and attempts to answer, in relation to them, similar questions to those raised about concepts in the last chapter: what do they involve, what is the nature of progression and what can we expect of younger and older primary school children?

Dimensions of progression

Before we look at separate process skills it is helpful to have in mind certain overall changes that we identify as 'progress'. They indicate the natural starting point for young children and the directions in which their learning should take them. The role of the teacher in promoting these changes is considered in Chapter 20. Three dimensions of change are:

1. From simple to more elaborated skills

This is the most obvious dimension, comprising the development of ability to perform more aspects of a skill. A parallel in another field, is the development from just being able to move round an ice-rink on skates to being able to jump, twist and dance and still land on your feet. Both might be called 'ice skating' but one is much simpler and less elaborated than the other. In the case of science process skills it is the difference between observing main features and observing details, between predicting what might happen in value terms and being more specific, between concluding that a change in one variable does affect another and identifying the direction and nature of the relationship.

2. From effective use in familiar situations to effective use in unfamiliar situations

As noted in Chapter 2, all process skills relate to some content and it is not difficult to appreciate that what the content is will influence the way children engage with it. Some children who may be able to make a reasonable prediction or plan an investigation about, say, how far paper darts will fly, may be less likely to do these things effectively in relation to the effect of resistance in an electric circuit. The reason is that some scientific knowledge is always involved in using science processes. Whether or not the required knowledge is the main obstacle in a particular case depends on familiarity with it. A consequence of this is that the extent to which young children can conduct scientific enquiries can only be assessed when they are engaged on enquiries about things familiar to them or ones they have thoroughly explored. However, as they have more experience and recognise the role of skills in helping to solve problems or answer questions, they become able to deploy the skills more consciously in tackling less familiar problems.

3. From unconscious to conscious action

By unconscious action here is meant doing something without recognising just what one is doing. For example, noticing something without consciously observing it, or finding an answer to a question by enquiry without recognising the kind of question that is being answered in this way. This dimension of change is connected with the previous one, since becoming aware of one's thinking is necessary to applying deliberately certain thinking to unfamiliar problems. The kind of thinking that is at the conscious end of this dimension is meta-cognition, being aware of one's thinking and reasoning processes. It is often considered that primary children are not able to stand back from their enquiries or problems and reflect on how they tackled them and so opportunities to do this are not offered. Recent attempts to involve children in such thinking (AKSIS and CASE projects) have, however, provided evidence of some positive effects. Giving children more opportunity of this kind may well advance the development of their process skills and thus their ability to make sense of the world around. We return to this in Chapter 20.

The nature of progression in process skills

The following sections describe each of the seven scientific process skills, identified in Chapter 2, in terms of what anyone involved in using them would actually be doing. At the end of each section these observable behaviours are summarised for early stages of development (young children from the beginning of schooling up to about the age of about 8) and for later stages (children at the end of their primary education, at the age of 11 or 12 years), indicating some progression in these skills along the dimensions just discussed.

Observing

For an image of observing in action let's take the example of someone given an unknown object which resembles a sea shell; it might be a shell of a kind they have never seen before – or it might not be a natural object. After it is put into their hand they might just look at it and from this decide what it is: 'it looks like a shell'. Or, they might rub their fingers over it, hold it to the light to see the detail (or use a hand lens if there is one), they might smell it, even put it to their ear (as people do with shells); they might tap it and listen to the sound. They could be mentally, or actually, be comparing it with something known to be a shell, seeking points of similarity and difference. All these things add up to more careful observation in this particular situation and are signs of a more developed skill in observing. Recognising that useful information can be gathered in this way and deliberately taking steps to do so are further indications of development.

In another example, imagine a person watching a 'cartesian diver', made from a dropper floating in water inside a large plastic bottle (Figure 4.1).

When the bottle is standing, firmly capped, the dropper floats at the surface upright, with water about half way up the tube. When the sides of the bottle are squeezed the dropper slowly sinks to the bottom. More than this can be noticed, however, by looking carefully and noting the order in which events take place. The level of the water inside the dropper's tube rises when the bottle is squeezed and

Figure 4.1

this happens before the droppers starts to sink; indeed it could be the reason for the sinking (which would be a hypothesis based on the observation). At this point, however, we keep the focus on the observation. In this situation the careful observation of detail and of the order of events are important aspects of what we mean by observation in action.

Observing is the basis of all means of collecting data in a practical situation. Where attention to detail or to small differences is necessary it will be appropriate to extend senses by using an instrument such as a hand lens or stethoscope and to use measuring instruments to quantify observations. Data can also be obtained from secondary sources, of course, from books, displays, film, television, computer links, which are considered under communication skills.

From these considerations we can identify the kind of actions which indicate skill in observation:

- *At early stages*
  - using more than one of the senses to make observations;
  - identifying the obvious features of an object or event.

- *At later stages*
  - making conscious use of several senses;
  - noticing relevant details of the object and its surroundings;
  - identifying similarities and differences;
  - discerning the order in which events take place;
  - using aids to the senses for study of details;
  - making measurements or comparisons using appropriate instruments.

Raising questions

In science we are concerned with investigable questions, ones which can be answered by scientific enquiry. However, we should first make clear the value of children raising all kinds of questions, in order to avoid the impression that investigable questions are the only kind worth raising. Raising a variety of questions, including poorly expressed and vague ones, is important to children's learning, for questioning is the means by which they can create some links between one experience and another and can make sense of the world. Such learning is helped, however, if teachers, and eventually children themselves, recognise the distinction between the kinds of questions that science can answer and the questions that cannot be settled by scientific activity.

Given a wind-up toy as part of work on energy and movement, Andy immediately asked these questions:

How far can it go?
How fast can it go?
Where did it come from?
Is it very expensive?
What is it made of?
What makes the noise?

The first two and last two of these questions can be found by scientific enquiry, by doing something with or to the toy. They are investigable questions. 'Where did it come from?' is a matter of fact; it could be found out by investigation, but not scientific investigation. But 'Is it very expensive?' is not answerable by observation or logical argument; the answer depends on matters of value. Similarly questions that require aesthetic judgement are not scientifically investigable.

Of course Andy was not aware of asking different sorts of questions and that some could not be answered by scientific enquiry. The development of this awareness is a significant part of children's education, which comes rather slowly, through realising the kind of questions to which they can find answers for themselves. These are the questions that Elstgeest (1985b) suggests we can 'ask the object'. You can ask the toy how far it will go when wound up and find out the answer from what it does. You can ask an ice cube what is the best way of preventing it from melting – and find out the answer from doing something to it. You can ask three different fabrics which is most waterproof – and do something with them that gives you the answer. And so on. At the primary level we are particularly concerned with the sub-set of investigable questions that children can answer through their own activity (although these are not the only kind of investigable questions) because they give children opportunities to use and develop enquiry skills and also help them to recognise the difference between questions that are and are not answerable by science.

Many questions are potentially investigable, but not expressed in a form that can be turned into an investigation. For example, 'How far can it go?' needs clarification in relation to the clock-work toy, for it is likely that it can go different distances according to the number of turns of the key. But at least in this case it is clear what it to be observed or measured as an outcome, ie distance. In many cases, such as 'Which is best...?' questions, clarification is needed about 'best for what?' and how the difference will be observed, before any action can be taken. This is the beginning of planning an investigation and demonstrates the contiguous nature of process skills.

These are the things that we can expect of children in relation to raising questions:

- *At early stages:*
  - asking a variety of questions including both investigable and non-investigable ones;
  - discussing how their questions can be answered and identifying the ones they can answer for themselves.

- *At later stages:*
  - discussing how different kinds of questions (not just their own) can be anwered;
  - recognising a difference between an investigable question and one which cannot be answered by scientific enquiry;
  - clarifying questions by identifying what to change and what to observe or measure to achieve an answer.

Hypothesising

In the cartesian diver example a hypothesis was mentioned in the context of attempting to explain why the dropper sank. A hypothesis is a statement put forward to attempt to explain some happening or feature. When hypothesising the suggested explanation need not be correct, but it should be reasonable in terms of the evidence available and possible in terms of scientific concepts or principles. There always is some knowledge from past experience brought to bear on the evidence in making a hypothesis. In the case of the cartesian diver, the suggestion that the dropper sank because of the extra water inside it was based not only on the observation of the water level in the tube but also the knowledge that adding more mass to a floating object can make it sink.

Often there is more than one possible explanation of an event. This underlines the point that hypotheses are plausible but not necessarily correct.

Take for example the observation that one of two puddles of water left after a rain storm dries up more slowly than the other. The reason could be that there was more water in one than the other to begin with, that one is on more water permeable ground than the other, that the sun shines more on one, that there is greater air movement over one than the other. Several more ideas might well be thought up. In each case there is knowledge brought to bear – about the conditions which favour evaporation, about the differences in properties of materials with regard to water permeability, and so on. If the suggestion were that the water ran uphill out of one of them or that it dried up more quickly 'because it wanted to', these would not be scientific hypotheses because they conflict either with the evidence or with the scientific knowledge.

Even though one may not oneself be able to think of alternative explanations it is important to recognise the possibility of alternatives. In turn this brings the realisation that any hypothesis has to be regarded as provisional since there may always be another which is more consistent with the evidence.

So in relation to hypothesising we can expect the following of children at different stages:

- *At early stages*
  - making an attempt to explain something based on earlier experience.

- *At later stages*
  - suggesting an explanation which is consistent with the evidence;
  - suggesting an explanation which is consistent with some scientific principle or concept;
  - realising that there can be more than one possible explanation of an event or phenomenon;
  - realising the tentative nature of any explanation.

Predicting

A prediction is a statement about what may happen in the future, or what will be found that has not so far been found, that is based on some hypothesis or previous knowledge. For example, if you know how far a car will go on two gallons of petrol and how far it will go on four gallons, it is possible to predict how far it will go, say, on five gallons. In another cases, if your hypothesis about why a table lamp is not working is that the fuse has blown, then you predict that changing the fuse will make it work again.

A prediction is quite different from a guess, which cannot be justified in terms of an hypothesis or evidence. Given no information about how far the car goes on a certain amount of petrol the suggestion of how far it would go on five gallons would be a guess, not a prediction (except that evidence of other cars may be used, in which case the prediction would be based on that evidence). However, even when there is a rational basis for a prediction there is always the possibility that it will not be supported by evidence of finding out what actually does happen. This may be because a relationship assumed to hold does not do so indefinitely. For example, an elastic band may stretch 10cm under a force of 5 Newton, 20cm under a force of 10 Newton but break under 15 Newton! Caution is thus needed in making a prediction which depends on applying a relationship beyond the range of available evidence (extrapolating). Interpolating (predicting within the range of evidence), such as predicting how far the elastic band will stretch with a force of 8 Newton is much safer.

Young children don't realise the difference between a prediction and a guess. When asked 'what do you think will happen' or 'what do you expect to find?' they answer without necessarily making clear whether or not they are using evidence. For example, when asked to say how far she expected a clockwork toy to go if the key were turned five times, after seeing how far it went when the key was given two turns, four turns and six turns, Anya said her answer was a guess. However on probing, she said she worked it out as 'a bit more than four and a bit less than six'. Helping children to become aware of their reasoning and to use evidence more consciously is important to developing skill in predicting.

There is often confusion of the meaning of a hypothesis and a prediction, partly because the hypothesis on which a prediction is based may be implicit, not explicit. So, a statement such as 'I will be able to see myself better in that spoon than this one because it is shinier' is a prediction The related hypothesis is that shininess makes surfaces reflect better. Again, helping children to realise the distinction between the two enables them to identify the hypothesis being tested when they see whether or not there is evidence to support their prediction.

What we can expect at different stages is described as follows:

- *At early stages*
  - attempting to say what may happen or be found even though not being able to explain why;
  - making reference to some previous experience that is relevant to a prediction.

- *At later stages*
  - explaining how a prediction is based on a pattern in observations;
  - explaining how a prediction is derived from a hypothesis or possible reason or explanation;
  - recognising the difference between guessing and predicting.

Planning and conducting investigations

Planning and carrying out an investigation are very closely connected and it is difficult to know where one ends and the other begins. The two often occur together, particularly in the case of young children. Parts of the investigation are worked out along the way rather than being all thought through before taking action. In this discussion, planning is taken to be part of enquiry. It is not seen as involving writing something down before practical work begins; indeed most planning by primary children will be 'on the job' and not written down. Planning is implicitly, though not always explicitly, focused by a prediction based on an hypothesis. The suggestion that 'we want to find out if x happens when we do y' is implicitly a prediction that x follows from y and is based on the hypothesis that the two are connected.

As an example of planning, suppose you do decide to investigate possible reasons for one puddle of water drying up more than the other (page 37). The first hypothesis which you decide to test is that it could be caused by different movement of air over the water. The prediction is that when the air is moving over the surface of the puddle it dries up more quickly than when the air is still. But there are several things which can vary (variables) as well as the movement of the air. To find out whether air movement can make a difference, you must set up a test where this is the only thing which is different between the puddles which are compared. It is necessary to create experimental conditions such that other things can be kept the same. The 'puddles' need to have the same amount of water, be on the same kind of ground, receive the same sunshine and be the same in any other respect which is thought might affect their rate of drying. These considerations refer to the variables which have to be kept the same, or controlled.

It would be much easier to ensure that 'all other things are equal' by making 'puddles' in equal containers indoors. One variable, the amount of movement in the air, has to be different, of course, in the two cases. This is the independent variable, the one which is being changed by choice. An investigation set up in this way is described as 'fair' in the sense that there is (or should be) no difference in any other variable than the one we choose to change which will affect the result and so that result can be said to have been caused by the independent variable. What may change as a result of the change in the independent variable, in this case the amount of water left, is dependent on what is done and so is called the dependent variable. The change in this variable has to be compared or measured to obtain the result and this has to be done in a suitable way. Planning must involve deciding ways of doing this, using measuring instruments if necessary.

If the result shows that there is no difference resulting from varying the air movement, then an alternative hypothesis may be considered and used to create a different prediction. Then further investigation may be carried out with another variable, say the exposure to sun, as the independent variable. In that investigation the air movement would be kept the same and not varied for the puddles studied.

Developing the ability to plan and conduct these 'fair test' investigations, and other kinds of systematic enquiry, clearly takes time and experience. Young children are typically only able to take the first few steps or to suggest in general terms what to do to find out something. Talking through what needs to be done in order to be sure that the result will be able to answer the question is important for 'scaffolding' the development of planning investigations. Other ways of helping development are considered in Chapter 20.

Expectations of children at different stages in planning are:

• *At early stages*
  – proposing a simple investigation to answer a question or test a prediction;
  – saying what they would do to make a test 'fair'.

• *At later stages*
  – deciding which variable is to be changed (independent) and which are to be kept the same (controlled);
  – identifying what to look for, measure or compare (dependent variable) to find a result;
  – identifying the appropriate degree of precision of any measuring instruments to be used;
  – reflecting on plans and procedures to make improvements.

Interpreting

Interpreting involves putting results together so that patterns or relationships between them can be seen. The results of the water evaporation investigation might be in terms of the amounts of water present in two containers at various times. To interpret these would mean relating what happened to the different conditions in a statement such as 'the water went down more quickly when the air was moving than when it was still'. The further step of drawing a general conclusion, such as 'water evaporates more quickly in moving air than in still air' requires some caution, since it suggests not only that this relationship was found in one particular investigation but that there is reason to suppose that it would hold in other cases.

Where several pieces of information have been collected (as in seeing how far an elastic band stretches under various forces), interpretation involves looking for patterns in them. These patterns might be regular – as in the case of the elastic band, as long as it is not stretched too much – or merely trends – such as in the tendency for taller people to have larger hands and feet than shorter people. In a regular pattern all the information will fit the pattern without exception, but in the latter there is an overall association although there may be exceptions to it in some cases. This is a distinction that comes with experience of checking a conclusion against all the data.

It is typical of early development in the skills of interpreting that children jump to a conclusion on the basis of only some of the data, ignoring other information which conflicts. At a more advanced stage they consider all the data and only leave some out of account if there is good reason to do so. Even when all available data supports a conclusion, the possibility that more data, were they to be collected, might conflict with it has to be kept in mind. So expressing conclusions in the form of 'On the basis of our results…' is a way of indicating this awareness.

The development of this skills at early and later stages takes a form of this sort:

- *At early stages*
  - using information obtained to answer the question posed in an enquiry;
  - comparing what was found with what they predicted would happen.

- *At later stages*
  - putting various pieces of information together to make some statement of their combined meaning;
  - finding patterns or trends in observations or results of investigations;
  - identifying an association between one variable and another;
  - making sure that a pattern or association is checked against all the data;
  - showing caution in making assumptions about the general applicability of a conclusion.

Communicating

Talking, writing, drawing, or representing things in other ways are not only means of letting others know of our ideas but help us to sort out what we think and understand. It is also important to be able to express opinions and to set out arguments based on evidence. Thus communication is important in learning and applying scientific concepts. It takes various forms according to the subject being learned. In science, talking and listening are particularly valuable for making ideas explicit and for helping the understanding of scientific vocabulary. Children often use words which they pick up without necessarily realising the meaning which attaches to the words. Encouraging children to talk about what they mean by these words and to listen to what others say can help to reveal differences which can be the source of misunderstanding. Discussion also helps where children may have ideas but no words to put to them. There is more about the use of scientific words in Chapter 12.

The reports children write at the end of an investigation to present what they have found are only one form of writing, one which is most useful when it is seen to have a specific purpose and a specific audience. Notes or drawings made for themselves during the course of an investigation are valuable for jotting down ideas as well as findings and other information. They can take the same role as talking with regard to helping to sort out ideas.

Communication in science involves using various conventions of representation which help in organising information and conveying it efficiently. Graphs, charts, tables, symbols, etc. serve this purpose and have to be chosen to suit the particular kind of information. Children have first to become familiar with these as forms of communication. Further development shows in being able to think consciously about the nature of what is to be communicated and to whom and to select the best medium for the message. Communication is, of course, two way, and involves the ability to take information from written sources, to use information presented in graphical or tabular form, thus expanding the evidence which can be used in testing ideas.

Thus in relation to communication skills, what we can expect at different stages includes the following:

- *At early stages*
  - describing the main points of what has been done, observed and found out;
  - using models, actions, charts and drawings as appropriate to convey information.

- *At later stages*
  - talking, listening or writing to sort out ideas and clarify meaning;
  - making notes of observations in the course of an investigation;
  - using graphs, and tables and conventional symbols to convey information;
  - choosing an appropriate means of communication which is understandable to others;
  - selecting relevant information from secondary sources such as books, films, computer databanks.

Summary

- Some overall dimensions of change in the development of process skills are: from simple to more elaborated skills; from effective use in familiar situations to effective use in unfamiliar situations; from unconscious to conscious action.
- Added to experience of observing children, these dimensions of progress help in identifying the expectations at early and later development.
- Goals, in terms of these expectations, have been identified for the seven process skills: observing, raising questions, hypothesising, predicting, planning and conducting investigations, interpreting and communicating.

Chapter 5
Building the attitudes that promote learning in science

Introduction

This chapter is concerned with those attitudes, or habits of mind, that influence learning. Their importance is succinctly captured in these words of K. M. Evans:

> Ask a boy what he learns at school and he will tell you English and Mathematics, History and Geography, Science and Languages. But his teachers, if not the boy himself, will know that he learns far more than this. Models of thinking and acting, attitudes and interests are also acquired and developed during these school days, and these may become permanent, remaining effective and observable long after the greater part of the subject matter learnt has been overlaid or forgotten. It would be difficult to overstress the influence of attitudes and interests in the lives of individual people. They determine what a man will do or say in particular situations, what he will enjoy or dislike, his approach to other people, and his reactions to events in his own life and in the world around.
>
> (Evans 1965, p. 1)

As this passage suggests, there are many different kinds of attitudes which influence behaviour. Our concern is with those which influence children's learning and in particular their learning in science at an early stage. For reasons given in Chapter 2 (page 18) the focus is the attitudes that promote effective learning in science rather than the attitudes towards science and scientists.

We first consider the overall direction of progress in developing attitudes and then look at the nature and development of each of the five attitudes identified as most relevant to learning science.

Dimensions of progression

The formation of attitudes is influenced by many factors. Children and adults who feel they can succeed are more likely to do so, while those who anticipate failure are less likely to succeed. These attitudes affect not only what is learned but the effort put into the tasks given which in turn affects the likelihood of success. When the attitudes are negative there is a vicious circle created:

The child thinks he or she is no good at the task.
The child thinks it is not worth making an effort.
Little success results from the lack of effort.
The feeling of being 'no good' is reinforced.

School is all about tackling new tasks, so children's feelings about themselves in relation to different kinds of task are very significant. For the young child, ideas and feelings about the self are formed very largely from the ways in which he or she is treated by others. The picture the child has of him/herself grows from comments and actions of others around him or her, at home at school and in social groups. These things reflect the image others have of the child and have a strong influence on what (s)he thinks (s)he is. Parents often try to protect their children from failure by lowering expectations: 'You're not very good at drawing, are you, Jane, so you'd better leave it to Meg'; or talk about them to others in their hearing: 'Ali is like me, not very bright!' It is easy to see how these images which others have of children can become their self-images: they will see themselves as 'no good' at drawing, or whatever, and expect to be grouped among the 'not very bright'.

In school, teachers and other children make comments every day which reinforce the general trend of children's performance. The classroom organisation in which children are grouped by ability on different tables leads to children labelling themselves, even when the teacher uses neutral group names: 'We're the green table; we won't be able to do the same as the others.' Work becomes something to endure for such children, who then often attempt to preserve or boost their self-esteem in other ways; sometimes this can be positive but it also takes the form of 'rubbishing' others in order to show themselves in a better light.

Of course children do vary in achievement. The challenge is to cater for this without labelling them, to build up self-confidence so that there is always willingness to try and thus have the chance of success. When this happens the vicious circle can be turned into a benign circle, from which a positive self-image emerges; realising that one's achievement is less than others' can be accepted without bringing with it a sense of failure as a person.

The many influences on the development of attitudes, from maturation, social interaction, parents and other adults, make it difficult to define a pattern which can be regarded as the course of development across different attitudes. Nevertheless, certain common trends can be identified. The immature forms of attitudes, normal for younger children but found in older children and even in adults, are characterised by

- control of behaviour being external to the person;
- lack of appreciation of a point of view other than their own;
- a 'black and white' view of what is 'right' and 'wrong';
- regarding rules as given and unchallengeable.

The more mature forms are characterised by

- autonomy;
- the ability to see things from others' points of view;
- judging right and wrong by taking into account intention and motives and not just the results of an action;
- regarding rules as the result of agreement between people involved and subject to changes by agreement.

These themes suggest that genuine collaboration, for example, cannot be expected if children are at the stage where they do not appreciate the position or point of view of others, nor real responsibility if they regard the control of their behaviour as being external rather than part of themselves.

The following two dimensions of change are particularly relevant to scientific attitudes.

From orientation to self to orientation to others

This dimension describes the difference between focusing on one's own experience and ideas and being willing to take notice of what other have found and their views of it. Self-orientation implies looking at things from a personal point of view, being attracted by new objects and experience, but easily distracted when initial curiosity is satisfied since there is little willingness to take notice of input from others that might extend interest. Moving towards orientation to others is important in learning science, where many activities are collaborative and ideas are constructed in interactions with others. Being open to sharing with others and to their ideas extends the learner's thinking and experience.

From being externally motivated to being self-motivated

The word 'motivation' is used here in the sense of motivation to learn, acknowledging that all behaviour is motivated in some way. Those children whose motivation comes from outside themselves, engage in activities for reasons of gaining the approval of others and perhaps rewards that have little to do with the activities themselves. These children lack the willingness to undertake tasks, to persevere and to complete them because through this they gain satisfaction, that is typical of self-motivated learners. Encouraging children to take responsibility for their learning, to move control from outside to within, is essential for continued learning of all kinds. It is particularly important in science because the development of scientific ideas depends upon a desire to understand and to persist until satisfied. It is only the learner who knows when this point has been reached.

The nature of progression in scientific attitudes

Here we discuss the five attitudes most closely related to learning science. The first four: curiosity, respect for evidence, willingness to change ideas and critical reflection, influence the extent to which children take note of evidence and accommodate their ideas to it. The fifth relates to the process and impact of scientific and other human activities on the environment. Each is summarised in terms of the kinds of behaviour in children which show its development. These stages are, however, less tied to age than in the cases of concepts and skills.

Curiosity

Curiosity, while important for all learning, is particularly so for learning science since it leads children forward into new experiences and so is essential for learning from exploration of things around. It follows that for children to benefit from opportunities provided for first-hand investigation, their curiosity should be encouraged. To do this we need to know about how it develops and to encourage it.

Children apparently vary enormously in their curiosity; some always wanting to ask questions and seeming never to be satisfied, following one question with another; others seem 'switched off' and don't show interest in anything. We may, however, be making hasty judgements if we use only the evidence of the questions which children ask. Some children have been deterred from asking questions by previous experience (of being told not to do so or just by never achieving satisfaction from a response, for example), others may be unsure of what is appropriate behaviour, while others again may be just shy and reserved. Such children need positive encouragement which legitimates expressions of curiosity, not just in terms of asking questions but through other ways of getting to know; such as touching, watching intently, using books.

The curiosity of young children, once released, is inevitably immature. It is spontaneous and impulsive, easily stimulated by new things but just as easily distracted by something else. A child who has reached a more mature level shows greater powers of concentration and will be less impulsive. The number of questions asked is likely to decline but the ones which are asked will be more perceptive and relevant. There will be more thought behind them in the attempt to equate new experience with previous knowledge. Mature curiosity shows in wanting to 'come to terms' with each new experience and reach an understanding of it. Thus curiosity become an active component in learning with understanding.

In summary, we can expect children at different points in developing curiosity to show these behaviours:

- *At early stages*
  - noticing and being attracted to new things;
  - asking questions of all kinds and showing interest in finding answers.

- *At later stages*
  - showing interest through careful observation of details;
  - asking questions of all kinds including those which seek explanations;
  - spontaneously using information sources to find out about new or unusual things.

Respect for evidence

Respect for evidence is central to scientific activity. Although many new ideas have been born as a leap of the imagination, they would have a short life unless they could be shown to fit evidence and help make sense of what is already known to happen. Children's keen desire for things to 'be fair' provides a basis for respecting evidence. They will readily challenge each other to 'show me' and not be prepared to accept something as true unless they see evidence for themselves. There are many reasons why this behaviour does not carry over to their relationships with adults, and particularly teachers. Apart from status, one of the worrying reasons is that adults themselves appear to accept statements without questioning the evidence and expect children to do the same. So children build up an attitude of acceptance that what 'authority' says is true. Of course, it is impossible for evidence to be obtained for every statement and it is as immature to accept nothing as definite as it is to accept everything at face value. The sign of mature respect for evidence is willingness to place one's own ideas under test in relation to evidence, in the understanding that any ideas which are worthwhile stand up to such testing. As a corollary the understanding develops that no ideas are worthwhile unless the evidence is there to support them.

Actions which, if a general pattern of behaviour, indicate respect for evidence include:

- *At early stages*
  - reporting what has been observed.

- *At later stages*
  - reporting what actually happens even if this is in conflict with expectations;
  - querying and checking parts of the evidence which do not fit into the pattern of other findings;
  - querying a conclusion or interpretation for which there is insufficient evidence;
  - treating ideas or conclusions as provisional and as being open to challenge by further evidence.

Willingness to change ideas

Implicit in the use of evidence is the *willingness to change ideas* if they are not consistent with the evidence. This attitudes is sometimes described as *flexibility* but it is not to be mistaken for adopting whatever is the current way of thinking and having no ideas of one's own. At all times scientific ideas are changing with new experience. For example, recently identified holes in the ozone layer have extended many people's understanding of ecology and indeed introduced a new concept of 'ecocide'. However, for young children the rate of experience of new phenomena and events is particularly high and there need to be frequent adjustments in their ideas.

Unless there is a willingness to change ideas then there would be devastating confusion as new experiences conflict with existing ideas. The importance of legitimising these changes, making them open and acceptable and considered as normal, cannot be overemphasised. It is helpful to discuss with children how their ideas have changed, and to give some examples of how other people's ideas, including those of scientists, have changed. At first children may be prepared only to listen to others' ideas, without considering that any differences from their own ideas might have some relevance for them. Gradually they realise that other points of view are just as worthy of consideration as their own and, indeed, begin to see that they can be useful in helping their own understanding.

With maturity, and bolstered by greater experience, children's initial ideas need to change less often but it is important to retain the possibility of change and the tentative nature of any ideas. This can be facilitated by expressing conclusions in terms of the evidence available. 'So far we have found that all the pieces of wood float' lays a better basis for accommodating evidence that some wood (lignum vitae and ebony) does not float.

In summary, indications of children's willingness to change ideas include:

- *At early stages*
  - taking notice of others' ideas;
  - giving consideration to evidence which conflicts with their own ideas.

- *At later stages*
  - being prepared to change an existing idea when there is convincing evidence against it;
  - considering alternative ideas as seriously as their own;
  - spontaneously seeking alternative ideas rather than accepting the first one which fits the evidence;
  - realising that it is necessary to change or give up existing ideas when different ones make better sense of the evidence.

Critical reflection

In the context of science activities *critical reflection* increases the potential learning from experiences and class activities. It manifests itself in deliberate review of the way in which activities have been carried out, what ideas have emerged and how these could be improved. It is the beginning of reflecting on one's learning, but only the beginning, for this is a mature activity, requiring a degree of abstract thinking not available to young children. But as everything has a beginning at an earlier level than that at which it shows in its full form, we should begin to encourage critical review as a normal part of work. This requires teacher guidance at first; making time to talk through activities, to compare different approaches and to make suggestions of how thing might, with hindsight, have been tackled more effectively. The emphasis has to be on arriving at better ways of planning, investigating or collecting evidence which can be used in the future rather than criticising what has been done.

A more mature form of this attitude shows when children themselves take the initiative in reflection on what they have done and realise the pros and cons of various alternatives. Reflecting on processes of thinking does not come readily to young children, but a useful start can be made at the level of specific activities rather than through discussion of general approaches.

So, the kinds of actions of children which indicate this attitude include:

- *At early stages*
  - being willing to consider different ways of doing something.

- *At later stages*
  - being willing to review what they have done in order to consider how it might have been improved;

- considering alternative procedures to those used;
- identifying the points in favour and against the way in which an investigation was carried out or its results interpreted;
- using critical reflection of a previous investigation in planning and carrying out a later one.

Sensitivity towards living things and the environment

These attitudes are more obviously linked to particular concepts and understanding than the four just considered. The relationship between knowledge and personal attitudes and action is complex, however. We might hope, for example, that people who understand the effect of over-picking on wild flowers, or disturbing animals in rock pools, or collecting non-living souvenirs from sites of special geological interest, might desist from such practices. There is no certainty about this. On the other hand, if they are to be deterred from doing these things without the understanding, then it has to be through externally imposed restrictions and rules of conduct. In the case of children we should be developing understanding but meanwhile influencing behaviour by example and rules, so that they do not cause damage to the environment or injury to living things in their explorations.

Children readily show sensitivity to pets and living things that they look after in the classroom. Through these activities they recognise that living things have needs similar to their own and may suffer if these needs are not met. It is important to transfer this knowledge and the feeling towards living things beyond the furry attractive ones to others such as spiders and worms, and to plants as well as animals. Studying these things in their habitats enables children to realise how each depends on other living things and why it is necessary to preserve them. Living things collected from the environment for study in the classroom should afterwards be replaced where they were found. Helping to do this shows sensitivity to their needs.

With greater maturity children will extend their care for their environment to the non-living things. This also begins 'at home' by avoiding litter, recycling paper and other materials, activities which help children to realise that there actions make a difference to the environment. As their understanding of reasons for these actions grows, so will their responsibility.

So we can expect these kinds of behaviours of children as these attitudes develop:

- *At early stages*
  - taking part responsibly, with others, in caring for living things at home or at school;

- observing rules or codes of behaviour relating to caring for the living and non-living environment.

- *At later stages*
  - taking steps to reduce the impact of their investigations of the environment, by, for example, replacing animals taken into the classroom for study;
  - taking personal responsibility for caring for living things;
  - avoiding damaging or polluting the environment through their own action;
  - participating in creating and keeping rules and procedures that protect the environment.

Summary

- Consideration of the more and less mature forms of attitudes leads to identification of progression in terms of change from an orientation to the self to orientation to others, and from being externally motivated to being self-motivated.
- These dimensions, together with experience of observing children, help to identify expectations of behaviour at early and later stages of development.
- Goals in terms of these expectations have been identified for curiosity, respect for evidence, willingness to change ideas, critical reflection, and sensitivity towards living things and the environment.

Chapter 6

A view of learning in science

Introduction

This chapter is about the process of learning in science. It begins by presenting a model – or framework for thinking – about learning based on how we make sense of new experience and develop ideas that explain it. The framework proposes how both process skills and ideas from previous experience are involved in developing understanding. The second part uses the model to highlight the important role of process skills in determining whether ideas accepted really do fit the evidence. If the skills and reasoning are not scientific then ideas emerging will not accord with the scientific view. Thus we can understand how children can come to hold some non-scientific ideas, such as those illustrated in the third part of this chapter. Finally we acknowledge the importance of taking seriously these existing ideas as starting points for developing more scientific ideas and identify some of the implications.

A framework for thinking about learning

What happens when someone encounters something new and tries to make sense of it? This is a relevant way of approaching the description of the learning of children, since they are constantly faced with new experiences. However, the framework or model that emerges fits a good deal of adult learning as well. Indeed it in based on evidence from observing children and adults making sense of new happenings and on reflecting on what scientists do in trying to explain new observations.

Observing learning

In exploring this question of making sense of a new experience, I have often shown adults something that they are unlikely to have seen before. This is not so easy in these days of ready access to objects from all over the world. But for some time I had something that was novel to many people. It is a set of four translucent objects, roughly oval in shape but curved in two dimensions, each slightly small than the next, the largest being about 6cm long and 4 cm wide. A very common first reaction is that they are elephants' toenails! Indeed they might be if elephants had toe nails; so that idea is easily dismissed by those who suggest it. To many adults they look like something that has come from a living thing because of their texture and this is not very different from one's own finger nails. However, when tapped, they make a sound that could come from something made of hard plastic, but why would anything like that be made? Manufactured things usually have a purpose. Exploration goes on, using the sense of smell, touch and hearing, or previous knowledge to test out each idea that occurs. The way the four objects fit together and the pattern thus formed usually eventually provides a visual clue. They are in fact, scales from an enormous fish, only found in the water of the Amazon, and the scales are sold in markets in Brazil as nail files. But it is the process of making sense of the new experience that is of interest here. I refer to it as learning because not only is the result understanding something not understood before (perhaps trivial in the instance just given but not in other cases) but the ideas used in understanding it have been extended (again, in this case, it is perhaps not so important but still relevant).

The framework

This particular example, and others in quite different situations, seem to fit the framework of stages set out in Figure 6.1. Starting with an experience to be explained, the first two stages, (a) and (b) relate to making a link with something similar encountered in previous experience. The link may be made because of some physical property or something else that calls it to mind, such as a word or situation. Creativity and imagination also have a part. Indeed, in the case of the scientist faced with an unexpected phenomenon, it is the ability to try ideas outside the immediately obvious that may be the start of a 'breakthrough'.

The stages (c) and (d) are concerned with testing the idea by making a prediction and gathering evidence to see if the idea 'works' in terms of predicting something that actually happens. If the evidence is not there to support the prediction (e) it is probably necessary to think of another link that might lead to a better idea. If what is predicted is actually found, however, then we might cautiously accept that the idea helps to explain the new experience (f). The idea is changed by becoming one of wider application than before; just a little 'bigger'.

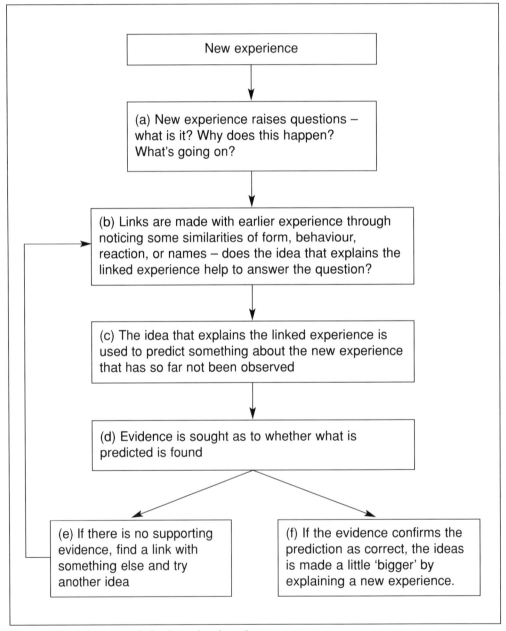

Figure 6.1 A framework for learning in science

An example: using alternative ideas

These stages can be seen in the case of some children who were investigating the difference felt in placing their hands on three surfaces in the classroom – one metal, one wooden and one of polystyrene foam. The metal felt considerably colder than the other two surfaces, which raised the question: why? This was stage (a). They immediately said that the metal was indeed at lower temperature, because that was usually the case when something was felt to be cold, as when touching an object just taken out of the fridge or touching things out of doors on a cold day, (b). Their teacher asked them what they would expect to find if they measured the temperature of the surfaces and they predicted that the metal would be lowest, the wood next and the foam about the same as their hands. Using a temperature sensor connected to a computer, they tested their prediction (d) and found almost no difference among the three surfaces. They were so surprised by this that they wanted to repeat it and to try it in different places. In particular they wanted to take the surfaces out of the classroom to where it was colder. The result was the same, no difference, although the metal still felt much cooler than the other surfaces. Stage (e) was reached and the question was whether there were other ideas that explained the differences felt.

The teacher asked them to think of things that had made their hands cold. One child remembered putting his hands in warm water after snow-balling. (Back to (b)). With a little 'scaffolding' by the teacher (see page 80), the children arrived at the idea that the warm water was replacing heat lost to the snow. Could this account for the hand on the metal getting cold? If so, then the hand would really be colder after touching the metal than after touching the other surfaces, (c). A fair test of this was devised by the children, involving someone placing one finger tip on the metal and another finger of the same hand on the foam, (d). The feeling of cold was confirmed by the temperature reading from the probe placed on the fingers straight afterwards. This had merely confirmed their original experience and although this was necessary as they had begun to doubt that feeling cold really meant that the hand was cold. The teacher challenged them to predict what would happen if the surfaces were all warmer than their hands rather than colder. This would be the real test of the idea. For safety's sake their predictions were not tested, but various experiences were collected that helped to provide supporting evidence – the handles of cooking pans being wooden or plastic rather than metal, the kinds of gloves that keep our hands warm, and so on.

Holding on to existing ideas

It is not always that children can find in their experience, ideas that 'work' in explaining new experiences. Their experience is limited and they take from it what seems reasonable to them. For example, faced with the evidence that varnished cubes of wood stick to each other when wet, several groups of eleven year olds concluded that the blocks became magnetic when wet (Harlen 2000, p. 34). The resemblance of a block sticking to the underside of another, without anything to hold them together, to a magnet picking up another magnet or a piece of iron was clearly very strong. An equally good alternative explanation was not available to them and so they held onto their view of magnetism, modifying it to accommodate the observation that the blocks only stuck together when wet by concluding that 'they're magnetic when they're wet'. Had they had experience, say, of 'suction cups' being held to a surface when air is forced out from under the cup, they might have used a different linking idea – that air pressure can 'stick' things together.

Here we have an illustration of a common way in which children deal with the situation of lacking experience to give them alternative ideas, this is to modify the idea they do have in order to accommodate the conflicting evidence. It seems characteristic of human beings to try to explain things and if ideas that really fit are not available then less satisfactory ideas will be used. It is more comfortable to modify an idea than to abandon it, especially if it is your only way of making any sense of an observation. It often happens that young children will hold on to their idea to the point where their modification in order to explain away contrary evidence renders the idea unscientific (because untestable), as the following examples show.

Luis had an idea about what made snow melt, which was that it was caused by the presence of air; he did not consider heat. He wanted to preserve some snow and said that it would not melt if it were put in jar with a lid on to keep out air. His first attempt led to the snow melting when the jar was brought into a warm room. He said that there was still some air there and that if the jar were to be packed with snow it would not melt. But however much snow was put into the jar he still said that there was room for air. He had, therefore, turned his claim into one which was irrefutable since it would never be possible to have only snow in his jar.

Another example was a child who was convinced that something that did not float would do so if the water was deeper. More water was added but it was never enough, all the same she maintained her claim that it would float in very, very deep water. Again, the idea had become untestable.

In such circumstances it may be helpful for the teacher to suggest another idea and to scaffold the children's application of it until they are satisfied that it makes sense to them. This may work if there is relevant experience that can be used with a little help (as in the case of thinking about cold hands in the earlier example). Alternatively it may be preferable simply to leave the matter until more experience is available which can be brought to bear to change these ideas by the mechanism suggested here. The issues of whether and, if so, how, to introduce alternative ideas is one which we shall pick up again in Chapter 19.

The role of process skills

As we have already noted, the process of linking that leads to ideas that explain new phenomena may not always be rational. But once the connection is made, by whatever process, the idea proposed as an explanation has to be tested. And the testing has to be done scientifically if the result is to be of value in making sense of the experience. If the testing is rigorous and systematic, in the way associated with scientific investigation, then ideas which do not fit the evidence will be rejected and those which do fit will be accepted and strengthened. But it may not be the case that the testing has this quality. The skills of young children – and those of some adults – may not have developed to the appropriate degree. Children may ignore contradictory evidence in interpreting findings and hold on to their initial ideas even those these do not fit the evidence. Thus the extent to which ideas become more scientific (by fitting more phenomena) depends both on the way ideas from previous experience are linked to new experience and on how the testing of possible explanatory ideas is carried out, that is, on the use of the process skills. *So process skills involved at all stages have a crucial part to play in the development of ideas*. This is one important reason for giving attention to helping children to develop their process skills and to become more conscious of using them with appropriate rigour. The other reason, of course, is that these skills are needed for making sense of new experiences in the future and for learning throughout life.

Children's own ideas

Children are trying to make sense of their surroundings all the time. When they do this using immature thinking and reasoning, as we have just suggested, it is not surprising that they form some ideas that do not accord with the scientific view of things. Immature process skills, as implied in Chapter 4, may mean that:

- children take account of only some factors that are relevant;
- things are considered from only one point of view, their own;
- inappropriate links are made (as in the case of the magnetic wood blocks);
- predictions may be no more than restating what is already known, so that they are bound to be confirmed;
- evidence may be selectively used to support an existing idea, ignoring what may be in contradiction.

So it is not surprising that children have some non-scientific ideas, or limited ones, arising from this kind of thinking and reasoning about their experiences. Some examples from research into children's ideas illustrate what this means in practice.

Ideas about growth inside eggs

Research in the SPACE project studied the ideas of children about what was happening inside hens eggs that were being incubated in the classroom. The most popular idea was that there was a miniature but mainly complete animal inside the egg, feeding on what was there. This is evident in the drawings made by the children when asked to depict what they thought was inside an egg while it was incubating.

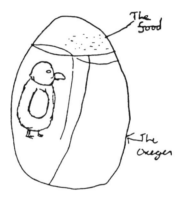

Figure 6.2 (Russell and Watt 1990, p. 31)

An alternative was that the complete animal was inside simply waiting to hatch.

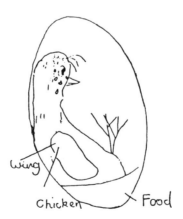

Figure 6.3 (ibid., p. 10)

There was also the view that the body parts were complete but needed to come together.

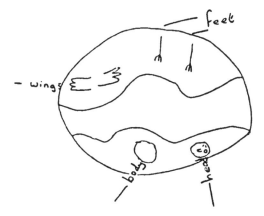

Figure 6.4 (ibid., p. 26)

The more scientific view that transformation was going on was evident in some children's ideas and it was also clear that they used knowledge derived from experience of reproduction of pets and observations of human babies when trying to understand what was going on inside the eggs.

Ideas about growth in plants

When asked 'What do you think plants need to help them grow?' infant children generally mentioned one external factor. For example, Figure 6.5 suggests that light in necessary.

Figure 6.5 (SPACE research, unpublished)

Other young children mentioned soil or water or sun, but rarely all three. Characteristically the younger children made no attempt to explain why these conditions were needed or by what mechanism they worked. Junior children, however, made efforts to give explanations, as in Figure 6.6.

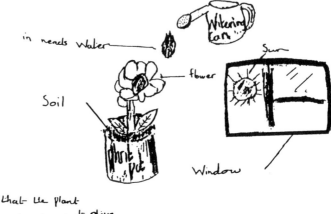

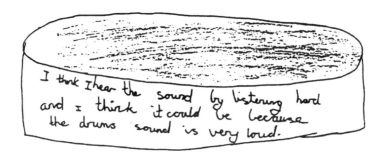

Figure 6.6 (SPACE Research unpublished)

Ideas about how sounds are made and heard

Children's ideas about sound were explored after they had opportunity to make sound with a variety of instruments. The example in Figure 6.7 suggests no mechanism for sound being produced by a drum or for it being heard; it is as if being 'very loud' and 'listening hard' are properties which require no explanation.

Figure 6.7 (Watt and Russell 1990, p. 36)

The simplest mechanism suggested is that the impact of hitting produces 'sound'. In contrast, Figure 6.8 explains the sound in terms of vibration. But notice that the vibration comes out of the drum through 'the hole'. A very common understanding of children was that sound travelled through air, or at least through holes in solid objects and not through the solid itself.

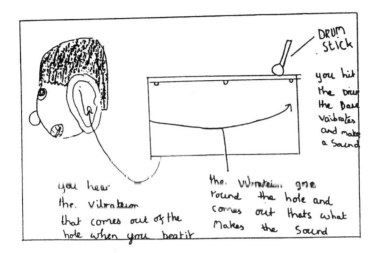

Figure 6.8 (SPACE Research unpublished)

The notion of 'vibration' was associated with sound in ambiguous ways, sometimes sound being the same as vibration and sometimes having some cause and effect relationship to it. Figure 6.9 illustrates this struggle to connect the two.

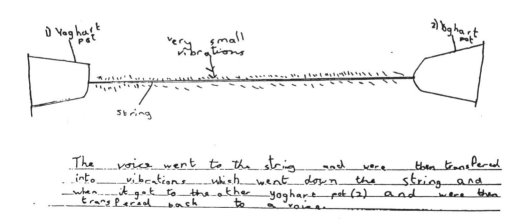

Figure 6.9 (SPACE Research unpublished)

Ideas about forces

Children's ideas about how things are made to move and what makes them stop were explored in various contexts including the 'cotton reel tank' which is propelled by the energy put into twisting a rubber band. Again the younger children found no need to explain more than 'it works because you're turning it round' and 'it stops because it wants to.' Another six year old could see that the pencil (used to twist the rubber band) was important but the idea of why went no further than its presence:

> When we wind it up it goes because of the pencil. When the pencil goes to the tip it stops.

Energy was mentioned in the ideas of older children (Figure 6.10) but the meaning the word was given is not entirely consistent.

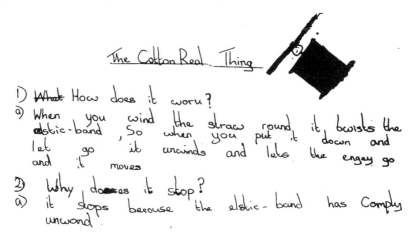

The Cotton Real Thing

1) ~~What~~ How does it work?
a) When you wind the ~~elastic-band~~, So when you put it round, it twists the let go it unwinds and lets the engey go and it moves

2) Why ~~doeses~~ does it stop?
a) it stops because the elastic-band has Comply unwond.

Figure 6.10 (SPACE Research unpublished)

Ideas about solids, liquids and gases

The idea that air is all around, including inside 'empty' containers, was expressed in some way by most junior age children but by a much smaller proportion of five to seven year olds. This statement by an eight year old shows a child who has not yet acquired an idea of air as a substance although its presence is accepted:

> You can't see the air, but sometimes you think there is nothing in there 'cos you can't see anything, but it isn't a matter of seeing, it's a matter of knowing.

Even young children have relatively little difficulty in identifying something hard, such as steel, as solid, and something watery as a liquid. A five year old, after activities with liquids, managed to give a general definition:

Liquids are all kinds of things that don't stay where you put them. They just run. If you put them on the table it runs along the table.'

But where does talcum powder fit? One explanation was:

Its something like a kind of liquid, but it isn't a liquid, its talcum powder. It goes fast like vinegar and its not a solid because you can put your finger through it. Its a bit solid, but not like a liquid. A liquid feels wet and this doesn't.

(quoted in Russell, Longden and McGuigan 1991)

The significance of children's ideas

It is not difficult to see some reasoning, albeit limited, in these ideas and that they may well make sense to the children themselves. It is precisely because of this that we must take these ideas seriously. If we just ignore them, the children may well hold onto them, since non-scientific explanations often seem more rational to children than the scientific ones. (For example, it makes more sense to conclude that puddles dry up because water seeps away through the ground, than that water particles fly off the surface into the air.) If their ideas are not taken into account and changed or replaced they may well hold on to them, learning the 'right' answer by rote but still believing their own version.

In helping children to develop scientific concepts, therefore, we need to start from their ideas and help them, through scientific reasoning or testing, to change them or replace them with ideas which fit the evidence better than their own.

Summary

- Observations of learning in various contexts leads to a model that describes how people try to make sense of new events or phenomena by using ideas from previous experience. If these existing ideas are used to make a prediction, they may be found to fit (and so explain) the new experience; if not, alternative ideas have to be sought and tried.
- The role of process skills in linking and testing existing ideas is central to this process. If the skills are not developed to the point of being scientific, then ideas will not be properly tested and may be retained when they really do not fit the evidence.
- Examples of the ideas children express through their talk, drawing and writing suggest that the ideas are the product of reasoning, even if not of scientific reasoning, and so make sense to the children. It follows that these ideas have to be taken seriously and addressed in helping children to come to hold more scientific ideas.

Chapter 7

Experiences that promote learning

Introduction

This chapter is concerned with some initial answers to the questions: What kinds of experience are needed to give children opportunity for developing scientific ideas, process skills and attitudes? How can children be helped to interact with materials in ways that support learning with understanding about the world around? What is attempted here is an overview of these matters, since much of the rest of the book is concerned with addressing them more fully. The first part considers how thinking about children's learning can help in making classroom decisions. This is followed by a discussion of the implications for learning of decisions about the content of activities and of the procedures and climate of the classroom. This lead to the identification of criteria that should be met by activities that support learning of the kind described in the framework in Chapter 6. Finally the use of the criteria in adapting and improving activities is exemplified.

Making decisions about science activities

Knowledge and understanding cannot be passed to children directly. All that was said in Chapter 6 indicates that understanding is not developed by rote learning: for example, children do not come to know 'that light passes through some materials and not other, and that when it does not, shadows may be formed' simply by being told this and asked to memorise it. So much is agreed. But in providing more genuine opportunities for learning there are still many aspects to be decided: for instance

- *The context of the activities:* Should the science be studied in the context of real life events, which provide interest and stimulate curiosity, but are complex and present ideas often intertwined together, or in 'tidied up' activities which demonstrate scientific relationships and concepts in a more direct form but which then have to be related to real situations? Questions here relate to teaching within a topic which may draw in studies across the curriculum or at least across those parts of it included within environmental studies.

- *The role of the learners.* Should they be addressing their own questions, and so have a part in deciding their activities, or questions proposed by the teacher or work sheet, which will lead them more directly to intended experiences?
- *The role of the teacher during activities.* Is this to show the way to work through prescribed steps in the most efficient way or to challenge them to make decisions about what they do and to justify their actions in the light of the evidence available to them?
- *The attention to be given to development of process skills.* Given that the development of process skills is as much an objective as knowledge and understanding, how does this affect decisions about the form of activities? Should children be directed to observe, predict and plan in a way that makes them conscious of what they are doing and why, or encouraged less explicitly to use these skills?

It is, of course, false to express these as 'either...or' choices and they are contrasted only to show that there are different ways to be considered. In reality the decision will most often lie somewhere in the middle between the two extremes positions and will vary from one activity to another. There is no single answer, but an approach that is relevant in deciding what to do in particular cases is to anchor the decision to the view of learning and of science which we wish to underpin teaching. In the next section we apply this approach to establish criteria that can be used to evaluate activities in planning and in practice.

Activities that provide opportunities for learning

What children experience in their activities is a combination of content, the way in which they interact with that content, and the general classroom climate which influences all activities.

Content

The scientific ideas or concepts that can be developed in classroom activities depends on the content or subject matter. However, while the ideas to be developed are generally chosen to meet the requirements of the curriculum standards or guidelines, the choice of particular subject matter is generally left to the school and teacher. So, for example, in the case of the National

Curriculum, the programme of study refers to children learning about the properties of materials, but does not specify which materials, apart from referring to them as 'everyday' materials, or how these activities should be carried out. However, if the children are to engage with the activities in ways that give opportunity to learn, it follows that the content should:

- be sufficiently accessible to the children so that it is possible for them to make links between their activities and previous experience. Among other things this means using simple, robust and safe equipment rather than complex science apparatus that may come between the children and the observations to be made;
- relate to their environment, not only so that is it familiar but so that they are learning about the things around them;
- stimulate interest of all the children, both boys and girls and those of different ethnic and social backgrounds. It is important that all children should be able to find links between new experiences and their previous experience;
- provide the potential for children to acquire some ownership of the questions they answer through their enquiries.

Classroom interactions

The development of process skills and attitudes, which should be an aim of all science activities, is dependent on the way they encounter the content. This is influenced by the classroom organisation, whether children work in groups, and if so of what size and composition, whether they follow instructions on workcards or sheets, etc. These are matters taken up in Chapter 9. Here we focus on the nature of the interactions between teacher and children, between children and the materials they are studying, and among children. These interactions should be such that children are encouraged to:

- observe and raise questions and develop hypotheses based on their ideas;
- share ideas and listen to other points of view;
- test ideas of their own or of others;
- use evidence in coming to conclusions;
- compare initial ideas with emerging ones;
- review their investigations to suggest improvements.

Classroom climate

The view of learning as change in ideas means that there has to be willingness to propose ideas in the first place, and then to put the ideas to the test to see if they work in explaining things and so face the possibility of finding that they don't work and having to find alternatives. This involves some risk on the part of learners and some may be uneasy about exposing their idea in case it is found not to work. Thus teachers have to take positive steps to avoid a classroom atmosphere that would inhibit children airing and sharing ideas. For example it is important for teachers to show genuine interest in what the children think, by phrasing questions carefully (see pages 76 to 80) and allowing time for children to give considered answers.

It is all too easy to indicate that some ideas are more welcome than others. The result is that children try to guess what the teacher wants rather than say what they really think. To avoid this teachers find two courses of action effective: making no judgemental comment on the ideas children provide, accepting all as worthy of attention; and avoiding identifying ideas with particular children. When all ideas are drawn together for discussion, then children's own comments will eliminate the 'far out' ones, which can be dropped by common consent without anyone losing face.

In a supportive classroom it should be not only accepted but expected that ideas change. Teachers can help by talking about how their own ideas have changed and by encouraging children to recognise the changes in their ideas and to value this as evidence of learning. When discussion of this kind takes place the teachers can encourage children to reflect on what made them change their ideas, thus helping them to reflect on the process of their learning.

A classroom that supports learning is also one that enables children to take some responsibility for their own learning, through access to materials and sources of information. This can only happen without chaos ensuing if the expectation has been set up that children will use these things with care and thought for others.

Criteria for evaluating activities

From these arguments we can identify criteria that need to be met if activities are to provide real opportunities for learning. The following are adapted from Harlen and Elstgeest (1992). They take the form of questions that can be asked about planned or possible activities.

Does the activity:
- give the opportunity for children to apply and develop their ideas about scientific concepts, that is, is the content relevant and interesting to them?
- enable children to use and develop science process skills, that is, is there room for the children to do the thinking or is it all done for them?
- encourage scientific attitudes, that is, give opportunity for children to exercise some choice?
- engage the interests of the children and relate to real life and their everyday experience?

- appeal equally to boys and girls and to those of all cultural and ethnic backgrounds?
- provide experience of learning through interaction with things around?
- involve the use of simple and safe equipment and materials which are familiar to the children?
- use readily available materials and equipment?
- involve children in working cooperatively and in combining their ideas?

The process of developing and deciding how to use criteria such as these is most helpful when undertaken by the teachers who will use them so that they are committed to the values they embody. Such criteria are useful in several ways. They can be used to evaluate activities to find out to what extent intended learning opportunities have been provided and intentions put into practice. They provide justifications of the experiences given to children. If shared with parents and others involved in children's education they help to communicate reasons in terms of learning outcomes for the way of working in science.

A further advantage of making explicit the criteria on which we evaluate and select activities is that it provides a basis for adapting and improving activities at the planning stage, as in the following example.

Using criteria in adapting activities

Take the example of the activity presented to children on the workcard in Figure 7.1

There are some obvious reasons why this is limited as a learning experience although it is certainly an activity most children would enjoy. It is perhaps useful to recognise what is valuable about the activity before criticising it. It is capable of relating to children's interests across a broad spectrum, with no obvious gender or cultural bias. It uses simple and safe materials, which are familiar and cheap and it would be an easy activity for teachers to manage. On the other hand there are many ways in which the activity could be changed to meet other criteria. For example:

- *Encouraging attitudes – stimulating curiosity.* The activity might begin with the experience of throwing several parachutes, of different sizes and even shapes, and noticing how they fall. The question as to why the differences would inevitably be raised.
- *Opportunity for skill development.* Opportunities for children to develop their process skills are limited by the lack of any investigation once the parachute is constructed. There are many variables which affect the fall of the parachute, such as shape, area, length of strings, which children should explore in a controlled way as they test out various ideas about why there are differences between one and another.

Parachute
- Cut a 14-inch square from sturdy plastic
- Cut 4 pieces of string 14 inches long
- Securely tape or tie a string to each corner of the plastic
- Tie the free ends of the 4 strings together in a knot. Be sure the strings are all the same length
- Tie a single string about 6 inches long to the knot
- Add a weight, such as a washer to the free end of the string
- Pull the parachute up in the centre. Squeeze the plastic to make it as flat as possible
- Fold the parachute twice
- Wrap the string loosely around the plastic
- Throw the parachute up into the air

Results The parachute opens and slowly carries the weight to the ground

Why? The weight falls first, unwinding the string because the parachute being larger, is held back by the air. The air fills the plastic slowing down the rate of descent if the weight falls quickly a smaller object needs to be used.

Figure 7.1

- *Working cooperatively and combining ideas.* There could be instructions for pooling ideas within a group, planning how to find out 'what happens if…' and preparing a group report to others. At intervals in the work the children should meet together as a class to listen to reports of each others' progress and share ideas.
- *Opportunity for scientific concept development.* A main point of the activity is to enable children to recognise the role of air in slowing down the fall of the parachute. With this in mind it would, therefore, be useful for children to observe how quickly the parachute falls when it is not allowed to open. Exploration of larger and smaller parachutes might further children's ideas about the effect of the air. The question of why the parachute falls at all could also be discussed leading to a recognition of the main forces acting on the parachute when it is falling. Giving the 'answer' to why the parachute moves slowly is not allowing the children to use and explore their own ideas; so this part should be omitted.

- *Relating to real life and everyday experience.* The uses of air resistance are many and not restricted to parachute descents from aircraft. Children should be encouraged to think about air resistance in relation to horizontal movement, in yachts and sailing ships as well as in slowing aircraft in landing on short runways and aircraft carriers. They can be challenged to think about the kind of materials and construction which is needed in each case. They will also be able to relate to more everyday events, such as riding a bicycle in a strong wind and the 'helicopter' wings of sycamore seeds seen drifting gently down to the ground.

There are two main consequences of modifying the activity in these kinds of ways:

1. First it will depend more on the teacher than on a workcard, although careful wording of worksheets or workcards can go a long way in encouraging children to use their own ideas and think things out for themselves (see Chapter 9).
2. Second, it will undoubtedly take up more time. This has to be balanced by the much greater learning which takes place. Further, had the same time as required for the modified activity been used for several of the kind of the original there would still be no opportunity for some of the learning which is required.

Fewer activities, with more opportunity for different kinds of learning, for discussion and for developing skills will be a greater contribution to learning with understanding. Using criteria such as the ones above will help in making this case.

Summary

- The aim of helping children to learn with understanding – that is, to make new ideas part of their way of thinking – raises many issues about the kind of activities and classroom interactions that should be provided.
- Criteria for selecting content include equal relevance to the interests and environment of all children regardless of gender and social and ethnic background, and accessibility to understanding through children's own enquiries.
- Interactions between children and teacher, children and materials and children with each other should stimulate the use of process skills and foster scientific attitudes.
- As an overall context for learning, it is important to establish a classroom climate that encourages children to express ideas, accepts that ideas change and helps children to take responsibility for their learning.
- These criteria can be used to select the most useful activities and to adapt others to make them richer learning experiences.

Chapter 8

Teachers' and children's roles in learning

Introduction

In Chapter 7 the spotlight was on the nature of children's science activities and the way in which their design influences children's interaction with the materials they study and consequently what they can learn from them. In this chapter we shift the focus to the roles in learning of the main actors – the teacher and children.

Among the characteristics of effective teaching in science, widely recognised by inspectors (OfSTED 1998, SEED 1999) and by researchers (Monk and Osborne 2000, Harlen 1999), the following are invariably included (there are others which are relevant to later chapters):

- teachers being well prepared and clear about the objective of the lesson and the learning outcomes intended;
- teachers sharing this information with children in ways appropriate to age and stage, so the children are clear about expectations;
- lessons having a clear structure of phases in which different kinds of activity take place, such as introduction, discussion, practical work, and ending with whole class discussion of outcomes and opportunity to reflect on procedures and learn from mistakes;
- raising expectations of children and asking questions that require higher levels of thinking;
- structuring group work to promote collaboration and discussion.

The intention here is to look at what these mean in practice. We do this in the context of specific activities and summarise in general terms. We then consider two important procedures that teachers use to advance children's learning: asking questions and scaffolding new ideas and procedures.

The teacher's role

It is useful to have an example of classroom science activities in mind in this discussion. For this we return to Graham's lesson, described in Chapter 1. The main soil investigation activities occupied a whole afternoon and some of the next morning (when they observed the soil and water mixtures after time for settling), while the growth trials were spread over the following weeks. The main soil activities in the first afternoon can be divided into six phases involving the teacher and four involving the children.

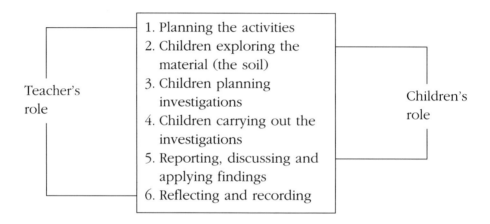

Teacher's role

1. Planning the activities
2. Children exploring the material (the soil)
3. Children planning investigations
4. Children carrying out the investigations
5. Reporting, discussing and applying findings
6. Reflecting and recording

Children's role

The first and last of these phases take place out of lesson time. Phases 2 to 5 involve both teacher and children.

Planning the activities

This phase involved thinking through all parts of the lesson, keeping in mind the ideas that the teacher wanted the children to develop (about the structure and composition of soil and how this relates to its properties) and the enquiry skills that they would need to use and develop. He consulted sources of ideas for classroom investigations and decided to adapt these so that the children had a chance to plan their own enquiries. He decided against making work cards and instead wrote on a large piece of paper the four things for the children to focus on in their initial exploration. He planned the kinds of questions to ask in each phase of the lesson and how he would find out the children's ideas. (See later in this chapter, page 78). He also planned to make particular note of observations of one group in order to assess their progress in developing process skills (see Chapter 16).

Exploring

While the children were engaged in exploring the soil samples, the teacher visited each group. The questions he asked were carefully phrased to reflect his interest in what the children were finding and what they were thinking about it. Where necessary he reminded them of the four points to guide their explorations.

Children planning investigations

This phase was begun by collecting observations from each group, asking for evidence to support the statements made. Ideas about what plants need from soil in order to grow were then pooled, Graham writing them on a large sheet of paper as the children suggested them. When they had given all their ideas he helped the children to think about air in the soil, scaffolding their thinking so that they agreed that this should be added. The question of which soil was 'best' was then discussed in terms of what evidence would be needed to decide this. The children quickly saw that the best soil would be the one with the most of the things that had been listed. In this way, the question was turned into an investigable one. Each group selected one of the features to investigate, knowing that they would need to share findings with others to arrive at an overall result. So communicating in an effective way to others was part of their task. Graham helped them with their planning by asking questions that made them think about the variables that should be controlled and what was to be measured. Again he introduced ideas about how to do these thing by scaffolding.

Carrying out the investigations

While the children collected equipment they needed and made a start, Graham was busy making sure that their requirements were met (he anticipated most needs but there were other things suggested by the children). He then observed the practical work of all the groups, focusing on the children's enquiry skills and paying particular attention to the group chosen as targets for on-going assessment. He asked questions to probe the children's understanding of the ideas involved. The investigations did not take very long and when completed the groups settled to deciding how to report what they had found.

Reporting, discussing and applying findings

In the whole class discussion after each group reported its findings, different views were expressed about the outcome of combining results. Graham insisted that they should use evidence to support their views. He then asked them to apply their combined findings in considering the garden soil samples. This led to another investigation, this time a whole-class activity, children from each group helping to set up the jars of soil and water. The next day, before continuing, he made time to involve the children in reflecting on what they had learned from the afternoon's work.

Reflecting and recording

Following the activities, Graham annotated his lesson notes to record what had been done. He also used other records to note the observations of individual children during the practical work. He noted weaknesses in understanding and in enquiry skills that would need attention in future lessons.

The children's roles in learning

What role did the children play in this? What they did physically is clear, but their role was more than carrying out the required actions; they also had to think, to make decisions, to reflect and to communicate. Without these there would have been no learning. What was learned depended not only the ability to do these things but the willingness to become involved, to use evidence and to modify their ideas. The children's role was in response to the teacher's actions, so it is helpful to place what they did beside a summary of the teacher's role in the activities.

Teacher's role	Children's role
Planning the lesson	
• Decide the main ideas, skills and attitudes to be developed • Plan how to introduce the topic, linking with previous activities • Plan how to find out children's ideas • Plan questions to ask • Consider possible activities from various sources • Select target group for observations	

Teacher's role	Children's role
Exploring	
• Provide experiences which encourage exploration • Set the scene and indicate purpose of activities • Ask questions to find out children's ideas	• Make sure they understand the purpose of the exploration • Engage with the materials and try to explain observations • Raise questions where not understood
Children's investigation planning	
• Involve children in deciding investigations • Clarify questions until they are investigable • Help children to plan effective investigation	• Put questions into investigable form • Make predictions based on possible explanations • Suggest ways of collecting evidence to answer question or test hypothesis
Carrying out investigations	
• Provide equipment needed • Observe children's procedures and note process skills • Ask questions to probe understanding	• Carry out investigation systematically, collecting evidence using measurement where required • Record results in suitable ways • Interpret results • Try to explain findings
Reporting, discussing and applying findings	
• Arrange for sharing of results • Hold discussions on the interpretation of results • Ask question requiring application of findings	• Report their work, individually or as a group • Use evidence in interpreting results • Be prepared to change ideas if there is convincing evidence
Reflecting and recording	
• Record activities undertaken and observations during practical work • Reflect upon progress made and further help needed.	

Teachers' questions

Questioning is frequently mentioned in the teacher's role and is perhaps the main means of encouraging children's thinking and use of process skills. But what kinds of questions? Elstgeest (1985a) distinguished between 'productive' and 'unproductive' teachers' questions. The latter are questions that ask directly for facts or reasons where there is clearly a right answer. The former are far more useful in helping children's investigation and thinking. There are different kinds of productive question which serve different purposes in encouraging enquiry:

- *Attention-focusing questions*, which have the purpose of drawing children's attention to features which might otherwise be missed. 'Have you noticed . . . ?' 'What do you think of that?' These questions are ones which children often supply for themselves and the teacher may have to raise them only if observation is superficial and attention fleeting.
- *Comparison questions* – 'In what ways are these leaves different?' 'What is the same about these two pieces of rock?' – draw attention to patterns and lay the foundation for using keys and categorising objects and events.
- *Measuring and counting questions* – 'How much?' 'How long?' – are particular kinds of comparison questions which take observation into the quantitative.
- *Action questions* – 'What happens if you shine light from a torch onto a worm?' 'what happens when you put an ice cube into warm water?' 'What happens if . . .', are the kinds of question which lead to investigations
- *Problem-posing questions* give children a challenge and leave them to work out how to meet it. Questions such as 'Can you find a way to make your string telephone sound clearer?' 'How can you make a coloured shadow?' require children to have experience or knowledge which they can apply in tackling them. Without such knowledge the question may not even make sense to the children. It is in relation to this point that the matter of the right time for a question arises.

Cutting across these categories are differences in the form and wording of questions. Chief among these are differences between open and closed questions and between 'person-centred' and 'subject-centred' questions.

Open and closed questions

Although the distinction between open and closed questions has become familiar there are many occasions where closed questions are asked when open ones would be more appropriate. The research of Galton, Simon and Croll (1980) showed that on average only 5 per cent of all teachers' questions were open, while almost 20 per cent were closed and 30 per cent requesting facts. Therefore it is perhaps the value of open questions which needs to be pointed out rather than their nature. Open questions give access to children's views about things, their feelings and their ideas, and promote enquiry by the children. Closed questions, while still inviting thought about the learning task, require the child to respond to ideas or comments of the teacher. For example these questions:

'What do you notice about these crystals?'
'What has happened to your bean since you planted it?'

are more likely to lead to answers useful to both teacher and children than their closed versions:

'Are all the crystals the same size?'
'How much has your bean grown since you planted it?'

Closed questions suggest that there is a right answer and children may not attempt an answer if they are afraid of being wrong.

Person-centred and subject-centred questions

Another way of avoiding the 'right answer' deterrent is to recognise the difference between a *subject-centred* question, which asks directly about the subject matter, and a *person-centred* question, which asks for the child's ideas about the subject matter. Subject-centred questions are such as:

'Why do heavy lorries take longer to stop than lighter ones?'
'Why did your plant grow more quickly in the cupboard?'

which cannot be answered unless you know, or at least think you know, the reasons. By contrast the person-centred versions:

'Why do you think heavy lorries take longer to stop than lighter ones?'
'Why do you think you plant grew more quickly when it was in the cupboard?'

can be attempted by anyone who has been thinking about these things (and we assume the questions would not be asked unless this was the case) and has some ideas about them, whether or not correct. Where there is interest in children's reasoning, person-centred questions are clearly essential, but at other times they are a more effective, and more friendly, way of involving children in discussions which help in making sense of their work.

Questions to promote thinking and action

We shall be considering here questions which are designed for three purposes: finding out about children's ideas, developing their ideas and leading to the use

and development of process skills. The kinds of questions which seem best suited
to these purposes can be described in terms of the categories and forms above.

Questions for finding out children's ideas

The following questions were among those designed to be used by teachers to find
out children's ideas. These particular question were used when children had been
involved in handling, observing and drawing sprouting and non-sprouting potatoes:

'What do you think is coming out of the potato?'
'What do you think is happening inside the potato?'
'Why do you think this is happening to the potato?'
'Do you think the potato plant will go on growing?'
'Can you think of anything else that this happens to?'

(Russell and Watt 1990, p. A-10)

They can readily be seen to be open, person-centred questions, since there was
a need for children to be given every encouragement to express their thoughts
at that time before investigations started, so that the teachers would know the
children's initial ideas.

Questions for developing children's ideas

According to the kinds of ideas the children start from, activities to develop them
may take various forms: testing ideas by using them to make predictions and
then devising an investigation to see if there is evidence of the prediction being
correct; applying ideas in problem-solving; making further observations or
comparisons; discussing the meaning of words; consulting secondary sources.
Questions can be used to initiate these activities and to encourage children's
participation in them.

Encouraging children to test their ideas means that these ideas have first of
all to be in a testable form. 'It's the rudder which make this boat go better than
before' is not testable until the particular aspects of the rudder and the meaning
of 'go better' are specified. Questions of the kind:

'How would you show that your idea works?'
'What would happen which showed that it was better?'
'What could you do to make it even better?'

require the specification of variables which are only vaguely identified in the
initial statement. When it comes to carrying out a test then many of the questions
for developing process skills, in the next section, could be used.

When the development of children's ideas seems to require further
experience and comparisons between things, then attention-focusing, measuring
and counting and comparison questions are the most useful. For applying ideas,

the problem-posing questions are appropriate. For discussing the meaning of words, it is best to ask for examples rather than abstract definitions. One of the words which children often use imprecisely is 'dissolving'; indeed they often talk about their own actions as 'dissolving' things, when they probably mean mixing together. These uses can be clarified through questions such as:

'Show me what you do to 'dissolve' the butter?'
'How will you know if the sugar has dissolved?'
'How can you make something dissolve?'

and other questions for clarifying words, discussed in Chapter 12.

Questions for developing process skills

These examples of questions relating to some of the process skills are set in the context of children investigating a collection of different seeds. They are designed to require children to use the process skills in providing an answer.

Observing

- What do you notice that is the same about these seeds?
- What differences do you notice between seeds of the same kind?
- Could you tell the difference between them with your eyes closed?
- What happens when you look as them using the lens?

Predicting

- What do you think the seeds will grow into?
- What can we do to them to make them grow faster?
- What do you think will happen if they have water without soil?
- What do you think will happen if we give them more (or less) water/light/warmth?

Planning

- What will you need to do to find out . . . (if the seeds need soil to grow)?
- How will you make it fair (to be sure that it is the soil and not something else which is making the seeds grow)?
- What equipment will you need?
- What will you look for to find out the result?

Interpreting

- Did you find any connection between . . . (how fast the plant grew and the amount of water/light/warmth it had)?
- Is there any connection between the size of the seed planted and the size of the plant?
- What did make a difference to how fast the seeds began to grow?
- Was soil necessary for the seeds to grow?

Questions that ask children to think require time to answer. Teachers often expect an answer too quickly and in doing so deter children from thinking. Research shows that extending the time that a teacher waits for children to answer increases markedly the quality of the answers (Budd-Rowe, 1974). This is a case where patience is rewarded and time saved overall by spending a little more in allowing children to think about their answers before turning to someone else, or rephrasing the question.

Scaffolding

Too much attention to teachers' questions can give the impression that all the ideas used come from the children. If this were the case there would be a danger of recycling ideas from limited experience and not making the headway that an input of new ideas might make possible. It is part of raising the expectations of children to offer them more advanced ways of thinking and more scientific ideas to try out. Indeed there were at least three occasions when Graham (see pp 2–3) supplied ideas to his class, but in each case he was careful to 'scaffold' their use by the children.

Scaffolding means supporting children in considering an idea or a way of testing an idea that they have not proposed themselves but are capable of making 'their own'. The judgement of when this is likely to be possible has to be made by the teacher, taking into account the existing ideas or skills of the children and how far they are from taking the next step. It often means the teacher making links for the children between experiences and understanding they already have but have not linked up for themselves.

In theoretical terms, it means finding what Vygotsky (1962) introduced as the 'zone of proximal development'. This is the point just beyond existing ideas, where the learner is likely to be able to use new ideas with help. What the teacher does in scaffolding is to suggest the new idea and provide support for the children while they use it and, finding it helps to make sense, begin to incorporate it into their thinking. The teacher might ask children to 'Try this idea' or 'Try looking at it this way' or 'Suppose…' An example might be 'Suppose the water that disappears from the puddle goes into the air?' or 'Suppose the sun is not moving but the Earth is turning round…' Each of the 'supposed' ideas can be used to make a prediction that can be tested and as a result children can see that they do help to explain experience.

Analogies often provide the new idea when the link to something that children are trying to understand is pointed out by the teacher. Scaffolding can be used to develop skills, too. It is indeed familiar in teaching new skills such as using a microscope or a calculator. In these cases the learner needs to be told what to do at first, may need a reminder later and eventually uses the skill confidently.

It is important to underline that scaffolding ideas is not the same as telling children the 'right answer'. It is essentially enabling children to take a further step in progress that is within their reach. It depends on teachers having a good knowledge of their children's ideas and skills and using this in deciding the next steps and helping children to advance their thinking (see Chapter 19).

Summary

- The teacher's role in helping children's learning through enquiry begins before the children's activities, in planning of intended learning, how to introduce the activities, questions to ask to find out about children's ideas, and observations to make.
- During the activities the teacher helps children through questioning and scaffolding, ensuring that equipment needs are met and holding discussions of results in groups and with the whole class.
- Teacher's questions that are open and person-centred in form are best suited to encouraging children to use their ideas and process skills. It is equally important for teachers to allow time for children to think about their answers.
- An important part of the teacher's role is to scaffold children's thinking, that is, to suggest an idea or way of reasoning and help children to use it and take it into their own mental framework.
- The children's role is to engage with the materials, raise questions, apply process skills in answering them through investigation and use evidence to review and possibly change their ideas.

Chapter 9

The role and organisation of practical activities

Introduction

Practical activities are at the heart of primary science because they provide first-hand experience, the channel through which a great deal of learning takes place in the early years. Interaction with materials is important to learning, but it has far greater value if it is accompanied by social interaction that helps in making sense of it and making links between ideas from one situation and another. This chapter begins by elaborating this point, placing practical activities in the context of learning activities in general. The second part mentions briefly some problems associated with practical work in secondary school science that might well provide warnings to heed in primary science. We then look at different kinds of practical work, beyond 'fair testing', and finally consider the issues arising in the organisation of practical activities relating to group size and composition and the use of work cards.

The role of first-hand experience in children's learning

Seeing for oneself is the most direct way of knowing that something exists or happens. This still applies to adults even though our experience makes it more likely that we can learn about new things in other ways, by reading or hearing others tell about them, for instance. We can used our experience of similar things or events, and our imagination, to envisage something we have not seen. For children, who have much less experience, things are different. Words can conjure up false images and misunderstandings are common unless children see for themselves. We only have to recall the children who link milk with cartons and supermarkets rather than cows, and those who have no idea of the size of objects that they have only seen in photographs.

Seeing, or more widely, observing, is only one kind of direct experience. More significant for learning science is physical 'interaction', when you see the results of carrying out some action on an object. Interaction opens up the possibility of explaining things in terms of cause and effect; and science is about explaining, not just describing, things. But physical interaction alone is not enough to develop ideas that help children understand the things around them. Social interaction has an important part to play. The give and take in sharing ideas has a double benefit. It is a very common experience for adults as well as children to clarify their own understanding by explaining to others what they think. In addition, listening to others, particularly peers, brings the further benefits of access to alternative views and of using these to create a shared understanding.

In the classroom, therefore, the value for learning of direct experience and physical interaction with materials is vastly increased by discussion among children as well as between teacher and children (see also Chapter 12.) This has important consequences for the organisation of practical work. It is not enough for children to use and investigate materials; time must be spent on discussing what sense they are making of what they have found. This may mean less time for doing, but increased learning from what is done. It becomes even more important to select and plan activities carefully with a clear idea of the learning intentions. In this context it is useful to note some criticisms of practical work arising from research into secondary school science.

Lessons from secondary science

Research into the impact of conventional laboratory work involving the use of scientific equipment has provided little support for the ambitious claims made about its value in learning. Among these claims are the development of students' skills and conceptual understanding and increased motivation for learning science. Although most secondary students report that they like practical work, what they say they like about it is the freedom to work in groups at their own pace rather than appreciating that it helps their understanding. Indeed some practical work is found confusing rather than illuminating.

Some of the reasons for this appear to be that:
• A great deal of students' attention in laboratory work is absorbed by details of procedures rather than the purpose of the practical activities. Students are mainly concerned with how to set things up, what to do in what order, how to write up their work, etc. and spend little time talking about the meaning of what they are doing.

- Many tasks require quite complex procedures, often because of the specialised equipment being used, and students have to follow closely the instructions for the steps to take but do not always know why they are taking these steps.
- Often students don't understand the purpose of the practical work and so may not pay attention to the significant events.
- If the result that the teacher intended is not achieved, students lose interest and see the practical work as purposeless.

These points don't always apply, of course, but where they do they indicate a lack of ownership of the work on the part of the students and an ineffective use of time and other resources.

But these findings do not constitute an argument against practical work *per se*. There remains a strong case for claiming that practical work can be effective in giving students experience that they can get in no other way. In particular the potential learning is

- about the world around, from first-hand experience of the phenomena that have to be explained. As Hodson (1992) pointed out:

  It isn't enough to read about magnesium burning with a brilliant white flame or about light bending as it passes through a prism. Students need to experience these things at first-hand and to handle objects and organisms for themselves in order to build up a stock of personal experience. (p. 110)

- about how evidence is collected and used in science and how scientific theories and experiments are related. This learning should be implicit in the way science is taught, but made explicit through reflecting on how experiments help to build theory and how, in turn, theories lead to experiments (Hodson 1993)
- about what is involved in undertaking a scientific enquiry. The only way to know how to do a scientific investigation is to do one from beginning to end. This means having some experience of taking through a complete investigation, though this might be an occasional rather than a regular experience.

The messages from the research, however, do point to the need to consider what learning is intended and to decide whether practical experience is the best way of achieving it and, if it is, what kinds of activities are most appropriate.

So what lessons for primary science can we learn from this? Some obvious ones are:

- Decide whether first-hand experience is the best way of achieving the learning intended. There are many other kinds of activity that can help children's understanding besides direct interaction with materials, for example, games, simulations, drama and acting out, visits, and demonstrations.

- If first-hand experience is appropriate, decide what kind. While all practical work should involve investigation, not all investigations are of the same type.
- Share with the children the purpose of the work and ensure that it is answering a real question for the children.
- Involve the children in decisions about what to do and planning how to do it. There is then no risk that they don't know why they are doing things, since they decided this for themselves.
- Use simple and familiar equipment so that the complexities of its use don't present a barrier between the children and the phenomena they are studying.
- Organise small and whole-class discussion of what has been learned both from the findings and from the procedures used.

Types of investigations

The dictionary definition of 'investigate' is to 'observe, study or closely examine'. All the practical work involving first-hand study of materials would therefore be called investigation (or enquiry, since this is defined in terms of investigation). There are different kinds of investigation, however, which emphasise different process skills and are appropriate for investigating different kinds of questions. The main types are: information-seeking; comparing or fair testing; pattern-finding; hypothesis-generating; how-to-do-it investigations.

Information-seeking investigations

These are investigations carried out to see what happens, either as a natural process unfolds or when some action is taken. Examples are seeing eggs hatch, raising butterflies or silk worms, observing the expansion of water on freezing, seeing what things dissolve in water. Usually these concern the behaviour of particular living things or substances and there is no comparison between things. They emphasise observation and communication skills. They are relevant at all stages but particularly for younger children since they help to build the 'stock of personal experience' that is needed for making sense of later experience. Sometimes an information-seeking investigation is the first step to another type of investigation. For instance, seeing which things float or sink can be an end in itself or it can lead to a hypothesis-generating investigation about what it is about things that make them sink or float.

Comparing or fair-testing investigations

This type of investigation often begins from a 'which is best?' question. Which detergent washes the clothes best? Which fertilizer is best for the plants? Which paper towel is best for mopping up water? The first step in these investigations is to turn the question into an investigable one by specifying the meaning of 'best' in a way that identifies the basis of comparison. So 'which type of sugar dissolves best?' has to be turned into, for example, 'which type of sugar dissolves most quickly?' These are popular and useful investigations since they involve children in identifying and controlling variables (amount of sugar, amount of water, temperature of water, presence or absence of stirring, etc). They also have the appeal of yielding information about real things from the actions carried out by the children. However it's necessary to avoid a routine or formulaic approach, when the value for thinking becomes diminished. This is avoided and the investigations given increased value when they lead on to questions about *why* one thing is 'better', in the way defined, than another.

Pattern-finding investigations

These apply where there is a relationship to be found between variables associated with the behaviour of a thing or substance. Examples are: the note produced by blowing across the top of a bottle with different amounts of water in it; the direction of a shadow cast by the sun and the time of day; the number of turns given to a wind-up toy and how far it will go. These investigations involve the same skills as 'comparing' investigations since the effect of changes in one variable have to be tested fairly, with other variables or conditions kept the same. However, there is additional emphasis in these investigations on the interpretation of findings and they provide valuable opportunities for considering the extent to which conclusions about cause and effect can be drawn. Generally there is not a direct relationship, and there is another step in the chain of events. So while the clockwork toy car may go further the more turns of the key, the effect of turning the key is to give the car different amounts of energy which enable the car to move different distances. Similarly the fact that trees of the same kind with more growth rings tend to be taller does not mean that one causes the other; there is another factor that links the two. So these investigations provide experiences that help children to distinguish between an association between things and a cause and effect relationship.

Hypothesis-generating investigations

These are investigations which seek explanations to things such as: the appearance of dew on grass overnight; the misting of windows in certain conditions; the echo of foot-steps in some places; the behaviour of a 'Cartesian diver'. At the primary level the explanations are often in terms of the conditions or events that are associated with these observations rather than general scientific principles. The investigations begin with open-ended exploration of the phenomenon leading to the generation of a range of possible explanations. These can be checked against the evidence so far available by using the hypotheses to make predictions. For example, if the hypothesis is that the echo is caused by the kind of surface of the path, do you find an echo in all places where there is this kind of surface? The hypotheses surviving this first testing are then the subject of further investigation, which might well involve some fair-testing. Sometimes the end product is making something happen, such as a making an object that sinks in water float, or vice versa. This involves trying different things based on possible explanations of why things sink or float.

How-to-do-it investigations

These are investigations where the end product may be an artefact or a construction that meets particular requirements – a model bridge that will support a certain load, for example. These are problems of a technological nature though involving many scientific process skills and ideas. As discussed in Chapter 24, it is not necessary to make a clean distinction in children's activities between science and technology, but it is important for the teacher to be aware of the difference and of the particular learning that can be developed through these activities.

Organising practical work

In making decisions about organising the practical work it is important to keep in mind the features that enhance the value of first-hand experience; the physical interaction with materials and social interaction.

Group size and composition

Group size has to be a compromise between what is desirable and what is possible in terms of the size of the whole class. Groups of four are ideal for the youngest children but 8 to 12 year olds can be in groups as large as six if this is necessary, although a smaller number is desirable. The potential for genuine collaborative work, where the work is a combined effort and not a collection of individual efforts carried out by children working in proximity, diminishes the larger the group size increases above the optimum, but it can also be influenced by the way a task is set up and the encouragement of the teacher.

In relation to the composition of groups, there are quite different approaches practised and advocated both by teachers themselves and by others For example, a teacher writing in *Primary Science Review* (no 17, 1991, p. 8) described her preference for grouping by 'the level of understanding each child has of a particular concept'. In the same publication another teacher wrote 'children of differing abilities would work together easily – they only needed to be able to communicate with each other'. Advice from inspectors in Scotland is that 'Allocating pupils to a small numbers of attainment groups for science allows them to apply their understanding at an appropriate level...' (SEED 1999, p. 21). Conclusions from research, however, point clearly in the direction of favouring mixed ability groups.

In an important study of group composition and learning, researchers compared the change in ideas of groups of children some of whom were in groups of similar initial ideas and some in groups composed of children with different ideas about the topic of the task to be undertaken. The research provided strong and consistent evidence that children in groups whose ideas were initially different progressed markedly more that those in the groups with initially similar ideas to each other. The findings enabled the researchers to conclude with confidence that there was more advance in the ideas of those children who worked with others of different ideas from their own than in the groups where the ideas were the same.

What is particularly noteworthy in this research is that the differential progress was more apparent at a later date than during the group work. When children were assessed immediately after group work as well as six weeks later, there was no evidence of immediate change in ideas, but this did appear, to a significantly greater extent in the groups with differing ideas, later. 'Thus, there is a strong suggestion that progress took place after the group tasks, indicating that interaction when concepts differ is a catalyst for development and not the locus of it' (Howe, Primary Science Review, no. 13, 1990, p. 27).

So if we judge only from the way the group work goes then there is very little to choose between one basis for grouping and the other. However the exposure to different ideas from their own appears to lay the foundation for greater learning in all children over a longer period of time.

The researchers followed up the obvious alternative explanations for the differences (for example that further work at school, or experience at home was responsible) but found nothing which could account for them.

Allocating group activities

The questions here are:

should all groups be working on science at the same time?
should groups be working on the same activities as each other?

The questions are interconnected and so best considered together.

Again practicalities will modify any theoretical ideal. Where specialised equipment is needed and available only in limited quantities, or requires close teacher supervision, then there is no alternative to having one group at a time using it. What other children will be doing and whether groups will take turns at the same activities remain more open to teachers' decisions.

Where these restrictions do not apply, which is for most of the time, opinions vary about these questions. One school of thought advocates that the amount of science going on at one time is best limited to one or two groups, with others engaged on non-science activities. However, some arguments against this arise from experience: the science work can be a distraction to others; the teacher's attention is too widely divided; and there is no opportunity for whole-class discussion of experiences shared by everyone.

A more effective alternative is to have groups working on science all at the same time, with the activities of each being different but all linked to a single theme (as in the case of Graham's class, page 2). The reasons for this being preferred are easy to see, since it solves the problem of distraction and enables class discussions to take place on a shared theme with enough differences between groups to create interest in each others' findings.

Work cards

The role that work cards might have in children's investigations is best decided in relation to the purpose of the practical work. If this is to give first-hand experience of phenomena, a card can be an efficient way to ensure that children gather together the necessary materials and are guided by some with 'attention-focusing' questions and 'comparison' questions (see Chapter 8, page 76) or simple instructions such as the ones used by Graham (Chapter 1). Activities which invite children to explore materials may be selected from published cards but teachers may prefer to produce their own, particularly if they want to use these activities to gain access to children's ideas.

Where the purpose is to enable children to find things out from manipulating materials, a work card, if used, should contain some 'action' questions and 'problem posing' questions, but not give instructions for what to do. In producing or adapting workcards, the questions should be a written form of the teachers' questions suggested in Chapter 8 for finding out children's ideas and for promoting thinking and action.

Instructions on cards can also give children ideas about how to organise themselves to share ideas. Varying devices can be suggested, such as: *Get one person to write down all the ideas in the group and then decide which you all agree with and which you don't.* Or: *Each write down your ideas on a slip of paper and stick them on one piece. Make sure you understand all the ideas even if you don't agree with them.*

However, when the purpose of the practical work is to give children an experience of carrying through a complete investigation of their own, a work card is unlikely to be appropriate. Such investigations have to be drawn from the children's own questions and ideas and guidance is best given in discussion with the teacher, when new ideas for procedures or explanations can be 'scaffolded' by the teacher as necessary. The action to be taken coming from the discussion could then be written down as an aide-memoire or as a check-list to remind children of what had been agreed. This is a useful device to ensure that matters relating to safety and care of equipment will not be forgotten. Such 'tailor-made' work cards are specific to particular groups of children and should be prepared by the teacher and children together, not written by the teacher beforehand.

Summary

- Children of primary school age learn best from first-hand experience and so practical work has a central role in their science education. The value of the practical experience is, however, increased by discussion and sharing ideas about how to make sense of what is seen or done.
- Research in secondary schools provides a warning that practical work may not improve learning unless its purpose is clear to children and teacher and children are involved in the planning, so that they know why certain steps have to be taken and what to look for in finding results.
- Although fair tests are the most popular types of investigation they are not always appropriate for answering a question. Other types are information-seeking, pattern-finding, hypothesis-generating and how-to-do-it investigations.
- Practical work is best organised, if possible, with children working in mixed ability groups of four or five, engaged on aspects of a common problem. They achieve more than any one group alone by sharing their findings and adding to a wider understanding of the problem.
- Work cards, if used, should pose questions that provoke enquiry and should avoid giving a set of instructions to follow. They are best seen as aide-memoires of planning in which children have been involved.

Chapter 10
Equipment and visits to support learning in science

Introduction

Objects and materials from the environment, and equipment for use in investigating them, are the basic essentials of scientific activity in the primary school. The materials have to be there for reasons discussed in the early chapters of this book – the importance of first-hand experience for children. What is fashioned from this basic raw material follows from the role which the teacher plays and the role which the children are given in the learning; matters discussed in other chapters. Here we are concerned with three aspects of the provision of materials for exploring and for use in investigations: selection and storage of equipment and materials in the school; access to those things outside which cannot be brought in and need to be studied in situ; and matters relating to safety both within and outside the classroom.

Equipment and materials

The effective use of equipment and materials means that storage and access have to be convenient and efficient from the point of view of time and maintenance. First, however, we consider what sorts of things have to be provided and stored.

Selecting equipment and materials

If we have in mind activities such as those with parachutes, with string telephones, with soil and rocks, with plants, with things that dissolve, things that float or sink, the equipment needed is what might be called 'everyday' rather than 'specialised'. A great deal of science work depends on using materials and equipment which will be available in an active primary classroom, such as:

boxes, plastic bottles and other containers, string, scissors, rulers, paper clips, drawing pins, elastic bands, glues, paper, card, plasticine, straws, marbles, pieces of fabric.

Specialised equipment is needed, particularly for the activities of older children and for topics relating to electricity, magnetism, reflection, forces and for the measurement of time, volume mass and temperature. This equipment will include:

torches, mirrors, coloured acetate sheets, glass blocks, triangular prisms, hand lenses, spirit thermometers, night lights, tuning forks, stop clocks and watches, springs, bathroom scales, pulleys, filter paper and funnels, insect cages, aquarium tanks, wood working and gardening tools, magnets, bulbs and bulb holders, wire, crocodile clips.

The list is not extensive. It could be very much longer, if laboratory equipment were purchased instead of employing 'everyday' things where they can be used. There are good reasons for keeping specialised equipment to the minimum. As noted in the last chapter, research involving observation of secondary science classes shows that the manipulation of laboratory equipment can absorb so much of students' attention that they spend little time attending to the events from which they can learn. If this happens in the secondary school it is even more likely to happen in primary schools. Thus using simple equipment is important not only because it is easy and cheap to obtain but because it does not create a barrier between the children and what they are exploring.

A third type of material that is needed is consumable; the flour and soap powder used in dissolving activities, the wood which is hammered, the wire used up in the home-made sonometer, the batteries, the aluminium foil, the fruits which are cut open, the seeds which are sown, etc. Shortage of these things causes the greatest frustration because they are what many of the children's activities are all about – the stuff of exploring materials from their surroundings. Some of these things can be obtained free, but by no means all. Furthermore, they cannot all be bought at one time of the year and stored. Schools need to set aside sums for these purchases and to establish, generally through the science subject leader or head teacher, a means of access to and control of, these funds.

Storing equipment and materials

Access is the key word in deciding a system of storage for equipment and materials. There are various possibilities and the advantages and disadvantages of each in a particular case will depend on the size, physical layout and curriculum planning of the school. We can do no more here than point out options.

A decision has to be made about central storage versus distribution of the equipment among classes. Apart from physical availability of a central store a major consideration is having someone to look after it. There are obvious advantages in sharing expensive items which are only infrequently used but some of these advantages are lost if the equipment is not kept in good order. Clearly the science subject leader, or coordinator, has to be willing and able, in the sense of having the time, to organise a central store and to check that items are not 'lost' by being put back in the wrong place or in an unsatisfactory condition.

Another decision is whether children should have access to the equipment as well as teachers. The problems of maintaining an orderly central store can be exacerbated by too many having access, yet the teacher will want children to help in the collection and return of equipment. The suggestion of appointing a few children to be 'monitors' or 'storekeepers' may be a solution. If the store is within each class the same considerations apply. If children are to have access then the labels used to classify the equipment should be ones that they will relate to and understand. There are considerable dividends for the initial investment of time when children are, perhaps, involved in drawing up lists of what equipment there is and creating rules for using the store.

Whether or not there is a central store, within a class the equipment for a certain session needs to be accessible to the children. The demands of providing group activities for all the children at once are of course considerable and require preplanning and preparation. The materials and equipment needed for a set of activities can be anticipated and a suitable selection made available without limiting what the children will be able to do using their own ideas. It is handy to have these materials on a trolley if possible so that they can easily be put safely out of the way when not being studied. When the equipment is being used the teacher should be able to depend on the help of the children to take responsibility for choosing, collecting and later returning it to its proper place. Building up a system for this is important in developing children's ability to take a part in facilitating their own learning as well as for the teacher's sanity. It involves making sure that children know what is available, where, and how to look after it and keep it tidy.

A third major decision point, which applies where a school or class organises science within topics, is whether equipment should be boxed by topic or stored as separate kinds of items. The topic box is a great convenience, but can tie up equipment which could be used for work outside the topic. This can lead to 'plundering' from the box with the chance of the item not being there when that topic is being used. The effort put into developing topic boxes is also a disincentive to changing topics, when perhaps they have outlived their freshness. The device of temporary topic boxes is a useful compromise. The box exists for as long as the topic is being used and is dismantled when moving onto another topic.

Visits and field trips

Visits to locations out of school provide important opportunities for children to make links between their classroom activities and everyday life and to see science in action. Places to visit can be divided into:

- natural locations (parks, seashore, wood, etc.) where there is no formal structure for visitors;
- places of work (factories, farms, airports, etc.) where there will be someone at the visit location to accompany the children on the premises;
- science museums or centres, where groups can be supervised by teachers with or without help from museum staff, but where there is usually available some material to help plan a visit;
- other locations (castles, historic buildings) which do not at first appear to link to science but where there is potential for a science focus.

In addition, where a visit involves a journey by bus or train, this should be regarded as a valuable experience in its own right for observing, questioning and gathering information.

In all cases, the first step is for the teacher to make a visit well in advance of taking the children. Whether the place to be visited is a wood, a section of coastline, a small factory or workshop, a church, an airport or a row of houses or shops, there will be an immense wealth of possible things to notice, to do and to follow up. It is essential for the teacher to consider it all and plan out beforehand answers to the following questions:

- What do I want the children to notice?
- What do I want them to investigate (on the spot and back in the classroom)?
- Which ideas do I want to help them develop?

Based on the answers to these questions, more detailed planning need to include:

- questions to ask the children to stimulate their observation, their investigation, their questioning (as suggested in Chapter 8);
- preparation in terms of skills they will need (such as the use of a hand lens or pegging out a minifield);
- equipment they need to take with them;
- matters relating to safety.

The school will have procedures and regulations relating to out-of-school visits. In additions to following these rules, there must be time before the visit for the teacher to work with the children to:

- set the scene
- collect all the necessary equipment and ensure the children know how to use it;

- explain, and insist upon compliance with, safety measures, parts of the countryside code and considerate behaviour;
- introduce sources of information for use in the follow-up work after the visit;
- undertake some classroom activities before the visit to raise questions and whet appetites.

Natural locations

When the teacher is wholly responsible for the kinds of activities the children will undertake during a visit to a natural location, it is useful to plan experiences rather as a 'nature trail' so that attention is drawn to particular objects or features. The activities and questions at these places have to be thought out beforehand. They might invite children to observe or investigate, for example, different kinds of vegetation, folds or cracks in rocks, evidence of erosion, fossils, animal tracks or holes, living things in a pond, etc. Whether or not work sheets are prepared beforehand with questions and spaces for answers or drawings, depends on the circumstances, aims of the visit and age of the children. But if worksheets are used they should not be so structured that the children have no invitation to raise questions of their own or to observe other than to answer the questions. Taking a disposable camera, or better still, a digital camera, is a useful way of making a record of special events to discuss later in the follow-up classroom work.

Places of work

Visits to factories, small industries, supermarkets or farms involves liaison with those at the site. During the pre-visit it is as important for the teacher to tell those involved at the place of work about the children and the aims for the visit as it is for the teacher to find out what the children can do and experience. This avoids unrealistic expectations on either side and will enable the teacher to set the scene for the children and prepare focusing questions. Safety is always important on visits, but never more so than in work places. Farms present both physical hazards (from machinery and slipping on mud) and health hazards (infections can be picked up by stroking animals or touching surfaces that might be contaminated with dung). These risks may be small but should be taken seriously and can be largely avoided by ensuring that children follow safety codes, such as those set out in the ASE's publications on safety, *Be Safe* (1991, Scottish Edition, 1995) and *Safety in School Science for Primary Schools* (1994).

Science museums and interactive science centres

Visits to interactive science museums or children's museums have an important part in children's experience, for they provide opportunities which are not available in school. They are most effective when planned to complement what the school provides and to focus on phenomena round the themes or topic being studied. For example, if the theme involves sound, there are, in most interactive centres, opportunities for children to experience sound focusing by hollow reflectors, to create echoes in long tubes, to use models of compression wave motion, to experience the effect of changing the frequency of their voice, to hear different things in each ear, and so on. To encounter a small selection such as this at one time is the best way to use these facilities. Museums contain an overwhelming number of exhibits and little is gained if children flit from one to another without really interacting with any at more than a superficial, button-pressing, level. It will benefit their future learning as well as their present understanding to experience the museum as a place to explore new events, to try out their ideas and to find information, rather than as an amusement arcade.

Most museums have an education sections which will often provide a service tailored to the needs of a particular group. However, the pre-visit by teachers is essential so that full advantage can be had from the visit, which, except for schools close by, will probably require all the organisation and incur the cost of a field trip.

Other sites

In a useful discussion of 'Science out of school', Katherine Hann pointed out that science can be learned from visits to a number of museums and sites other than those obviously connected to science (*Primary Science Review*, 45, December 1996, pp. 11–14). These require a more focused approach so that attention is drawn to such things as the fabrics used in clothing, the way stones or bricks are laid in arches, the materials used for different purposes today and in the past, how durable these materials are, and so on. Children can compare the way homes or castles were heated in the past with what we have today and the implications for daily life of other developments in science and their technological applications over the past centuries.

In the same article, Hann also provides some ideas for making use of the journey to a site. Children might be asked to note the different forms of transport they observe, decide on the source of energy used to power each one and think about how the energy is transferred at different stages to move the vehicle, whether bicycle, car or aeroplane. These activities can also be followed up later back at school.

Safety in and out of school

Fortunately science at the primary level is not, in practice, a source of danger to children; very few accidents related to science activities have occurred.

However, now that virtually every teacher is involved in science, and technology, activities, there is a need for precautions to be spread more widely and to become established in routine practice. The Association for Science Education's publication *Be Safe* (ASE, 1991) and the inset pack (1994) bring together the best advice which primary teachers can find on the subject. *Be Safe* contains essential safety codes for using tools, glues, sources of heat, chemicals and electricity. It also covers the preparation of food in the classroom and the related matters of hygiene. Precautions to take in studying 'ourselves' are set out. There are important sections on the selection and care for animals kept in the classroom and a list of those that should not be kept. Advice is also given about growing micro-organisms. Finally, there is information about poisonous plants and safety codes for working out of class and for visits and field trips.

Safety is not only a matter for teachers to consider in obtaining and using equipment; these considerations should be shared with children. Most curriculum guidelines and standards now require explicit development by children of ideas relating to road use, mains electricity, health hazards or smoking and the abuse of drugs and solvents. Children need to come to an understanding of the dangers these present so that self-discipline replaces obedience to rules. Rules and obedience to them is necessary where safety matters are concerned but the sooner compliance becomes voluntary the sooner the temptation to break them is eliminated.

Developing a willingness in children to use their understanding and to take sensible safety precautions requires the teacher to take the same role as in the development of other attitudes. The suggestions to be found in Chapter 21 apply, with particular emphasis on setting an example. The prime importance of safety should not operate to curtail children's investigations but to ensure that the necessary precautions are taken and that children gradually come to understand the reasons for them.

Summary

- In selecting the materials and equipment that are necessary for children to have first-hand experience of things around them, simple and familiar utensils and containers are to be preferred to laboratory apparatus
- There are pros and cons relating to keeping equipment in a central store and a clear allocation of responsibility for maintaining it is important if a central store is to operate effectively; children should be involved in keeping all the things in good, orderly condition.
- Teachers need to be able to purchase consumable materials for study at the time they are needed.

- There are many different locations for out of school visits, but they all require
  - a thorough pre-visit by the teacher;
  - careful planning of questions that will help children to engage with the new experiences;
  - attention to safety;
  - follow up work after the visit.
- A wide view of safety has been taken, so that the risks involved in certain activities can be minimised without unduly inhibiting children's experience. Helping children to understand reasons for safety codes has to be seen as an important part of their learning in science.

Chapter 11
The role of computers and ICT

Introduction

In this chapter we look at the fast changing roles of the computer and of information technologies in science education. In particular the concern is with the roles that these new technologies can play in furthering the kind of learning discussed in Chapter 6, that is, learning with understanding constructed from within. Such learning does not require the computer to be an instructor or to replace the teacher, but to provide additional and more effective means for children to study and come to understand the scientific aspects of the world around. There is a world-wide move towards providing children with access to computers at school and at home. The growing evidence that this access does lead to higher levels of achievement in basic skills will only serve to increase the pace of development in the use of ICT.

Here we are concerned with the roles that computers can take in learning science, and the implications of these for the teacher, looking first at these roles in general, as they are being developed in both primary and secondary education. In the second part the focus is on the particular applications, reflecting current experience, in learning science in the primary school. This is in two parts; the role of computers in enhancing classroom-based enquiries and their use in bringing experience from outside into the classroom. In the third part we look at the role of ICT in supporting the professional development in science of primary teachers.

Overview of the role of computers in science education

The main uses of computers in science education are for word-processing, data-logging, data handling, simulations, modelling, analysing data through databases and spreadsheets, and accessing information through the Internet and from CD-ROMs. The National Curriculum for Science (DfEE 1999) provides examples of where each of these can be used in teaching. We look briefly at them in turn.

Word-processing

Word-processing in science has all the advantages shared with other areas of curriculum of enabling children to edit and redraft their work and attain a well presented report. There are also further advantages when children begin to use the computer to make notes during practical work and not just to produce a report at the end. Clough (1987), a primary headteacher, observed the impact of the introduction of word-processing on his children, noting that:

> when the writing up stage is seen as an integral part of the scientific process it can be used to develop an awareness in children of the importance of attention to detail and to promote a more thorough understanding of what they are doing...
>
> Before word processing, relatively little was done in terms of planning and improving scientific writing in spite of regular encouragement by teachers to do so. The need to make notes and extract information tended to be overlooked in the excitement of the investigation and the eagerness to get on.
>
> (David Clough, PSR No 5, 1987, p. 5)

Data-logging

Data-logging uses a computer to record information sent to it from a probe or sensor. It has considerable advantages over data-logging by hand in terms of speed, memory, accuracy and perseverance. Probes which respond to temperature, light, sound, rotation, pressure, humidity, and so on, open up to children direct experience of some variables that would not be available to them through conventional measuring instruments. Connecting probes to computers, using suitable software, provides a screen display of data which changes in real-time. This means that the children's attention can be given to the trends and patterns as they appear, whereas, if they are, say, using a thermometer to take temperatures at different times, their attention has to be on the mechanics of using the instrument and reading the scale. However, children still need to make sense of what is happening and to maintain the essential link between what they see on the screen and the real events taking place. There is, therefore, a key role for the teacher in ensuring this link.

Data-handling

Data-handling software can create bar charts, line graphs or pie charts from quantitative data which is either input directly from a probe or input by the children via a keyboard. In either case, using the computer to produce the graphical display removes the time and possibility of error that is associated with manual graph plotting. It is particularly useful for less able children who can to proceed to the stage of interpreting data which they otherwise might not reach. However, the ease of changing from one form of graphical display to another means that it is important for children to appreciate the kinds of graph or chart that are appropriate for different kinds of data. So, again, the teacher has to ensure that the children understand what they see on the screen.

Simulations and modelling

There are various kinds of computer simulation, from direct reproduction of classroom or laboratory activities, to models of industrial processes or to representing theoretical ideas (such as frictionless surfaces) which do not exist in the environment. They are useful at the secondary level for giving students opportunity to investigate processes which are not accessible or dangerous or would involve expensive equipment. In a simulation users can only manipulate the variables that are built into the program. In modelling, users are able to work out for themselves how variable relate to each other and so build their own model of what is going on. There is more opportunity for students to work out and test their own ideas.

Spreadsheets and databases

Databases are organised collections of information which can be used to record the information children collect for themselves or to use information collected by others. In either case the program allows users to look for patterns in data, make predictions and test hypotheses. Their use encourages children to work collaboratively, sharing data and ideas about data interpretation. Spreadsheets have some functions in data manipulation that are similar to those of databases but can also help in modelling, since they allow the effect of change in one variable on another to be seen.

Use of the Internet

This is a fast growing area of ICT where anything said is likely to be out of date before it is published. The Internet is not only a major source of information, but a medium for trade, advertising services, vacancies, etc. An equally rapidly expanding field of activity is providing easy access to find one's way round in cyberspace. As Jackson and Bazley (1997) point out, the Internet is 'potentially the most powerful aid to the educational process yet developed, but its use for educational purposes still needs to be structured and managed' (p. 41). Some schools and local authorities have created an intranet, a closed network, which makes available to schools selected information from various websites (Diffey 1997). Children and teachers can access this information just as if it were on the Internet. The Schools On-Line website provides a library of links to useful sources of information and a facility for e-mail links for question-and-answer interaction and for collaborative projects. Increasingly museums, such as the Science Museum and the Natural History Museum in London, provide resources to support science education via the Internet. The STEM project is designed to facilitate use of the resources of the Science Museum, while the QUEST resource enables children explore and investigate from a distance museum objects presented to them on the screen (see page 105).

CD-ROMs

As CD-ROMs become easy and cheap to produce, incorporating video, sound and animation, they are assuming a major role in providing information. For certain kinds of information, such as is needed by children learning science, they are preferable to the use of the Internet, being more reliable and 'safe' for children to explore. When first used, children may need some help in navigation, otherwise this may absorb more of their attention than the subject matter they are seeking. However children quickly become used to finding their way around and the important point is then to ensure that they do this with an aim in mind. Well-selected CD-ROMs enable children to test their ideas. For example, Govier (1995) describes the use by nine-year-old children of information on a disc about animals to test their ideas relating to the position of the eyes of mammals and predator–prey relationships.

Using computers in classroom investigations

The importance of first-hand experience to primary children's learning means that the greatest value of using computers will be in enhancing their interaction with real things and developing the skills that enable them to develop understanding through enquiry. This points to data-logging, data-handling and the use of databases as having considerable potential value.

Data-logging using sensitive probes can extend children's observations to include evidence of the kind that would otherwise be imperceptible to them. They can, for example, using a light sensitive probe, investigate the intensity of light before and after it passes through a coloured filter, helping them test out the idea that children often have that the filter adds something to 'colour' the light. The reduction in intensity after passing through the filter may lead them to consider the alternative idea that some light is absorbed in this process.

Computers also help to obtain data which is difficult to collect (because things happen too quickly for human reactions, for example) or which require tedious repetition of observations. An example of the latter is the observation of animal behaviour under different conditions. Clough (1985) describes the construction of a temporary home for a mouse so that the mouse's movements could be followed. The device involved pressure pads at the four corners, forming switches which sent signals in various combinations to a computer programmed to turn these into a plot of the position of the mouse. Data could then be collected around the clock. This illustrates an advantage of data-logging, that children don't need to be present for all the data collection and this extends the range of questions they can ask and answer through their enquiries. An activity for primary children studying changes in the length of day and night is to record the level of light throughout a complete cycle of 24 hours so that they can identify the exact time of sunrise and sunset and see how this changes when repeated at different times of the year. Other methods of detecting movement, fast and slow, use interrupted light beams and light sensitive resistors.

The interpretation of evidence is essential to deriving the most benefit from practical investigations. Some advantages of using computers in this context were reported by Warwick and McFarlane (1995), in a study of seven and eight year olds. The children were in four classes where they were all comparing the cooling of warm water in identical bottles covered with different materials. In two classes the children were using thermometers and representing the falling temperatures by drawing line graphs. In the other two classes the children were using portable computers, temperature sensitive probes and software which recorded and plotted graphs of their findings. Before the work started all the children were asked questions to assess their ability to identify events from a temperature-time graph. The researchers found that, at the start, 'most children were completely unable to gain meaning from line graphs, with many unable to identify the data line as the significant part of the graph'.

Those using the temperature probes then explored their surroundings with them and were encouraged to find ways of making the line on the screen go up and down. They quickly discovered how to do this and were able to make predictions as to the effect on the line of placing the probe in certain places. They then devised an investigation to compare the effect of the covers on the bottle. The other children in the other two classes had help from their teachers who were 'extremely inventive in getting children to present data in an imaginative way'. On questioning both groups after their investigations, all had showed improvement in ability to interpret line graphs but those using the computer significantly more so. In addition to this advance, the researchers concluded that:

it was apparent that using IT reaped advantages in terms of the children's observed ability to work in a genuinely investigative way. They became more accepting that it is 'OK' to make predictions that turn out to be incorrect. They were willing to adapt and re-run their investigations, as they could immediately see the outcomes of changes made. Perhaps most crucially, they demonstrated a sound understanding of the relationship between variables, together with the ability to manipulate them for various purposes; this might not, perhaps, have been anticipated in children of this age.

(Warwick and McFarlane 1995, p. 24)

Computer databases provide opportunities for children to manipulate the data they collect, to find patterns in it and use it to test predictions. Various programs allow the user to define their own fields relating to the variables of an experiment. Many are suitable for children from the age of seven or eight. For example, in an investigation of parachutes (reported by John Meadows, 1988) the fields included the independent variables of the canopy material, the canopy shape, canopy area, the number of strings, the length of strings, the material of the strings, the mass of the load added, and the dependent variables relating to the way the parachute descended, the stability, direction and rate of fall. Once data had been entered about all the models used in the class the database was used to answer questions such as:

- Is there a discernible pattern between the time for descent and the canopy shape, length of string and mass of the load?
- Is there a relationship between mass of the load and stability?
- What factors seemed to be related to stability?

This example seems to show that the main benefit from the considerable work of setting up this database would be the appreciation of what a database is and how it can be used. Once established as a tool, however, and used in other contexts, it can help children to test ideas about associations between variables and so further their development of understanding of the things being investigated. They will then be in a position to use databases prepared by others to extend the range of data on which they can test their predictions and hypotheses beyond those which they has been able to collect themselves.

Using computers to bring the outside world into the classroom

CD-ROMS and websites designed for children provide information that children can use in a variety of ways. When seeking factual information, as already noted, it is important for the children to have clear questions in mind if they are to locate what is useful to them. The process of clarifying questions in seeking information via a computer is as important as is the identification of investigable questions when seeking answers through enquiry. But these sources do far more than provide readily available factual information. For example, the Natural History Museum's QUEST website creates an environment in which children can explore and investigate objects that actually exist in the museum but are presented on the screen. They can use a selection of 'virtual tools' to investigate them. The website also provides an on-line notebook where 'children can record their ideas, thoughts and questions about an object. They can read those of others and respond to them' (Hawkey 1999, p. 4).

In other situations, too, children are using computers to communicate via e-mail with other children or with scientists or other experts. This can expand their experience in a particularly friendly way. For example, the children recording the precise time between sunrise and sunset would probably find it intriguing to exchange this kind of information with children in another part of the world. There are many opportunities for children to learn from each other by using e-mail about the variety of animals, plants and habitats in different places. This is less formal and more immediate than conventional correspondence and has far more impact than reading about such things in books. Direct links to scientists are sometimes arranged but obviously have to be used with consideration for the adults involved. In some cases, however, schools can help to collect survey data of value to scientists. In the US the National Geographical Society's Kid's Network program offers elementary and middle school children opportunities to learn about globally significant science topics. In another US example, middle-school girls use e-mail to connect with women scientists who act as role models and encourage the girls' interests in science and technology.

The role of ICT in professional development

Increasingly CR-ROMs and on-line programs are being developed to support science teaching and to supplement conventional courses for professional development and TV programmes. The ease of access when and where required, rather than at the time and place where a course is being offered, makes these alternatives extremely attractive to busy teachers. Often there is opportunity for occasional face-to-face encounters with a tutor or with other teachers, but even without this the popularity of web-based courses is rapidly increasing. Of course, much depends on the construction of the website and the facilities offered. It is certainly not enough to transfer course notes to an electronic form. It is generally advocated (e.g. Bober 1998) that the website should provide at least e-mail links to tutors and fellow participants, activities on-line and off-line, interactive activities, many relevant examples, frequently asked questions, lists of resources, opportunities for participants to contribute ideas and examples, and, if the course is for credit, assignments, sample projects and assessment details.

A site with some of these facilities exists in Scotland to support primary science teachers. It was initially developed as an on-line facility to be used beside some material on CDi. It provided e-mail connection to science educators who acted as helpers, providing answers to questions asked by teachers. There was a 'library' of selected documents that could be downloaded as required and the opportunity to share ideas, lesson notes, children's work, and general information (Harlen and Schilling, 1998). Access and hardware problems led to the support being transferred to a CD-ROM and at the same time incorporating more structured plans and classroom activities. A move back to on-line provision is likely following the better provision of access to the web in the schools.

Another development, aimed specifically at upgrading teachers' science knowledge and teaching of the topic of 'forces and motion', has been developed in England at Exeter University. A website was established to deliver professional development tasks and other materials to teachers and to provide for teachers to exchange ideas and experiences. In the US, too, there are many web-based initiatives to improve the teaching of science and technology. In both countries, however, rigorous evaluation of these innovations has yet to be undertaken to identify the advantages and disadvantages as compared with conventional face-to-face professional development. Although the results of such evaluations are needed in order to avoid the weaknesses and build on the strengths, they are unlikely to reverse the tide that is running for the provision of courses on-line.

Summary

- The main used of Information and Communications Technology (ICT) in science education are for word-processing, data-logging, data handling, simulations, modelling, analysing data through databases and spreadsheets, and accessing information through the Internet and from CD-ROMs.
- At the primary level, data-logging, using probes sensitive to temperature, light, pressure, etc., have particular value in extending the range and accuracy of children's observation.
- Using computers for data-handling and manipulation frees children from repetitive work and enables them to focus on the meaning of their data.
- The use of the Internet, intranets and CD-ROMS has extended children's access to information and, through interactive sites, given them the ability to conduct investigations at a distance using 'virtual' tools.
- The use of ICT in the classroom makes as much demand on teachers' understanding and mediation as non-computer activities.
- ICT has a fast expanding role in supporting primary science teachers and providing professional development.
- E-mail is enabling both teachers and children to exchange information and ideas and to find answers to their questions.

Chapter 12

Talking, listening and using words in science

Introduction

This chapter is concerned with spoken language and discussion, which we have mentioned several times as having a valuable role of discussion in children's learning. It complements the section in Chapter 20 about communication on paper. We first look at the role of talk in children's learning, drawing on the writing of Douglas Barnes, who contributed so much to the understanding of communication in the classroom and whose ideas are as relevant today as they were when they were first written. In the second part, the teacher's role in encouraging productive discussion is considered through reflection on a classroom example. We then turn to the organisation of classroom discussions. The fourth part considers the matter of words used in science and the uncertainty which is often felt about whether and when to use 'correct' scientific words. The role of words and phrases used metaphorically is also discussed.

The roles of talk in learning

It is useful to draw a distinction, following the ideas of Douglas Barnes, between speech as communication and speech as reflection. Already many references have been made in this book to the value of children discussing with each other, exchanging ideas and developing their own views through the act of trying to express them and explain them to others. This involves both communication and reflection. The reflective part is sorting out their own ideas aloud, indeed 'thinking aloud'. The communication is sharing with others and involves listening as well as presenting in a way which is coherent and understandable by others. Barnes claims that both are needed and that it does not serve learning to focus only on the more formal communication since 'if a teacher is too concerned for neat, well-shaped utterances from pupils this may discourage the thinking aloud' (Barnes 1976, p. 28).

Speech as reflection

We have all probably had the experience where talking to someone has resulted in developing our own understanding, although apparently nothing was taken from the other person in terms of ideas. The effect is even more striking when you are the one against whom ideas were 'bounced' and are thanked for helping in sorting out ideas when all you have done is listen and perhaps question in a neutral manner. The presence of one or more other people is essential in these cases, not only to legitimate thinking aloud but for offering the occasional comment or question for clarification which has the effect of provoking reflection on what we think as we express it.

The same things happen with children though often less tidily, since the reflection is going on in several minds at the same time. The following example of interaction in a classroom involved the teacher, but acting as one of the group rather than as an authority figure.

Deidre and Allyson were investigating the way in which three whole hens' eggs, labelled A, B and C behaved in tap water and in salty water. They knew that one was hard-boiled, one soft-boiled and one raw. They had to find out which was which.

This is how the eggs landed up just after being placed in the salty water. The transcript begins with the teacher approaching them after they had been working alone for some time.

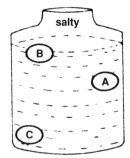

Deidre	. . . hard-boiled.
Allyson	I know
Teacher	(*coming up to them*) Can you tell me how you're getting on?
Deidre	I think that C is raw.
Allyson	We both think that C is raw.
Teacher	Do you?
Deidre	B is ...
Teacher	(*to Allyson*) Why do you think that?
Allyson	Because when you put eggs in water bad ones rise to the top.
Deidre	(*at the same time*) Because it . . . we put them all in . . .
Teacher	Bad?
Allyson	Yes, I think so – or it is the good ones? . . . well, I don't know.
Teacher	Yes?

Allyson	...they rose to the top, so...
	(*Deidre is putting the eggs into the salty water*)
Deidre	...that's the bottom (pointing to C)
Allyson	...if it's raw it should stay at the bottom.
Teacher	I see.
Deidre	So that's what we think, C is raw and B is medium and A is hard-boiled.
	(*Allyson starts speaking before she finishes*)
Allyson	...and I think that B is hard-boiled and she thinks that B is medium.
Teacher	Ah, I see. (*to Deidre*) Can you explain, then why you think that?
Deidre	If we put...er...take C out, (takes C out, puts it on the table, then lifts A and B out) and put these in, one after the other. Put A in – no B first. That's what...Allyson thinks is hard-boiled, I think it's medium. If you put that in...(she puts B into the salty water)
Allyson	...'cos it comes up quicker.
Deidre	It comes up quick. And if you put that in...
	(*She puts A into the salty water. It goes to the bottom and rises very slowly*).
Allyson	And that one comes up slower.
Deidre	So, I think that one (*pointing to A*) is hard-boiled because it's... well...
Allyson	I don't. I think if we work on the principle of that one (*pointing to B*). Then that one comes up quicker because it's, you know, not really boiled. It's like a bit raw.
Teacher	A little bit raw.
Allyson	So, therefore, it'll come up quicker.
Deidre	Yes, but it's not bad.
Teacher	What'll it be like inside?
Allyson	Runny
Teacher	It'll be runny still, I see.

Having agreed that C is the raw egg, Deidre and Allyson disagree about the identity of the other two eggs. Allyson has a reason for considering B is hard-boiled on the basis that 'bad ones rise to the top', so she considers that B behaves as if it had had something done to it. But she does not articulate the consequences of this until Deidre attempts to give her reason. Then it is as if Deidre's reason, which she interrupts, sparks off her own thinking.

Although they respond to the teacher's request for an explanation what they do is to continue their interaction and struggle to work out their own reasoning. Deidre's response in particular is hesitant and disjointed, not at all like a straight answer to the question. Barnes call this 'exploratory talk' and he argues that it is very important whenever we want the learner to take an active part in learning, and to bring what he learns into interaction with that view of the world on which his actions are based. That is, such exploratory talk is one means by which the assimilation and accommodation of new knowledge to the old is carried out.

(Barnes 1976, p. 28)

We can see from this interchange about the eggs how the girls use evidence to check their ideas. This comes through most clearly in Allyson's 'if we work on the principle that...' where she relates what she predicts on the basis of her judgement to the observation of how quickly the egg floats up in the salty water, bit it also occurs throughout. It is worth noting in passing that the origin of her idea is previous knowledge about how to distinguish good from bad eggs.

It is difficult to deny that Deidre and Allyson learn from this experience and from their discussion of it. But this does not always happen. For instance see how June and David, in the absence of the teacher, seem to regard the task as one where giving an answer is more important than having a reason for the answer. June, particularly, seems keen to move to early closure.

David	Look at that one, this one, look, June.
June	That one's the one that's not boiled.
David	How do you know?
June	Oh, I'm not stupid
David	Shall I put them in there, or in there? (*On the table or in the container where they were first*)
June	Put them in there.
	(*David puts the one he took out in the container and June brings out the other two eggs*)
June	There's B... (*as she passes them to David who places them carefully*). Now put them in the salty water.
	(*David picks up A and puts it in the jar of salty water*)
David	A floats. A.
June	B (*She puts B in. It sinks*) Sinks.
David	C.
	(*He puts it in the salty water. It goes to the bottom and slowly begins to rise again.*)
June	Sinks.
David	Yea, look...no, it doesn't.
June	No...that one (she points to C. Pauses, uncertain for a moment) No, how are we going to tell...

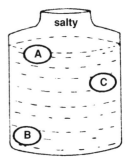

David	That one's . . .
June	Hard-boiled. The one at the bottom's hard-boiled. Put C hard-boiled. *(She instructs David to write. But it isn't C which is at the bottom.)*

Even here, though, there are signs that they are close to becoming more involved. David's 'How do you know?' could have sparked June into explaining her ideas, had she been less defensive. Later on, when an egg which she declares 'sinks' begins to float upwards, there is questioning in the air. The potential seems to be there. The question is then how this potential can be exploited; how, more generally, can we encourage interchanges which involve reflective thinking?

> The quality of the discussion – and therefore the quality of the learning – is not determined solely by the ability of the pupils. The nature of the task, their familiarity with the subject matter, their confidence in themselves, their sense of what is expected of them, all these affect the quality of the discussion, and these are all open to influence by the teacher.
>
> (Barnes 1976, p. 71)

The role taken by Deidre and Allyson's teacher gives several clues to positive encouragement of reflective thinking:

- joining in as part of the group, without dominating the discussion;
- listening to the children's answers and encouraging them to go on ('I see', 'Yes?');
- asking the children to explain their thinking;
- probing to clarify meaning ('what'll it be like inside?').

Not all aspects of the teacher's role can be illustrated in one short interchange and indeed much of it is in setting a context and a classroom climate which encourages exploratory thinking and talk. Important in this respect are:

- expecting children to explain things, which involves valuing their ideas even if these are unformed and highly conjectural;
- avoiding giving an impression that only the 'right' answer is acceptable and that children should be making a guess at it;
- judging the time to intervene and the time when it is better to leave a children-only discussion to proceed.

The presence of the teacher changes a discussion quite dramatically, for it is difficult for him or her not to be seen as an authority. Left alone, children are thrown on to their own thinking and use of evidence. But, as we see with June and David, the absence of a teacher does not always lead to productive interchange and it is not difficult to imagine how a question from a teacher could have supported the move towards enquiry which David seemed to be making. The teacher needs to monitor group discussions, listening in without intervening, before deciding whether 'thinking aloud' is going on usefully or whether it needs to be encouraged.

Speech as communication

This is the more formal side of using talk, where shared conventions and expectations have to be observed if others are to be able to make sense of what is said. It is part of socialisation to be able to tell others in a comprehensible way about what has been done or thought about and to be able to listen to others, attending not only to the words but to the implicit messages conveyed by tone of voice and manner. In order to develop necessary skills, children need opportunity for reporting orally to others in a setting where they know that others will be listening and where they have to convey their information clearly. Such situations do not occur naturally in the classroom and have to be set up. The role of the teacher in creating the right climate as well as the specific opportunities is clearly a central one.

For children to learn from each other's experience and ideas they have to be helped to structure and compare their contributions so that they are understandable and interesting to others. The children also have to be prepared to listen to others, to participate in questioning and to value each other's contributions. The teacher can help them in this by providing guidelines for preparing presentations and a structure for ensuring that each can be heard and given consideration. The teacher's own response, by showing interest, asking questions for clarification, making positive comments, etc. provides guidance in the form of an example. Then the telling and listening can have a role in the development of children's ideas as well as in their communication skills. It means that they go back over their activities and make sense of them for themselves so that they can make sense of them for others.

In this way oral reporting has value for the development of children's ideas as well as communication skills, and both purposes are served better if the purpose of discussion is perceived by both teacher and pupils as part of the activity. To further this a teacher needs to:

- make use of children's ideas in comments, thus encouraging children to do the same ('That's an interesting idea you have about...' 'Tell us how you think it explains...');
- encourage children to respond to each other and not just to make statements of their own ideas;
- listen attentively and expect the children to do so;

- set up expectations that children will put effort into their presentations to each other and try to make them interesting; give time and help in preparation with this in mind.

These things have to become part of the general way of working, since expectations that children will respond to what their classmates say are set by the pattern of previous lessons as well as by the response on a particular occasion.

Organising class and group discussions

In setting up discussion the (perhaps obvious) point is to ensure the attention of all involved. For a whole-class discussion the location of the children is significant in avoiding distractions. Occasionally it may be necessary to hold a brief discussion during the course of practical activities, for the purpose of bringing together observations which have been made, reporting progress, or sharing information which will help everyone (including instructions about safety if unexpected hazards have arisen). On these occasions it may be advisable to move the children away from the materials they are working on in order to ensure their attention. The discussion will only last a few minutes and it will be no hardship for the children if they are cramped in a small space for this time. It is intended to help them with their work when they return to it, otherwise there is no justification for the interruption.

Apart from these infrequent interruptions, whole-class discussion will be at the beginning and end of the group work.

The initial discussion is the key to setting up group work which is sufficiently clear and motivating to ensure that children begin work promptly and with enthusiasm. Whether the purpose is for children to continue work already begun or to start on fresh activity the essential function of the initial discussion is to ensure that children know what they have to do and what role is expected of them.

Group discussions will be part of practical work; children should be encouraged to talk freely among themselves. The presence of materials and equipment gives them the opportunity to use evidence to support their points and claims (as Deidre and Allyson did). The noise which this inevitably generates is part of the working atmosphere. If the noise level becomes unacceptable it should be possible to spot the reason:

- too much excitement about certain activities?
- children waiting for equipment and not 'on task'?
- 'messing about'?

Once diagnosed, appropriate action can be taken – for example, by diluting the excitement by staggering work on certain activities, organising equipment for easier access, checking the match between the demand of an activity and the children's readiness to respond.

When the teacher is involved in a group's discussion the purpose may be to monitor progress, to encourage exchange of views, to offer suggestions, to assess. Since it is almost impossible for teachers to 'hover' without their presence affecting the children, it is best to make clear what is intended. 'I'm not going to interrupt; just carry on' or 'Tell me what you've been doing up to now'. During a teacher-led group discussion, the teacher should show an example of how to listen and give everyone a chance to speak. The group might also be left with the expectation that they should continue to discuss, 'Try that idea, then, and see if you can put together some more suggestions.'

Holding a whole-class discussion at the end of a practical session, whether or not the work is completed, should be the normal practice. The reasons for this strong recommendation have been well articulated by Barnes, who points out that learning from group activities:

> may never progress beyond manual skills accompanied by slippery intuitions, unless the learners themselves have an opportunity to go back over such experiences and represent them to themselves. There seems every reason for group practical work in science, for example, normally to be followed by discussion of the implications of what has been done and observed, since without this what has been half understood may soon slip away.
>
> (Barnes 1976, pp. 30–1)

The teacher should warn the children in good time for them to bring their activity to a stage where equipment can be put away and to allow five or ten minutes for reviewing and reporting on-going work. At the end of the activities on a particular topic a longer time for whole-class discussion should be organised and children given time beforehand to prepare to report, perhaps with a demonstration, to others.

Introducing scientific words

Children pick up and use scientific words quite readily; they often enjoy collecting them and trying them out as if they were new possessions. At first one of these words may have a rather 'loose fit' to the idea which it is intended to convey.

Take for example the child's writing in Figure 6.9 (p. 61) where, in describing how the sound is transmitted in a yoghurt pot and string telephone, he explains how vibrations go down the string. The word 'vibration' is certainly used in a manner here which suggests that the child understands sound as vibration, until we notice that he writes that the voice is 'transferred into vibrations' at one end and 'transferred back to a voice' at the other. It seems that the sound we hear is not understood as vibration, but only its transmission along the string. It may be that ideas both of sound and of vibration have to be extended, so that vibration is something which can take place in air and occur wherever sound occurs, which will take time and wider experience, but he has made a start.

The question as to whether the child should be using a word before he can understand its full meaning is a difficult one. But first we have to ask what we mean by 'full meaning'. Most scientific words (such as evaporation, dissolving, power, reflection) label concepts which can be understood at varying levels of complexity. A scientist understands energy in a far broader and more abstract way than the 'person in the street'. Even an apparently simple idea of 'melting' is one which can be grasped in different degrees of complexity: a change which happens to certain substances when they are heated or an increase in energy of molecules to a point which overcomes the binding forces between them. This means that the word melting may evoke quite a different set of ideas and events for one person than for another. Now to use the word 'melting' in a restricted sense is not 'wrong' and we do not insist that it is only used when its full meaning is implied. Indeed the restricted meaning is an essential step to greater elaboration of the concept. Therefore we should accept children's 'loose' use of words as a starting point to development of a more refined and scientific understanding of the word.

Two questions of importance then arise:

- when is it useful to introduce a word, knowing that it can only be used loosely at first?
- how are we to know the meaning that a child has for a word?

The second question is considered only briefly here. Children will, of course, pick up words without being given them by a teacher. It is important for the teacher to know what a child means by a word, for confusion can be heaped upon confusion if meanings differ. But since finding out children's meaning of words is an integral part of finding out their ideas we will deal with practical suggestions in Chapter 15.

The first question causes much concern. Teachers seem to be caught between, on the one hand giving new words too soon (and so encouraging a verbal facility which conceals misunderstanding) and, on the other, withholding a means of adding precision to thinking and communication (and perhaps leading children to make use of words which are less than helpful).

The value of supplying a word at a particular time will depend on:

- whether or not the child has had experience of the event or phenomenon which it covers;
- whether or not the word is needed at that time;
- whether or not it is going to add to the child's ability to link related things to each other.

These points apply equally to a teacher supplying the word consciously and overtly as to providing it indirectly by using it. That means that until the moment for introducing the word is right, the teacher should use the language adopted by the children in discussing their experiences. Then, once the word is introduced the teacher should take care to use it correctly. For example if children have been exploring vibrations in a string, drum skin, a tissue paper against a comb, and wanting to talk about what is happening to all these things, it may well be useful to say 'what all these are doing is called "vibrating"'. Before this the children and teacher may have called it by descriptive names: trembling, jumping, moving, going up and down, etc. A useful way of ensuring that the new word and the children's words are connected to the same thing, suggested by Rosemary Feasey (1999), is to use them together ('the thing that's trembling or vibrating') until the new becomes as familiar as the old.

All this can be summed up by saying that *if a word will fill a gap, a clear need to describe something which has been experienced and is real to the children, then the time is right to introduce it.* With young children one of the conditions for the 'right time' is the physical presence or signs of the phenomenon to which the word refers. Only then can we hope to fit the word to an idea, even loosely. Much more experience of a concept has to follow so that the word becomes attached to the characteristic or property rather than to the actual things present when it was first encountered. But there is no short cut through verbal definitions in abstract terms.

Metaphor and learning in science

There are many words in science which are used metaphorically and with a non-literal meaning, often having been 'borrowed' by scientists because they helped the understanding of a new phenomenon by linking it to an already known one. For example the word 'nucleus' was adopted by physicist to help describe the structure of an atom by analogy with the nucleus at the centre of a living cell, although the functions of the nucleus in the two contexts bear no relation to each other. The process of using language in this way is on-going, as witnessed by the recent use of the word 'virus' in connection with computers.

As Sutton (1992) points out

> Expressing a new thought often involves putting words together that would not normally be linked. For example, millions of people have experienced successive nights of winter frost followed by a clouding over of the sky and a realisation that it is suddenly less cold. Someone, sometime, made sense of this situation by speaking of a blanket of cloud over the land. Other people, recognising the aptness of the image, have accepted and used the phrase ever since.
>
> (Sutton 1992, p. 17)

Sutton goes on to discuss the subtle effect of putting these two words – blanket and cloud – together: 'both the generator of the phrase and its later recipients gain a means of understanding the cloud and of thinking about the experience of the cold evening and warmer ones'.

There is a danger, of course, in using phrases like this with young children who may not recognise the unspoken '*like* a blanket' and take the word too literally. The particular properties of a blanket which enable it to restrict heat loss have to be appreciated if the metaphor is to help in understanding the action of clouds in this context. Moreover the properties of blankets which are not relevant have also to be realised. This suggests caution in using such phrases with children and the need for thorough discussion of what they mean to the children when they are used.

There is a more general point here about using physical analogies as well as metaphors. For example, a common way of illustrating the water cycle in secondary schools is to use a boiling kettle and allow the water vapour to condense on a cold surface. When this is used in the primary school, however, it is often difficult for children to envisage the water cycle without a kettle, which not uncommonly appears in their drawings hovering somewhere in the sky. Often the models which adults think up to represent difficult concepts, such as water flow in pipes as an analogy of flow of electricity in a circuit, can cause more problems in understanding the analogous situation in the first place. A small-scale research (Jabin and Smith 1994) which involved trying different analogies for electric circuits, seemed to show that it was the effort made to create a link with something already familiar to the children which had an effect rather than the nature of any particular analogy.

Summary

- Talking serves an important purpose in helping the speaker to sort out his or her ideas as well as for communicating ideas to others.

- The teacher's role in encouraging speech as reflection among small groups is to avoid giving the impression that there is a 'right' answer, probe for clarity of meaning and value different ideas.
- Speech as communication takes place in a more formal setting, requiring some structure and time for preparation; children should be encouraged to listen to each other and respond positively.
- A time for communicating and sharing results at the end of activities increases emerging understanding and the development of enquiry skills.
- Scientific words are best introduced when the children have experienced the event or phenomenon that they represent. Children pick up scientific words and use them loosely at first, so it is important for teachers to find out the meaning a scientific term has for a child who uses it.
- Analogies and metaphors should be used cautiously in giving explanations to children and only if they link to something already familiar to the children.

Chapter 13

Encouraging and handling children's questions

Introduction

One of the aims of science education, as noted in Chapter 2, is encouraging curiosity since this is so important in continuing attempts to learn about and understand our environment. In Chapter 5 the relationship between curiosity and asking questions was discussed; curiosity is often, but not always, expressed in terms of questions. Questioning helps to bridge the gap between what we already know and what we do not understand. Children's questions are thus very important to teachers since they help to indicate the boundary between where children feel that they can and cannot make sense of something. So, the first part of this chapter is about how teachers can encourage children to ask questions. The necessary corollary to this is being able to respond to the questions, for unless teachers feel confident about this they will inevitably be reluctant to invite yet more questions. Thus the second part of the chapter deals with handling children's questions, which does not necessarily mean answering them directly, but using them to encourage children's thinking and enquiry.

Encouraging children's questions

Asking questions is an important means for adults as well as children to try to understand the things around us. When engrossed in the study of something new we use our existing knowledge to make sense of it and try out the ideas we already have to see if they fit. When we find a gap between what we already know and making sense of something new, one way of trying to bridge it is to ask questions. We might do this immediately by asking a question if there is an authority present, as might happen at an exhibition, on a guided tour, or in a class or lecture. At other times the question may remain unspoken but guides us to a source of information which is then more efficiently used because we know what ideas or information we are looking for.

However, the ability to pose questions in a way that helps understanding develops gradually and young children do not always express their questions clearly enough to indicate what kind of answer is required. The old story about answering a child's question 'where did I come from?' illustrates this well. Frequent 'why' questions often indicate that a child is not accepting things uncritically but is not able to express the query in the form of an easily answerable question. The more mature ability is shown by clear and often detailed questions which focus on the nature of the gap between present understanding and what is needed to understand something new. The child who can identify in this way the cutting edge of his or her learning is taking an important part in that learning. Thus is it very important for teachers to encourage the development of this ability.

Although we are in the main concerned with questions expressed verbally, it is the case that questions at all levels of maturity can be expressed in other ways. Indeed it is through action that very young children express curiosity.

> Tiny Niels, beaming, bare and beautiful, crawled on the wet sand on the beach. He moved where the sea reaches out for the land, where the ocean barely touches the continent, where the exhausted waves drag themselves up the incline and withdraw or sink into the sand. Whenever this happened in slow and steady rhythm there appeared, all around Niels, tiny holes in the sand which bubbled and boiled with escaping air. These little marvels drew his attention, and with immense concentration he poked his finger in hole after hole . . . The bubbling holes invited Niels: 'Come here, look at us, feel and poke.' And Niels did exactly that. He could not talk yet, not a word was exchanged, no question formulated, but the boy himself was the questions, a living query: 'What is this? What does it do? How does it feel?'
>
> (Jos Elstgeest 1985b, p. 9)

It happens also with older children when they need to take more planned action to answer their questions:

> Some junior boys were using three sand-timers of different durations. During their activity they found that turning over the one-minute timer five times did not take as long as the five-minute timer. They then checked the one-minute timer against the classroom wall clock, which had a second hand. As there was a difference there was then a problem of deciding which was correct. The question in their minds was clear from their action, of going into other rooms in the building to check the timer against different clocks.
>
> (Match and Mismatch Raising Questions 1977)

Which kinds of question?

We all, adults and children alike, ask a number of different kinds of question as well as those seeking information or ideas. Some questions are rhetorical and some just show interest; neither of these expects an answer. Some questions are asked to establish a relationship with someone, or to gain a response; some to attract attention; some even to irritate or harass (as in Parliaments). Questions which arise from curiosity and the desire to understand have the main part to play in learning science but it is important not to discourage any questions by implying that only some are worth answering. At the same time, while we recognise the value to children of encouraging the expression of their questions, including the vague and unspoken ones, it is helpful to their learning if they begin to recognise the kinds of questions which can be addressed through scientific activity.

Science is concerned with questions about the 'what, how and why' of objects and relationships in the physical world. The most productive kinds from the point of view of learning science are those which enable children to realise that they can raise questions and answer them for themselves. These are the questions which keep alive the close interaction (as between Niels and the holes in the sand) between child and environment, between question and answer.

Children who realise that they can find out answers to 'what, how and why' questions by their own interaction with things around have made the best start they can in scientific development. They realise that the answer to 'Why do daisies spread out their leaves?' 'Why do paper tissues have three thin layers rather than one thick one?' 'What happens when you turn a mirror upside-down?' are to be found directly from observations and actions on the daisies, the tissues, the mirror.

Two useful and tested ways of encouraging questions are now discussed. We will consider later (p. 126) how to turn questions into ones that children can answer through investigation.

A classroom climate which invites questions

The close dependence of questioning on curiosity means that the classroom where questions are stimulated must be one where there are plenty of opportunities for direct exploration of interesting materials. Materials and objects brought in by children have built-in interest at least for those who collected them and sharing this interest is very likely to spread it to others. As with materials brought in by the teacher with a particular view to creating interest in a topic to be studied, they need to be displayed so that it is obvious to the children that they are invited to touch, smell (where appropriate and safe), look carefully, find out, etc. In the same vein the expectation that children will ask questions should be built up. Sheila Jelly has the following suggestions for ways of encouraging questions, through displays and other tactics:

1. By making sure that displays and collections have associated enquiry questions for the children to read, ponder and perhaps explore incidentally to the main work of the class.
2. By introducing a problem corner or a 'question of the week' activity where materials and associated questions are on offer to the children as a stimulus to thought and action which might be incorporated into classwork.
3. By making 'questions to investigate' lists that can be linked to popular information books.
4. By ensuring that in any teacher-made work cards there is a question framed to encourage children to see their work as enquiry-based and which also provides a useful heading for any resultant work displayed in the classroom.

(Sheila Jelly 1985, p. 51)

Positive reinforcement

Although it is the new or unusual which is normally a stimulus to curiosity, more familiar objects may be ones which are more productive in encouraging children to express questions for investigation, perhaps because they are likely already to have raised queries in their minds. A display of different tools, nuts and bolts and screws could be set up with a 'question box' enabling children to post their questions on small pieces of paper. The apparently sex biased subject matter produced no bias in the interest and questions when this was put into practice. When the box was opened and each question considered, girls were as ready as boys to come up with reasons for different sizes and shapes of heads of screws, why screws had threads but nails did not or whether the length of the handle of a screw driver made any difference. They followed up some suggestions through practical investigations and others were left pinned to the display board awaiting information from an 'expert'. The work added considerably to their experience of materials and their properties as well as showing that questions were valued.

Another way of stimulating questions without constant recourse to things which the children will not have seen before, is to draw attention to important aspects by putting things together with very different properties. For instance, when investigating bouncing balls, what do children think of how a ball of plasticine 'bounces'? Questioning why the plasticine becomes flattened gives an important clue to why balls bounce back. Children can also be made to think about the presence of air in an 'empty' bottle by questioning why they can blow the pea into one of the bottles in Figure 13.1 but not into the other:

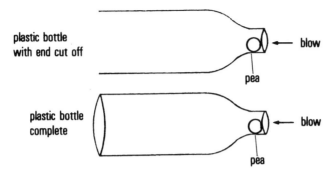

Figure 13.1

Setting aside time for children to describe what they have done is an important part of science experiences which can be used to encourage questions and make it legitimate for children to express questions and admit that there are things they don't know but want to know. It is best for the questions to come from the children rather than the teacher. So instead of the teacher interrogating the children, they should be invited to respond to 'What do you still want to know about...?'

More generally, the simple invitation 'What questions would you like to ask about...' can be regularly extended, either orally in writing, on work cards or sheets. Resisting the temptation, as a teacher, to do all the question raising is also a simple but important guideline. Raising questions is something children must learn to do for themselves, and this won't be encouraged if all the questions they pursue are raised for them.

Handling children's questions

Despite the value to children's learning of encouraging their questions, many teachers are worried about answering children's questions and, perhaps unconsciously, adopt classroom strategies that reduce opportunities for children to ask questions. So if questioning is to be encouraged, being able to handle the questions that children raise has a high priority.

Fortunately handling questions is a skill which can readily be developed. It requires thought about the kind of question being asked, about the likely motive for asking it and knowledge of how to turn a question into one which can be a useful starting point for investigation. The word 'handle', rather than 'answer' is used deliberately here. One of the first things to realise – perhaps with some relief – is that is often better not to answer children's questions directly (even if the teacher does know the answer). But it depends on the kind of question which is asked and so we start by identifying important differences.

Type of questions children ask

Most questions children ask in the context of science activities fall into one of five categories which have been chosen because they group together questions requiring different kinds of responses.

(i) Comments expressed as questions

These are questions which children ask when they are intrigued or excited. The questions don't really need to be answered but there has to be some response which acknowledges the stimulus which gave rise to the question. For example, here is how an infants' teacher handled a question from a six year old when she and a group of children were examining a birds' nest:

Child:	How do they weave it?
Teacher:	They're very clever…
Child:	Birds are very clever with their beaks
Child:	Nobody would ever think they were because they're so small
Teacher:	Yes, it's wonderful isn't it? If we turn this right round and let you have a look at this side…

The child's question was used to maintain the close observation of the nest and a sense of wonder. She might have replied 'Look carefully and see if you can tell how it is done?' but perhaps she judged that this was too early a stage in the exploration for focusing on one aspect, but her response leaves open the possibility of returning to the subject in this vein if the children's interest is still there. Another way of putting this is that she judged the question to be a way of expressing wonder rather than a genuine query. The child might just as easily have said 'Look at how it's woven!'

(ii) Philosophical questions

This is another category of questions to which the response has to be of the 'yes, isn't it interesting/intriguing' kind, sharing the wondering behind the question. 'Why do we have birds and all different things like that?' is such a question. Taken at face value the only answer is to say that there is no answer. However, not all children's questions are to be taken at face value; the reason for asking has also to be taken into account (see page 121). Neither should we read too much into the exact words children use. They often phrase questions as 'why' questions, making them sound philosophical when the answer they are wanting is much more related to 'what makes it happen' rather than 'why does it happen'. When children's question seem philosophical the initial step is to ask them to explain their question. It may well then turn into a question in a different category, but if not it should be treated as an interesting question but one to which no-one can give a definite answer.

(iii) Requests for simple facts

These are questions which satisfy the urge to name, to know, to identify. The children looking at the bird's nest asked 'Where did it come from?' 'What kind of stuff is this that it's made of?' 'How long do the eggs take to hatch?' These are questions to which there are simple factual answers which may help the children to give a context to their experience and their ideas about the lives of birds. The teacher may know the answers and if so there is no point in withholding them. In the case of the birds' nest she knew where it had come from and helped the children identify the 'stuff' as hair. But for the length of hatching she did not have the knowledge and the conversation ran on as follows:

Teacher	Well, you've asked me a question that I can't answer – how many days it would take – but there's a way that you could find out, do you know how?
Child	Watch it . . .
Child	A bird watcher . . .
Child	A book.
Teacher	Yes, this is something you can look up in a book and when you've found out . . .
Child	(who had rushed to pick up the book by the display of the nest) . . . I've got one here, somewhere.
Child	. . . here, here's a page about them.
Teacher	There we are . . .

The children were engrossed in the stages of development of a chick inside an egg for some time. The question was answered and more was learned besides. Had the book not been so readily available the teacher could have suggested that either she or the children could look for the information and report back another day.

Requests for names of things fall into this category, as do definitions which arise in questions such as 'Is coal a kind of rock?' While names can be supplied if they are known, undue attention should not be given to them. Often children simply want to know that things do have a name and, knowing this, they are satisfied. If work requires something to be named and no-one knows the proper name at that moment then children can be invited to make up a name to use. 'Shiny cracked rock', 'long thin stem with umbrella', 'speedy short brown minibeast' will actually be more useful in talking about things observed in the field than their scientific or common names. Later the 'real' names can be gradually substituted.

Some requests for simple facts cannot be answered. Young children often have a view of their teacher as knowing everything and it is necessary to help them to realise that this is not the case. When the children asked 'Where are the birds now, the ones who built the nest?' they were expecting a simple question to have a simple answer. In this case the teacher judged that the kind of answer they wanted was 'They've probably made their home in another shed, but I really don't know for sure' rather than an account of all the possibilities, including migration and whether or not birds tend to stay in the same neighbourhood. A straight 'I don't know' answer helps children to realise the kinds of questions that cannot have answers as well as that their teacher is a human and not a superhuman being.

(iv) Questions requiring complex answers

Apart from the brief requests for facts, most questions children ask can be answered at a variety of levels of complexity. Take 'Why is the sky blue?' for example. There are many levels of 'explanation' from those based on the scattering of light of different wavelength to those relating to the absence of clouds. Questions such as 'Why is soil brown?' 'Why do some birds build nests in trees and others on the ground?' 'How do aeroplanes stay up in the air?' fall into this category.

They seem the most difficult for teachers to answer but they are in fact the most useful questions for leading to investigations. Their apparent difficulty lies in the fact that many teachers do not know the answers and those who do will realise that children could not understand them. There is no need to be concerned, whichever group you fall into, because the worst thing to do in either case is to attempt to answer these questions!

It is sometimes more difficult for the teacher who does know the scientific explanation to resist the temptation to give it than to persuade the teacher who does not know not to feel guilty about not being able to answer. Giving complex answers to children who cannot understand them is underlining for them that science is a subject of facts to memorise that you don't expect to understand. If their questions are repeatedly met by answers which they do not understand the children will cease to ask questions. This would be damaging, for these questions particularly drive their learning.

So what can be done instead of answering them? A good answer is given by Sheila Jelly in the following words:

> The teaching skill involved is the ability to 'turn' the questions. Consider, for example, a situation in which children are exploring the properties of fabrics. They have dropped water on different types and become fascinated by the fact that water stays 'like a little ball' on felt. They tilt the felt, rolling the ball around, and someone asks 'Why is it like a ball?' How might the question be turned by applying the 'doing more to understand' approach? We need to

analyse the situation quickly and use what I call a 'variables scan'. The explanation must relate to something 'going on' between the water and the felt surface so causing the ball. That being so, ideas for children's activities will come if we consider ways in which the situation could be varied to better understand the making of the ball. We could explore surfaces, keeping the drop the same, and explore drops, keeping the surface the same. These thoughts can prompt others that bring ideas nearer to what children might do.

(Sheila Jelly 1985, p. 55)

The result of the 'variables scan' is to produce a number of possible investigable questions such as 'Which fabrics are good ball-makers?' 'What happens if we use other fluids, or put something into the water?' Exploring questions of these kinds leads to evidence which can be interpreted to test hypotheses concerning what it is about felt that makes it a good ball-maker (and can we use this idea to make it into a poor ball-maker?) and what extent it is something about water which makes it form balls (and how we can change this). These activities lead towards an explanation of the original question and can be pursued as far as the extent of the children's interest and understanding. It is not difficult to see that there is far greater educational potential in following up the question in this way than in attempting to give an explanation (which probably has to be in terms of a misleading 'skin' round the surface of the drop).

'Turning' questions into investigable ones is an important skill since it enables teachers to treat difficult questions seriously but without providing answers beyond children's understanding. It also indicates to children that they can go a long way to finding answers through their own investigation, thus underlining the implicit messages about the nature of scientific activity and their ability to answer questions by enquiry.

(v) Questions which can lead to investigation by children

Teachers looking for opportunities for children to explore and investigate will find these are the easiest questions to deal with. The main problems are:

- recognising such questions for what they are;
- resisting the urge to give the answer because it may seem so evident (to the teacher but not the child);
- storing them, when they seem to come at the wrong time.

Recognising potentially investigable questions

It is not often that a child expresses a question in an already investigable form; there is usually a degree of 'turning' to do and the 'variables scan' is a useful idea to keep in mind. A child's questions about snails' shells is an example. The question 'Why do snails have four rings on their shell?' was quite easily turned into 'Do snails have the same number of rings on their shells?' A slightly different approach is to turn a question from a 'why' question into a 'what would happen if' question. For instance: 'Why do you need to stretch the skin tight on a drum?' can become 'What would happen if the skin is not tight?'

Not only is this more encouraging for the child than a straight return of the question: 'Well, what do you think?' but it directs the child towards finding out more than the answer to the original question – in this case probably the relationship between the pitch of the sound and the tautness of the drum skin.

Resisting the urge to give an answer

'What are these?' (the eyes of sprouting potatoes)

'Where did these come from?' (winged fruits of sycamore trees)

'How can I stop my tower falling over?' (tower built from rolled newspaper with no diagonal struts).

These are questions which the teacher could readily answer, but in most cases to do so would deprive the children of good opportunities to investigate and learn much more that the simple answer. Certainly, there can be occasions when it is best to give the short answer, but in general the urge to answer is best resisted. Instead it is best to discuss how the answer can be found.

Storing questions

Questions which can be profitably investigated by children will come up at various times, often times which are inconvenient for embarking on investigations. Although they can't be taken up at that moment the question should be discussed enough to turn them into investigations and then, depending on the age of the children, picked up some time later. Some kind of note has to be made and this can usefully be kept publicly as a list of 'things to investigate' on the classroom wall, or just kept privately by the teacher. For younger children the time delay in taking up the investigations has to be kept short – a matter of days – but the investigations are also short and so can be fitted into a programme more easily. Older children can retain interest over a longer period – a week or two – during which the required time and materials can be built into the planned programme.

The five categories of questions and ways of handling them are summarised in Figure 13.2.

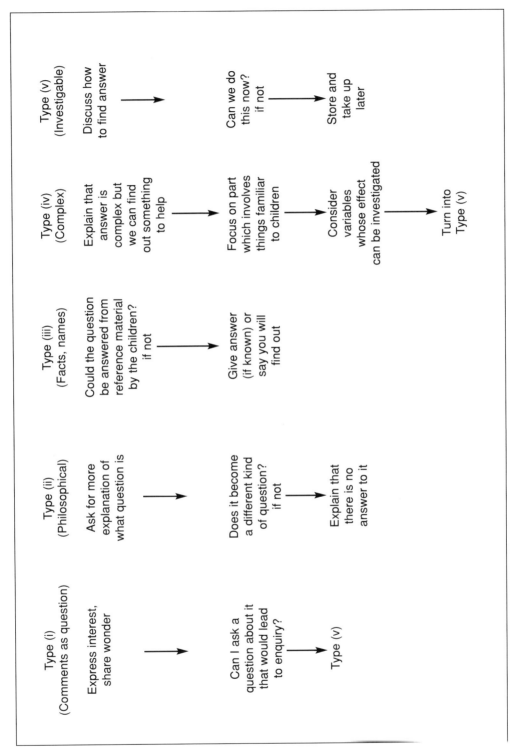

Figure 13.2 Flow diagram for handling questions

Summary

- Children's questions are valuable for a number of reasons: they show the gaps that the children feel they need to fill in their understanding; they can provide the basis for children's investigations; and they give children the opportunity to realise that they can find things out for themselves and satisfy their curiosity.
- Teachers can encourage children to raise questions by providing interesting and thought-provoking materials in the classroom, mechanisms for inviting questions, such as a question box, and an atmosphere that welcomes and does not deter questioning.
- Children will ask all kinds of questions and not just those which can lead to investigations. In order not to deter questioning, teachers need to be able to handle these different kinds.
- Questions that would require complex scientific answers, which the children would not be able to understand, may be able to be turned into simpler ones that the children can investigate. Other questions may require simple facts that the teacher may be able to supply or the children find out from various sources of information. Some questions do not require answers but a response in the form of shared interest, and children may have to be told that some questions can't be answered by scientific investigation. Responding appropriately helps children eventually to realise which kinds of questions are answered in science.

Chapter 14

The roles of assessment in teaching and learning

Introduction

Assessment has several roles in teaching and learning. Evidence about learning gathered by teachers can be fed back into their own teaching and also shared with the children so that they have a better idea of how to take their next steps in learning. This chapter provides an overview of the various roles of assessment and an introduction to the later chapters which take up some of the points raised here in more detail. We begin by discussing the purposes of assessment and clarifying the terms used to describe the main purposes in the primary school; to make decisions which are part of teaching, and to summarise what has been learned at certain times. We then consider in more detail what is involved in assessment: gathering, judging, interpreting and using evidence for particular purposes. The last section relates these to assessment formative and summative purposes, paying most attention to formative assessment on account of its proven potential for increasing levels of achievement. Children also have a role in reflecting on their learning and helping to decide their next steps, which is discussed in Chapter 18.

The meaning and purposes of assessment

Meaning

It is generally agreed that assessment in the context of children's achievements in relation to the goals of their learning *is a process of making judgements about the extent of these achievements*. The judgements are reached by bringing together evidence which has been gathered about performance and some standards, criteria or expectations. The combination of various ways in which evidence is collected and the various bases for judging it creates different methods of assessment. These include standardised tests, where information is gathered while children are tackling carefully devised tasks, under controlled conditions and, in contrast, assessment carried out almost imperceptibly during normal interchange between teacher and children.

The distinction between 'tests' and 'assessment' is not at all clear. Some use of the term 'assessment' excludes tests and refers only to various forms of informal assessment usually devised by, and always conducted by, the teacher. However, this distinction is not necessarily agreed and here we shall use assessment as a broad term, covering all ways of collecting and judging evidence and including tests. Tests are specially devised activities designed to assess knowledge and/or skills by giving precisely the same task to children who have to respond to it under similar conditions. Tests are not necessarily externally devised; teachers prepare tests (of spelling, arithmetic, for example) and some 'tests' can be absorbed into classroom work and look very much like normal classroom work as far as the children are concerned. It is therefore not at all helpful to characterise assessment differences in terms of methods but rather in terms of purposes.

Purposes

In their school career children may be assessed for a range of purpose, not all of which are intended to help their learning and indeed in some (national and international monitoring) they are simply representatives of a particular group. The purposes are:

- to help their learning (finding in what aspects they are and are not making progress, what particular difficulties they are having);
- to summarise achievement at certain times (for keeping records, reporting to parents, other teachers and the children themselves);
- to group or select children (both within a class and where there is streaming or setting, and, at later stages, for certification and progress to higher levels of education);
- to monitor the performance of children across a region or nation (as in national and international surveys of children's performance, where only a sample of children is assessed);
- to assist in research or evaluation of new classroom materials or educational reforms.

The concern in this book is with assessment for the first two of these purposes only, although reference will be made at times to some of the others. The first is described as formative assessment, aimed at helping the teaching and learning process. Evidence gathered regularly is used in making decisions about on-going work, assisting teachers in adjusting the challenges and support provided to children according to their existing ideas and skills. Its purpose is to help rather than to grade children. The term 'diagnostic' is sometimes used as distinct from formative assessment. Diagnostic assessment has a specific focus, being concerned with examining in depth a particular area of performance. But this is only a slight variant of formative assessment and can be considered part of it.

The second of the above purposes is described as summative. As the name suggests, it provides a summary judgement or a summing up of where a child has reached at a certain time. Quite often the information is obtained by a test (or examination), which may be teacher-made or externally produced, at the end of a term, year, or a certain section of work. The end of key stage tests in England and Wales fulfil this purpose as do national tests in other countries. But it is also possible to give a summative assessment as a result of reviewing records of on-going assessment, as teachers frequently do in reporting to parents, either orally or in writing, at the end of a year instead of, or in addition to, test results.

The process of assessment

As just noted, assessment involves making judgements based on evidence about children's learning, that is, about the ideas, skills and attitudes that are the aims of education. So the process has the following stages:

- gathering evidence about learning, using methods of appropriate reliability and validity;
- judging the evidence in relation to the goals of learning;
- interpreting the judgement;
- taking action.

How each of these stages is carried out depends on the purpose of the assessment. We look at the options in each case before summarising how they are combined in assessment for formative and summative purposes.

Gathering evidence

The main methods that teachers can use to gather evidence of children's learning are

- observing children carrying out their regular class work (this includes listening, questioning and discussing);
- studying the products of their regular work (including writing, drawings, artefacts and actions);

- introducing special activities into the class work (such as concept-mapping, diagnostic tasks);
- giving tests (teacher-made and externally produced).

The first two of these can involve children as well as teachers, a procedure that is particularly relevant in formative assessment (see Chapter 18).

The choice of methods depends on the purpose, which in turn indicates the balance to be struck between high reliability and high validity. Reliability and validity are important concepts for describing the outcomes of assessment, which should be taken into account in deciding the way evidence is gathered and interpreted. *Reliability* refers to how much you can depend on the result; that is, how likely it would be that the same result would be obtained if repeated. Reliability depends on the procedure that is used. Thus tests where children choose between fixed alternative answers, that can be machine marked, are more reliable than ones that ask children to provide answers which then require some judgement in the marking. However the latter may be a more valid test if the purpose is to find out what answers children can construct. *Validity* refers to the match between what is actually assessed by a procedure and what it is intended should be assessed.

Often reliability and validity point to different procedures. Increasing validity is likely to point to methods of gathering evidence about processes and actions in real situations, where high reliability is difficult to attain. Increasing reliability points to restricting the range of evidence to give closer control of the circumstances in which behaviour is assessed. There has to be a compromise and where it is struck depends on the purpose of the assessment. Assessment that serves a formative purpose has to be essentially valid. There can be less concern for reliability since the information is used to inform teaching in the situations in which it is gathered. Thus there is always quick feedback for the teacher and any misjudged intervention can be corrected. This is not to say that teachers do not need any help with this important part of their work, but the help required is not to be found in examples of work judged to be at different levels. This is needed for summative teacher assessment, but formative assessment is concerned with the future not with judgements about the past. Summative assessment, on the other hand, has to provide information about where children have reached in their learning that parents and other teachers can depend upon and so attention has to be given to increasing reliability as far as possible without endangering validity.

Judging the evidence

This stage is concerned with the reference point or basis used in judging evidence. The alternatives can be illustrated in terms of an example which is perhaps a little unlikely but enables us to look at the principles involved. Suppose that a teacher wants to assess a child's ability in knocking nails into wood. This can be described in different ways:

- The teacher may have some expectation of the level of performance (knocking the nail in straight, using the hammer correctly, taking necessary safety precautions) and judge the child's performance in relation to these. The judgement is made in terms of the extent to which the child's performance meets the criteria; that is, it is criterion-referenced.
- Alternatively, the teacher may judge in terms of how the child performs at knocking in nails compared with other children of the same age and stage. If this is the case there will be a norm or average performance known for the age/stage group and any child can be described in relation to this as average, above average or below average, or more precisely identified if some quantitative measure has been obtained. (The result could be expressed as a 'knocking nails age' or a 'hammer manipulation' quotient!) The judgement arrived at in this way is called a norm-referenced assessment.
- A third possibility is that the teacher compares the child's present performance with what the same child could do on a previous occasion – in which case the assessment is child-referenced, or ipsative.

It is important to recognise these different bases for judgements in assessment and to apply them appropriately. They each have their value in the right context but each have drawbacks outside these contexts. Child-referenced assessment is appropriate for formative assessment, for providing encouraging feedback to children, particularly slower ones who, if compared with criteria or with others' performance would always be seeming to fail, but can recognise progress in terms of their own previous performance. But it must be realised that it leads to one child being praised for work which, from another child, might be received with less approval. This is no problem as long as no comparisons are made between children, but where comparisons *are* being made, or performance in terms of external standards has to be reported, then one of the other bases for judgements must be used.

Interpreting judgements

The interpretation of assessment for all purposes, but particularly where tests are used, implies some generalisation of the result beyond the particular evidence gathered. It is only possible to assess a sample of behaviour, yet we tend to use it as if the results from this sample applied generally. Indeed unless we are assessing simple recall of facts, we have the expectation that the result will tell us more than just about the particular performance assessed.

The question of how far is it justified to generalise from assessment results touches on a matter of considerable debate among psychologists. On the one hand is the point of view that all learning is contextually bound, that is, what we can do in one context does not relate to what we can do in another even if the same skills seem to be involved. There is some support for this since we know that, for example, ability to use solve mathematical problems depends on the situation in which they are used. Boys regularly calculate batting averages in cricket but experience difficulty with the same calculations when decontextualised. Research in mathematics has shown a factor of three in the difficulty of different questions devised to assess the same mathematical skill (Wilson and Rees 1990). Similarly in science, the APU science surveys found wide variations in average performance (DES/WO 1985). Sometimes children performed better when the use of the scientific skill or idea was set in the context of everyday activity, while this kind of setting was associated with a depression of the level of performance in other cases. Some children anticipate failure in certain activities because of their self-image (see Chapter 5) and so make failure more likely. The poor performance of girls in some activities involving ideas of physics can be explained to an extent by the context and topics having a greater identity with boys' interests and triggering the reaction in girls that 'I can't do this' before even trying.

The other point of view supports the notion of generalisable skills that can be taught in one context and used in many others. There is evidence here, too, to support this view. The CASE project (Conceptual Acceleration in Science Education) provides activities for children that are directed towards problem solving and the manipulation of variables. Research results with secondary school children show that there are long-term effects which show not only in children's performance in science but in other subjects, including English (Shayer and Adey 1993). In this programme, deliberate efforts are made to encourage children to apply skills learned in one context to others.

It is likely that context does influence performance but to an unknown extent. Assessment results must therefore be interpreted cautiously, as guides to what children can do but not as indicating any kind of certainty about it. No assessment can be used predictively with certainty; it is best treated as a hypothesis, a tentative finding, to be modified by further evidence of the child's performance. Cautious interpretation should avoid labelling children, which results from over-generalisation of assessment results. When an assessment is taken to describe the whole child and not just a certain performance this can affect teachers', parents' and the child's views of what the child is able to do, often needlessly limiting expectations.

Taking action

According to the purpose of the assessment action may take the form of:

- Feedback into teaching, adjusting the challenge or support given to individual children to help them develop their scientific ideas, skills and attitudes (see Chapters 19, 20 and 21).
- Feedback to the children, given in a form that enables them to see how to improve their work and encourages them to take the necessary steps (see Chapter 17).
- Reporting progress made in learning over a particular time to parents, other teachers and the children themselves (see Chapter 23).

The characteristics of formative and summative assessment

We now bring these general points about assessment to bear on the characteristics of assessment for the two purposes being discussed.

Formative assessment

Formative assessment helps the process of learning. This statement is supported by both theories of learning and research into practice. The importance of formative assessment for learning follows from the constructivist view that the development of understanding starts from existing ideas and skills. Thus teachers need to know about how these skills and ideas are developing if they are to help children to construct scientific understanding in the way described in Chapter 6.

Evidence from research into assessment and classroom practice was brought together in a major review by Black and Wiliam (1998a) from which they concluded that improvement of formative assessment could lead to considerable gains in levels of achievement. They found that while all children's learning benefited, children with mild learning difficulties gained most, thus reducing the spread of attainment. However, improving formative assessment requires teachers to make considerable efforts and to have the confidence 'that they can make anyone learn as long as they go about it the right way' (Black 1993, p. 79). What this means includes sharing learning goals with children, feeding back the teacher's assessment to children in particular ways, involving children in self-assessment and using effective methods of helping children to take the next steps in their learning. These are all things we take up in later chapters.

Formative assessment has to take account of all the aspects of children which affect their learning – not only the progress being made in knowledge and skills, but the effort put in and the other aspects of learning which are unspecified in any curriculum. It must be positive, indicating what are the next steps to take, not pointing out what is missing. This means that formative assessment is not a pure criterion-referenced assessment. It is more ipsative or child-referenced. The teacher will have in mind the progression which (s)he intends for the child, and this will be the basis of the action taken. The teacher will be looking across several instances in which a particular skills or idea is being used and will see variations and possibly patterns in behaviour. It is these variations (that are, if the purpose of the assessment is summative, seen as sources of 'error') that, in the formative context, provide diagnostic information.

A further characteristic of formative assessment which is increasingly recognised as central to it, is the involvement of children. The developing theory of educational assessment, and various models within it emphasises the important role that children have to play in their own assessment, as they come to understand the process, to learn to work towards explicit standards or targets and to modify their performance in relation to constructive task-related feedback from teachers (Gipps 1994). We pick up these matters in Chapter 18.

So, to summarise, the characteristics of formative assessment are that:

- it takes place as an integral part of teaching;
- it relates to progression in learning;
- it depends on judgements which can be child-referenced or criterion-referenced;
- it leads to action supporting further learning;
- it uses methods which protect validity rather than reliability;
- it uses information from children's performance in a variety of contexts;
- it involves children in assessing their performance and deciding their next steps.

Summative assessment

Summative assessment has an important but different role in children's education. Its purpose is to give a summary of achievement at various times, as required. As noted in Chapter 22, it can be achieved by summing up (summarising evidence already used for formative purposes) or checking up (giving a test or special task) or a combination of these. Since its purpose is to report achievement to parents, other teachers, children, school governors, etc. then reliability of the judgements is important and the criteria have to be used uniformly. Thus if the summary is based on a review of evidence gathered during teaching some form of moderation, or procedure for quality assurance, is required. So the characteristics of summative assessment are that:

- it takes place at certain intervals when achievement has to be reported;
- it relates to progression in learning against public criteria;
- it enables results for different children to be combined for various purposes because they are based on the same criteria;
- it requires methods which are as reliable as possible without endangering validity;
- it involves some quality assurance procedures;
- it should be based on evidence relating to the full range of learning goals.

The difference between these two purpose of assessment should be kept very clearly in mind, especially when both are carried out by teachers. It is too often assumed that assessment that is carried out frequently is formative, or that all assessment by teachers is formative. Where this happens the true value of formative assessment will not be realised.

Summary

- Assessment involves judgements about evidence of children's achievement. How it is carried out depends on its purpose.
- The purposes considered in this book are assessment for a formative purpose (assessment *for* learning) and assessment for a summative purpose (assessment *of* learning).
- The process of assessment involves gathering evidence relevant to children's learning, judging it against expectations, interpreting and using the judgements for specific purposes.
- Judgements can be made by comparing against norms, criteria of performance or the child's previous achievement.
- Depending on the purpose of the assessment, different emphasis is laid on reliability (dependability of the judgement) and validity (how well it reflects what it is intended to assess).
- The characteristics of formative and summative assessment differ in timing and use of the judgements more than in the methods used for collecting information.

Chapter 15

Gathering evidence for formative assessment of children's ideas

Introduction

This and the next chapter are concerned with the first step in formative assessment: collecting evidence of children's ideas, skills and attitudes. The various methods described are ones which can be used as part of children's activities, for it is in this context that evidence is both gathered and used in formative assessment. It is for convenience only that we separate the discussion of methods relating to ideas and to skills and attitudes, beginning in this chapter with ways of accessing children's ideas and continuing the next with gathering evidence about process skills and attitudes. In practice both take place in the same activities and ideas for the planning how to do this in practice are taken up in Chapter 16. However, the selection of methods depends on what ideas and skills are to be assessed. So we begin by considering the selection of learning objectives for particular activities.

Deciding what evidence to collect

Teachers plan activities so that children can have opportunities that lead towards certain learning outcomes. Usually there are many activities that could provide particular opportunities and many kinds of learning that could be fostered through any one activity. In discussing the necessary decisions about these things it is helpful to distinguish between longer-term goals, or learning intentions, that are achieved over time and through several activities, and the short-term outcomes from specific activities.

The longer-term goals are generally related to the requirements of the national curriculum or standards; for example to 'describe how everyday materials can be change by heating, by drying or by mixing things' (Scottish CCC 1999) or to 'carry out a fair test with some help, recognising and explaining why it is fair' (National Curriculum DfEE, 1999). Each planned activity makes a contribution, expressed in terms of the ideas and skills specific to it, to one or more of these longer-term goals. In order to help children to develop these specific ideas and skills (and so make some progress towards the longer-term goals) a teacher needs information that is focused on the specific learning objectives for each activity. So the identification of the learning objectives of particular activities is essential if formative assessment is to be effective in helping learning. It is useful to have an example of what this means in practice.

Activities with ice-balloons

Ice-balloons (described in *Primary Science Review*, no. 3, 1987, p. 5) provide a spectacular way of enabling children to explore water in its solid form. An ice balloon (created by filling a balloon with water, freezing it and then peeling off the rubber when it is solid) is so much more likely to rivet children's attention than the more accessible ice cubes, that it is worth the effort to make.

Working with eight and nine year olds, a teacher prepared ice balloons and gave one to each group of children with a tank of water in which it could be floated. The children were fascinated and made many observations and raised questions, some of which were followed up on later occasions. Indeed the major set of objectives of the activities was to encourage children to explore, to question and then to set about answering the questions through more systematic investigation, in other words to use and develop almost all the process skills and attitudes identified in Chapters 4 and 5. In relation to the ideas that could be developed through the activities, the teacher decided to select these

* the meaning of 'hot' and 'cold';
* the notion of temperature as a measure of hot and cold;
* the idea that heat is needed to melt ice and that cooling causes water to solidify;
* the similarities and differences between solid ice and liquid water.

There were a few other ideas which children would no doubt be helped to develop in the activities but the teacher decided to focus on these four rather than spread more widely. They extend over a range of conceptual difficulty which the teacher judged would match the levels of development of children in the class with respect to this area of work.

The question then arises as to how evidence is to be gathered about the children's ideas, skills and attitudes. What methods can be used during the course of the activities? In attempting some answers to this question in this and the following chapter we deal with evidence about ideas separately from evidence about skills and attitudes. This is just for the sake of clarity in describing the methods. In practice these would be intermingled, often the same situation being used to gather different kinds of evidence.

Methods for gathering evidence about children's ideas

The main methods fall under four headings:

- questioning, discussion and listening;
- children's drawings, annotated by themselves or in discussion with the teacher;
- concept maps, which are a special form of drawing;
- and children's writing, which can range from being structured by the teacher in the form of questions to answer or an account of observations and ideas structured by the child.

Questioning, discussion and listening

Useful starting questions might be 'How does it feel?' 'Can you smell/hear anything?' 'Does it stay the same or change?' But in the case of the ice-balloons, there was no need to offer these 'attention-focusing' questions. Children eagerly made observations at the start and throughout the activities:

> The ice feels cold, and sometimes dry and sticky, when very cold; the surface is sometimes smooth and slippery, particularly on the clear part, but can feel rough on the frosted part.
> It feels heavy. It floats in water, but only just.
> In a tank of water the ice seems to prefer to float the same way up or sometimes in one of two alternative ways.
> If you leave the ice floating in a tank of water undisturbed, a ridge shape appears at the level of the water; it melts faster below than above the water, and eventually becomes unstable and capsizes. The water gets colder.
>
> (Ovens, *Primary Science Review*, 1987, 3, pp. 5-6)

Some action questions ('What happens when you…?') led to the following observations:

> The ice is very hard, and difficult to break. When it is broken it makes splinter-shaped pieces.
> If you put ink on top of the ice, it doesn't soak in, but runs down the side.
> If you put salt on the top, the ice melts, the salt mixes with the melted ice, and, if it runs down the side of the ice, it makes cuts in the surface.
> Larger pieces of ice slide down a slope more easily than smaller pieces.
> If you poke the ice with a metal object, a mark is easily made in its surface.
>
> (ibid.)

Open and person-centred questions (see page 76) focused on asking children for explanations, rather than just their observations, are appropriate when children have explored and begun to raise questions for themselves. It is the responses to these questions that indicate the links that the children are making and the ideas they are bringing to the new experience. In relation to the ice balloons, such questions are used to start discussions about why the ice melts, something which some children of this age may assume is 'natural' and does not need explanation:

- What do you think is causing the ice to melt?
- What would you need to do to stop it melting?
- What do you think is happening when you put water in a freezer and it goes solid?

Discussion within a group can be set up by asking such questions with a request to 'find out what everyone thinks and let me know your ideas later'. Then leave them to discuss. Children-only discussions are valuable in freeing children to express their ideas. To quote Douglas Barnes:

> The teacher's absence removes from their work the usual source of authority; they cannot turn to him [sic] to solve dilemmas. Thus . . . the children not only formulate hypotheses, but are compelled to evaluate them for themselves. This they can do in only two ways: by testing them against their existing views of 'how things go in the world', and by going back to 'the evidence'.
>
> (Barnes 1976, p. 29)

When the children report their observations, listening to the words they use will provide information about the way they are understanding concepts such as hot, cold, melt and perhaps temperature. For those children whose grasp of these is not clear some direct questioning will help to probe their ideas:

- How does the water feel compared with the ice?
- Touch your arm and then the ice – how does the ice feel in comparison?
- (If the word temperature has been used) Which do you think is at the highest temperature, your arm, the ice or the water?
- What do you think it means when the temperature of something goes up?

Children's drawings

Asking children to draw what they think is happening gives a permanent record of their ideas which has the advantage of being able to be perused after the event. Examples of children's drawings which reveal their ideas have been given in Chapter 3. It is not easy for anyone to draw abstract things such as ideas about melting, and the use of labels and annotation as a commentary on what is happening is necessary, but the drawing is essential for conveying the image that the child has in mind. For example, the drawing in Figure 15.1 by a seven year old shows very clearly that the child considered the direct action of the sun as important in causing the disappearance (by evaporation) of water from a tank.

(Age 7 years)

"The sun is hot and the water is cold and the water sticks to the sun and then it goes down"

Figure 15.1 A seven year old's ideas about evaporation of water

It is important to note that the value for opening access to children's ideas depends on how the drawing task is set. Merely asking for a drawing to show the water levels in the tank would not necessarily be useful in this respect. A request for a drawing of 'what you think makes the water level change' is more fruitful.

In the case of the ice balloon, useful suggestions for probing (and advancing) children's ideas through drawings might be:

• Draw what the ice balloon looks like now and what you think it will look like after dinner, at the end of the afternoon and tomorrow if we leave it in the water. (The same task could be given to predict what it would look like if left out of the water.)
• Put labels on your drawings to point out the things which have changed and what changed them.
• Draw a picture with labels to show all the differences you can between ice and water.

It is best, if at all possible, to talk to the children individually while they are doing their drawings and to clarify for your information things which are not easy to interpret.

Concept maps

Concept maps are diagrammatic ways of representing conceptual links between words. There are certain rules to apply which are very simple and readily grasped by children of five or six. If we take the words 'ice' and 'water' we can relate them to each other in this way by connecting them with an arrow to signify a relationship between them. If we write 'melts to give' on the arrow, we have a way of representing the proposition that ice melts to give water, but not vice versa:

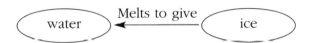

We can add to this by linking other words and so forming a map.

Asking children to draw their ideas about how things are linked up provides insight into the way they envisage how one thing causes another. The starting point is to list words about the topic the children are working on and then ask them to draw arrows and to write 'joining' words on them. Figure 15.2 shows the list and the map which a six year old, Lennie, drew after some activities about heat and its effect on various things. It is possible to spot from this that Lennie has not yet distinguished heat from temperature but that he has some useful ideas about what heat can do. As with all diagrams, it is advisable to discuss them with the child to be sure of the meaning intended.

energy
temperature
degrees Celsius
melt
boil
liquid
solid
friction
evaporate
heat
steam
insulate
food
water

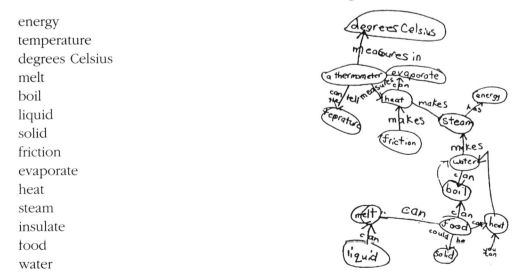

Figure 15.2 A six year old's concept map (Harlen *et al.* 1990)

Children's writing

While drawings can usually be made by even the youngest children, writing is most helpful when children become at ease in doing it. However, Figure 15.3 was written by a six year old to explain why the condensation from her breath on a cold window went away:

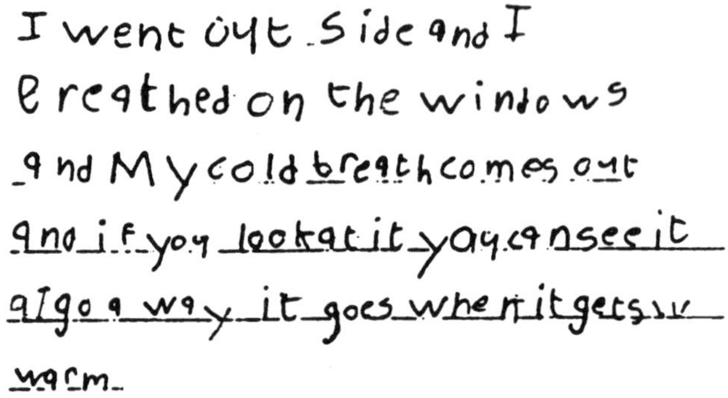

I went oyt side and I
Breathed on the windows
and My cold breath comes out
and if you lookat it yay can see it
algo a way it goes when it gets
warm

Figure 15.3 A six year old writing about condensation

In Figure 15.4, a ten year old's answer to how to slow down evaporation of water from a tank indicates the value of not just asking for writing about what has been observed but posing problems where ideas have to be used:

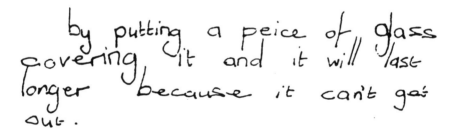

by putting a peice of glass
covering it and it will last
longer because it can't gas
out.

Figure 15.4 A ten year old using ideas about evaporation to suggest how to prevent it

The kind of writing task which may reveal children's ideas in the context of the ice balloon activity would be stimulated by questions and suggestions such as:

• What were the changes which happened to the ice balloon in the water?
• What would you need to do to stop the ice balloon changing?
• Describe what you think would make the ice melt more quickly and say why it would work.
• Describe to someone who had never seen ice and water what the differences are and how they would know which was which.

Many of the questions suggested earlier for discussion could also be turned into writing tasks for older children.

Summary

- It is important to be clear about the intended learning from specific activities and how this contributes to longer-term goals.
- Evidence gathered during activities is needed to help to ensure progress towards the intended learning.
- Methods of gathering evidence relating to the development of scientific ideas chiefly make use of:
    questioning, discussion and listening,
    children's annotated drawings,
    children's concept maps,
    children's writing.
- In all cases the question or task has to be expressed so that children are required to give explanations or predictions based on their ideas. Open and person-centred questions are appropriate here.

Chapter 16

Gathering evidence for formative assessment of children's process skills and attitudes

Introduction

Here we continue the description of ways of gathering evidence within classroom activities, turning attention to process skills and attitudes. We first discuss the different considerations that apply because process skills and attitudes can be used and developed in all enquiries. The second part of the chapter describes and illustrates the main methods of gathering evidence during activities: using observation and the possibilities offered by children's writing. In the third part we consider what is involved in planning the collection of evidence as part of lesson preparation.

What to assess

In Chapter 4 we identified seven process skills and in Chapter 5, five scientific attitudes. In theory all of these could be relevant in any activity, such as the one with ice-balloons. Unlike concepts and ideas, which are determined by the content of activities, the use and development of skills and attitudes is determined by the way in which children interact with the content. In practice, however, the emphasis given to various skills in different activities will vary, as indicated in discussing types of investigation in Chapter 9. Further, the activities of five- and six-year-old children will tend to give lots of opportunities to explore and gain experience; the skills most used will be observing, raising questions and communicating. The other skills will be used when the children begin finding ways to answer questions through their activity. Given plenty of previous exploring, children from the age of seven and eight will be covering the whole range of skills in simple activities. However, for teachers undertaking the assessment of process skills for the first time it would be advisable to keep to these three until becoming used to the procedures, then gradually extending to include more process skills.

The nature of the subject matter, as we have noted in Chapter 7, does have an important role in determining the extent to which children can use the skills they may have. We don't expect young children to be able to 'process' (that is, use process skills to make sense of) complex phenomena and events, particularly those which can only be understood using mental models. So the children must be engaged in the exploration, investigation or discussion of subject matter within their understanding when their process skills are being assessed.

Methods for gathering evidence about process skills and attitudes

The main methods come under the headings of observation by the teacher (including discussion and listening) and children's writing.

Observing children

Straight away we must acknowledge that the task of making useful observations of each and every child in relation to all the skills and attitudes, and at the same time fostering their learning, is not just a formidable one, but is impossible. This is not expected. Collection of evidence about process skills is made into a manageable task by planning and focusing. At the same time, it is made worthwhile by the benefits to teaching and learning. Knowing where the children are in their development is essential to deciding how to help them and the evidence gathered indicates the next steps to take (as we shall see in Chapter 17). So these are considerable benefits for teaching to add to the significant benefits for learning noted in Chapter 14.

We deal with planning the gathering of evidence later in this chapter. At this point we take up the matter of focusing observation.

The observation of children is not just a matter of seeing whether or not they are hypothesising, interpreting, showing critical reflection, etc. Such broad judgements would be impossible without thinking out what it means to hypothesise, interpret and so on. The descriptions of early and later development for each of the process skills and attitudes in Chapters 4 and 5 provide a useful start in focusing observation. They need to be 'translated' into the subject matter of the particular activities being observed. As an example, we return to the work with ice balloons mentioned in Chapter 15 and pick up the process side of these activities.

In their first exploration, the children made these observations:

> There are three types of ice: clear, lined and white, or 'frosted'.
>
> The lines are like spiky objects within the ice; they usually radiate out from a point near the centre; they are fairly straight.
>
> The ice has air bubbles in it. As the ice melts, they are released and, if the ice is in water, the air bubbles rise and pop at the surface.
>
> When the ice is just out of the freezer it feels very cold; a mist can be seen near it, a white frost grows on its surface, and if it is put into water straight away, cracking noises are heard and crack appear inside it.
>
> (Ovens, *Primary Science Review*, 1987, 3, p. 5)

They went on to explore and take certain actions which led to the comments quoted earlier (page 142). We now consider what the teacher would be able to observe (for one group of children) during the initial explorations and follow-up activities. Keeping in mind the behaviours identified in Chapters 4 and 5 as indications of the skills and attitudes in action, the observations made are likely to be as follows:

Observing

- Children made detailed observations (e.g. of 'lines' or air bubbles in the ice);
- used their senses (e.g. to feel the ice, its coldness, its 'stickiness' when just out of the freezer);
- noticed the sequence of events (e.g. which parts started melting first);
- used a simple instrument to aid observation (e.g. looked at the ice through a hand lens).

Raising questions

- Children asked 'what's in the middle?';
- wanted to see how long the ice could be kept without melting;
- asked if the water made it melt more quickly than if it was all in the air.

Hypothesising

- Children suggested why something happens or reasons for observations (e.g. why the ice seems to be cracked, why ink runs off and doesn't soak in);
- used previous knowledge (e.g. to explain what happens when salt is put on the ice balloon);
- realised that there were several possible explanations of some things (e.g. several reasons why there were air bubbles in the ice).

Planning and conducting enquiries

- Children used past experience in saying that something might happen that could be tested (e.g. that the ice would melt more quickly in warm water, or in other conditions);
- planned to change the independent variable (e.g. placing some ice in air and some in water to test the idea that this makes a difference);
- controlled variables for a fair test (e.g. keeping the initial mass of ice and the temperature the same in the above investigation);
- measured an appropriate dependent variable (e.g. the change in mass of the pieces of ice over the same time in this investigation).

Interpreting

- Children linked pieces of information (e.g. 'the larger pieces of ice slide down a slope more easily than the smaller ones');
- found patterns in observations (e.g. 'the more pieces an ice cube is broken into the more quickly the whole thing melts');
- showed caution in drawing conclusions (e.g. 'it isn't everything that melts more quickly in water than in air').

Communicating

- Children talked and listened in order to sort out ideas (e.g. sharing ideas about why a metal object will make a mark in the ice but a wooden one doesn't);
- made notes during an investigation (e.g. noting the initial mass of the ice cubes put to melt in different conditions; drawing and labelling the places where they are put);
- chose an appropriate means of communicating to others (e.g. drawing cubes of diminishing sizes to show how much melted at various times).

Curiosity

- Children showed interest (by making observations of the kinds reported on page 160);
- asked questions (e.g. 'Why does ice float in water?' 'Does it float in every liquid?' 'Why does salt make the ice melt?');
- spontaneously used information sources (e.g. to find out how much of icebergs are below the water).

Respect for evidence

- Children reported what actually happened despite contrary preconceptions (e.g. 'moisture still forms on the outside of the tank when there is a cover on the tank, but I thought it wouldn't');
- queried a conclusion when there was insufficient evidence (e.g. 'we don't know the bubbles are air, we just think they are').

Willingness to change ideas

- Children were prepared to change ideas in the light of evidence ('I thought the moisture on the tank came from the ice, but it can't be that if it happens when the tank is covered').

Critical reflection

- Children were willing to consider how procedures could be improved (e.g. 'it would have been better to have had larger pieces of ice to start with, because the difference would have been more obvious');
- considered alternative procedures (e.g. 'the cube in air ought to have been supported above the table – it was sitting in water half the time').

These items are a selection, based on the descriptions in Chapters 4 and 5, of those which seem applicable to the ice balloon activities. From these examples it is not too difficult see how these descriptions can be applied to other activities. Slightly different selections may be needed in different situations according to the opportunities they provide (e.g. whether measurement is appropriate or whether there are patterns to be identified). The descriptions are only guides to what may be significant; each and every one will not be applicable in every activity.

Using children's written work

Not all the evidence of process skills needs to be collected through on-the-spot observation. Children's written work often gives useful information, particularly in the case of older children, and if the tasks are set to require them to describe their observations, predictions, plans and how they carried them out. The examples in Figures 16.1 to 16.3 illustrate the value of the products. They all come from Paterson (*Primary Science Review* 1989, pp. 17–20).

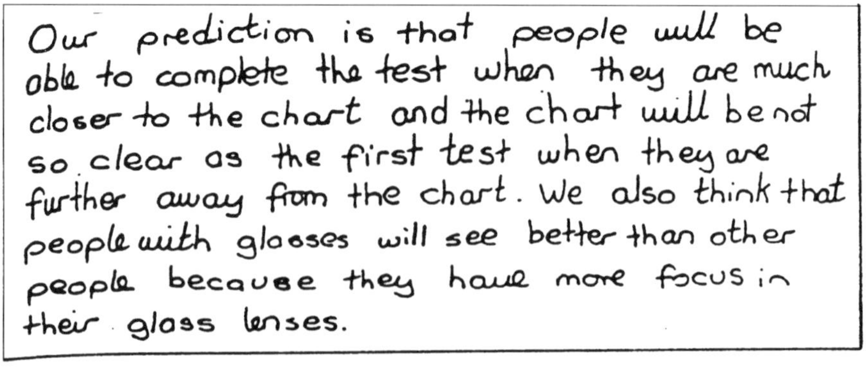

> Our prediction is that people will be able to complete the test when they are much closer to the chart and the chart will be not so clear as the first test when they are further away from the chart. We also think that people with glasses will see better than other people because they have more focus in their glass lenses.

Figure 16.1 An 11 year old's prediction based on ideas about spectacles and eyesight

In Figure 16.1 two predictions are made, both of which can be tested by investigation. The first prediction is based on the everyday experience that it is easier to see things which are closer than when they are far away. however. The basis of the second prediction, about people wearing glasses, is less easy to follow and deserves discussion.

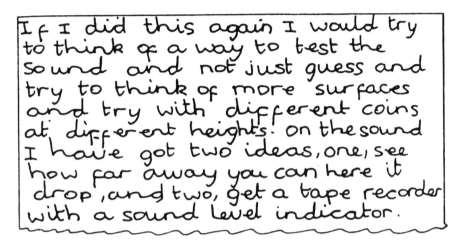

If I did this again I would try to think of a way to test the sound and not just guess and try to think of more surfaces and try with different coins at different heights. on the sound I have got two ideas, one, see how far away you can here it drop, and two, get a tape recorder with a sound level indicator.

Figure 16.2 A nine year-old's critical reflection on her investigation

Figure 16.2 shows a child's critical reflection on an investigation of how far away the sound can be heard of a penny being dropped. Not only does she identify the deficiencies of the investigation carried out, but shows some aspects of planning, including the ingenious use of an instrument to measure the sound level.

Figure 16.3 shows very detailed observation, using four senses, carefully and vibrantly described so that the reader can almost share the experience.

Planning to gather evidence during activities

As noted already, collecting evidence to build up a picture of all children in a class over all skills, concepts and attitudes, is a task which requires a thought out strategy and careful planning if the result is not to be patchy and only about the readily assessed parts of their achievement. Three points have to be considered in planning for assessment:

- which skills, ideas, attitudes will be assessed out of those which could be assessed;
- which children will be assessed;
- what part will children play, though self-assessment.

The third of these is the subject of Chapter 18. We consider the first two here.

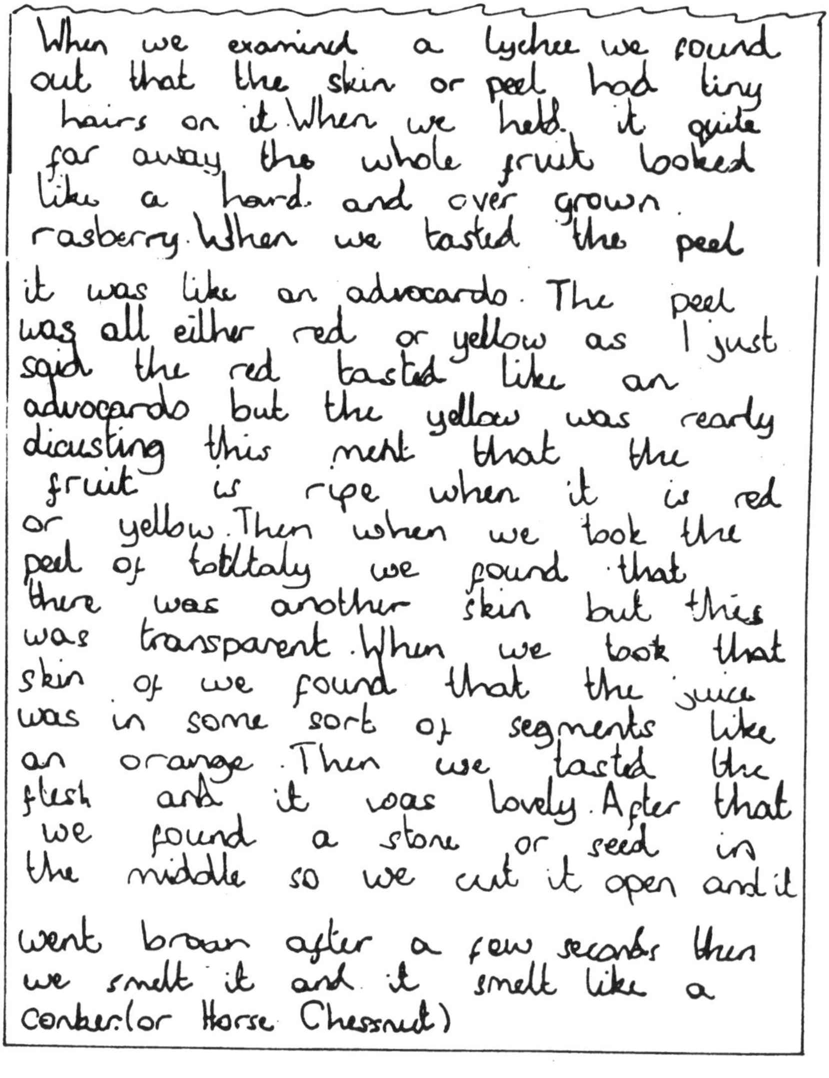

> When we examined a lychee we found out that the skin or peel had tiny hairs on it. When we held it quite far away the whole fruit looked like a hard and over grown rasberry. When we tasted the peel it was like an advocardo. The peel was all either red or yellow as I just said the red tasted like an advocardo but the yellow was rearly dicusting this ment that the fruit is ripe when it is red or yellow. Then when we took the peel of totltaly we found that there was another skin but this was transparent. When we took that skin of we found that the juice was in some sort of segments like an orange. Then we tasted the flesh and it was lovely. After that we found a stone or seed in the middle so we cut it open and it went brown after a few seconds then we smelt it and it smelt like a conker. (or Horse Chessnut)

Figure 16.3 Observations recorded by two ten year olds

When to assess what

Different aspects of achievement offer different assessment opportunities. Since the skills and attitudes relating to investigation can be assessed in many different investigations, the opportunity for their assessment will occur as frequently as children undertake investigations. These can be called 'frequently occurring' events. They do not need to be assessed for all children every time they occur, which is fortunate because this would be impossible. By their nature assessing these skills involves, particularly for young children, careful observation on the spot of how they carry out the activities.

Opportunities for assessing other aspects, however, do not occur so often. Ideas relating to specific subject matter, such as magnetism or seed germination, can only be assessed when activities relate to these things. These are 'infrequently occurring' opportunities for assessment. Information needs to be gathered about all the children working on a particular content while the opportunity exists. Fortunately these are the aspects of achievement which can be assessed through children's drawing and writing, things which can be studied after the event rather than assessed on the spot, so it is possible to collect information about several groups of children or even a whole class during the time the relevant activities are in progress.

In planning what to assess, therefore, it is best to consider: first, the *infrequently occurring* aspects and make sure that information will be obtained about these for all the children concerned, selecting the methods from those discussed in Chapter 15; then, the frequently occurring aspects, which will be assessed for some of the children, using methods suggested in this chapter.

Selecting the children

The greatest benefit of planning assessment is perhaps that it ensures that information is gathered equitably about all the children, not just the ones who need most help or claim most attention. It depends upon keeping records and carrying out the assessment systematically.

For *frequently* occurring aspects, the teacher might plan to observe and make notes about one group in particular during an investigation, which could spread over several sessions. The children in the target group should not be aware of special attention being paid to them; there is no suggestion of a teacher hovering with a clip board and refusing to interact with the children in a normal way.

The target group (of three to five children) should be selected according to the stage of their activities and the information the teacher wants to collect. The teacher may, for example, be filling in 'holes' in previous observation of these children, holes left when earlier activities did not give the opportunity to observe certain aspects as anticipated. The aim is gradually to collect evidence that can be used to help all the children to develop the skills and attitudes. In one lesson information may be collected about one group; later, other children may be observed, and missing information filled in, according to the opportunities provided by the activities planned. It may take a few months to cover all the skills for all the children. However, as the process becomes an established part of planning and interaction with children it becomes progressively more easy. The necessity for making notes about individual children, which may be felt at first, gives way later as the information fits into the mental framework which a teacher develops for assessing the children. The process is not in practice as demanding as it may seem in abstract, as an example may show.

This example of work with infants (5 to 7 year olds) is based on work quoted in Harlen *et al.* (1990). The teacher began the lesson by reading to the whole class a story about feet, in which a boy puts his Wellington boots on the wrong feet. After the story, still as a whole class, they talked about the events in the story, about their own feet, about shoes. This was followed by the organisation of group work, with six groups of four children, and the tasks of each group were described before they split up and went to the tables where necessary equipment had already been put out. So as soon as they reached their tables they could start on something, while the teacher began to pass round each group, helping, monitoring and observing.

The teacher had decided that her assessment focus would be group one, which had been given a collection of old plimsolls, Wellington boots, other shoes and slippers to investigate. (Other groups were taking up the subject of feet through different activities, including making shadows of their feet using a torch, measuring them, drawing round them and cutting out the shapes, making a graph, etc.) Group one had the task of discussing which shoes or boots they thought would be most waterproof and so this involved feeling and manipulating the materials. When they had made their choice and given their reasons, they were asked to find a way of showing that their idea was correct. So they planned a simple investigation and proceeded to carry it out. There was plenty of opportunity for the teacher, on her visits to this group to collect information about the detail of the children's observations, their identification of simple differences, their interpretation of the results (water drops stayed on the surface of smooth and fluffy materials) and the record they made of what they did. At the same time she made notes about individual children, for example: 'Lee – said water soaked though the plimsoll tongue because it's thinner that the other part. Tried out drips on sole and rubber edging – predicted that the water wouldn't go through'. Figure 16.4 shows Lee's record:

Figure 16.4 Five year old Lee's drawing

As well as the information about how group one went about observing and investigating, the teacher discussed the children's ideas about materials, particularly in relation to properties which varied among the ones they had been given. In this work on feet the other groups were not working with materials at this time, but the teacher ensured that such opportunities were given through other activities and so enabled her to complete her assessment of all the children's ideas on materials.

An aspect of this approach which may at first seem surprising is that accumulating information over time in this way means that children will be assessed in relation to the same skills, etc. while engaged on different activities. Does it matter that group one were investigating materials while group two might be investigating toy cars when their skills are assessed? Or that ideas about materials were assessed for group one using different materials than other children may be handling when their ideas are assessed? These are questions which need to be answered in terms of the purpose and use of the information, which we will take up in the next chapter.

Summary

- The main methods for collecting evidence about scientific process skills and attitudes are by observing how children go about their enquiries and listening to their discussions, and by studying their writing in tasks set to reveal their thinking.
- Observation has to the focused and so it is necessary to be aware of significant behaviours that indicate the skills in action.
- Evidence relating to skills and attitudes can be obtained from the writing of older children providing the tasks are presented so as to elicit their predictions, interpretations, reflections on methods used, etc.
- The collection of evidence has to be planned as part of the lesson, so as to ensure that opportunities for accessing ideas about the subject matter are taken when they exist for all the children and evidence is gathered systematically about process skills over time.

Chapter 17

Next steps: decisions and feedback

Introduction

How is the evidence gathered as part of teaching interpreted and used formatively in helping learning? This is the question we begin to address in this chapter. Although interpretation will happen at the same time as evidence is gathered, it is important to distinguish between these processes and so make sure that interpretations and decisions have a sound evidence base. After some examples, we look again at the nature of progression in the development of scientific ideas, process skills and attitudes and suggest ways of identifying next steps in children's learning. The question of feedback into teaching and learning is then considered. As well as feeding back into teaching (taking the kind of action discussed in Chapters 19, 20 and 21), feedback to children is considered in this chapter. This links with Chapter 18, which will take up the involvement of children in self-assessment.

Interpreting evidence of children's thinking

The process of interpreting evidence about children's thinking is similar to the process of interpreting evidence in scientific enquiry. We have to be careful to distinguish evidence from interpretations and to be as objective as possible about what the child actually says, writes, draws or does. As in scientific enquiries, interpretations are made in terms of the initial question, which might be 'what are the children's ideas about...?' or 'how well do they plan a fair-test investigation?' Conclusions are drawn tentatively about what the evidence means in terms of answers to these questions and the next steps in learning.

For example, if as part of exploring light sources children are asked to draw things that they think give out light, and they include a mirror and the moon in their drawings, the *evidence* is the drawings. The *interpretation* might be that the children do not distinguish between things that give out light and those that reflect it. Before deciding what action to take it would be wise to test out this interpretation. Is this really the problem, or did the children mistake 'things that are bright' for 'things that give out light?' Is there supporting evidence from other things the children have done or from what they say about the things they have drawn? Is it reasonable for children to be expected to know that the light from the moon is reflected light? If the interpretation is confirmed, the next step becomes clear – to provide opportunity for children to test their ideas by exploring what happens to a mirror in the dark, compared with a torch or other source of light, for example.

Similarly, if a child produces the drawing in Figure 17.1 of an electric circuit with two bulbs, it is necessary to make sure that the connection to the left-hand bulb is not just a mistake in drawing. If the child does not see anything wrong, then the next step might be to test the circuit in practice, following the diagram carefully.

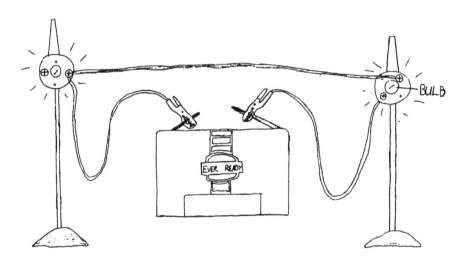

Figure 17.1 An 11 year old's drawing of lighting two bulbs from a battery

Another example concerns evidence about process skills. Figure 17.2 is the account produced by a nine year old girl of an investigation carried out by her group. There is evidence here of some process skills being used. Although the account does not allow us to judge how much of the planning came from the children, there is evidence of some attention to fair-testing, while the difference in the colour of the two thermometers was something that they could not control. Evidence relating to the initial question was collected, but the result is not interpreted in terms of the questions. It may be that the children assumed that it was 'obvious' in this case and so it would be important to check this in discussion. There is room for improvement in the structure of her report and for giving more information by labelling or annotating her drawing.

Does the colour of our clothes affect how warm we become. We put black tissue paper and white tissue paper round thermometers. We found that the thermometer with black tissue paper round it was 35 and the thermometer with white tissue paper round it was 29. The thermometer with black tissue paper was the colour white and the other thermometer was brown this was the one with white tissue paper. If we had put one thermom ter in the open and one in the shade this would not be fair.

Figure 17.2 A nine year old's account of her group's investigation

When problems can be spotted, as in these examples, next steps are easily identified in terms of remedial action. But evidence is useful not just to reveal problems; it also tells us what children can do well and when they can be helped to move on. Next steps follow from success as much as from errors. However, in order to identify where to go next it is necessary to have a map of progress in mind. So at this point we look again at the descriptions of progression in ideas and skills in Chapters 3 and 4 and consider how to use them to identify next steps.

Deciding next steps

Progression in ideas

In Chapter 3 the overall direction of progression was described in terms of three dimensions: from description to explanation; from 'small' to 'big' ideas; and from personal to shared ideas. The overall aim is to create more widely applicable ideas that are shared by others in making sense of the world around. These are formed by linking together ideas about specific aspects or the ideas that explain different events. We assume here that each small idea has been tested and fits the evidence but that it is limited to this evidence. Figure 17.3 represents the formation of idea D by the linking of ideas A, B and C, the formation of G from linking E and F and the formation of the bigger idea, H from linking D and G.

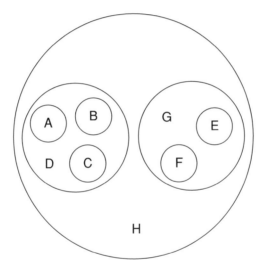

Figure 17.3 Formation of bigger ideas by bringing together smaller ones

The decisions about next steps follows from asking questions about ideas A, B and C:

Do the children understand A, B and C?

If 'no' then the next steps are to help the children to develop the ideas that are not understood

If 'yes', the next steps are to link them together and 'scaffold' idea D and help them to apply it where A, B and C were used previously and to explain things that could not be explained before.

For example, these ideas A, B and C, relevant to the force of gravity are needed to understanding why things don't fall off the side of the Earth or what happens to things dropped in places on the other side of the Earth:

A That things fall downwards
B That the Earth is spherical
C That 'down' means towards the centre of the Earth

If children have these ideas they may be helped to conceive gravity as a force that acts towards the centre of the Earth. If not, they need to be helped to develop these separate ideas before the one that brings them together can be grasped. Much later in their science education this bigger idea might be linked with others to reach the concept of gravity as a force of attraction between all bodies that have mass.

Progression in process skills

In Chapter 4 the general directions of progression in process skills were identified in terms of three dimensions: from simple to elaborate; from effective use in familiar situations to effective use in unfamiliar situations; and from unconscious to more conscious use of the skills. How this progression shows in each of the separate process skills was set out in terms of what can be expected of children at earlier and later stages of development. These statements are in effect indicators of development of each process skill. As such they help in the identification of next steps.

A useful approach is to turn each statement or indicator into a question. So, for example, for 'interpreting' the questions, derived from the statements on page 41, would be:

For early development

- Do the children obtain information relevant to answering the question posed in an enquiry?
- Do the children compare what was found with what they predicted would happen?

For later development

- Do the children put various pieces of information together to make some statement of their combined meaning?
- Do the children find patterns or trends in observations or results of investigations?
- Do the children identify an association between one variable and another?

- Do the children make sure that a pattern or association is checked against all the data?
- Do the children show caution in making assumptions about the general applicability of a conclusion?

To identify next steps, the evidence gathered about the interpretations the children are making in their work is scanned in relation to each question for early development. If answers are a clear 'yes', for the early stages, then the same things is done for the questions for the later stages. Where answers are a qualified 'yes' (sometimes, but not always) it is useful to consider where the skill is and is not shown, leading to identifying the kind of help needed. These are indeed the most useful answers since they identify the points where development is fluid. An answer 'no' signals where future help is needed, focusing first on using the skills in more familiar situations.

Progression in scientific attitudes

A similar approach to that described for process skills is applicable here. The overall dimensions of development were identified as: moving from orientation to self to orientation to others, and from being externally motivated to being self-motivated. It is useful to keep these in mind while considering the descriptions of children's behaviours relating to each kind of attitude at early and later stages (pages 47 to 51). These descriptions can be turned into questions and used to indicate the aspects for which there is or is not evidence of achievement, and from the 'yes and no' responses, where help can be most effective.

Feedback

The essential feature that makes assessment formative is that information from the evidence gathered is used to help children take the next steps in learning. This requires information to be fed back into the teaching-learning process. There are, however, at least three different ways of doing this, all of which need to be considered:

Teacher → (feedback about next steps) → teaching → → learning
Here the teacher uses the feedback as an input into teaching, to adjust the content and interaction with children with the intention of helping further learning

Teacher → (feedback about next steps) → children → → learning
Here the teacher feeds back the information to the children in a way that enables them to recognise the next steps they need to take and how to take them

Child and teacher → (decisions about next steps) → → learning
Here the children are involved in gathering information about their own progress and in using this to recognise the next steps they need to take and how to take them.

Feedback into teaching

So far in this chapter we have dealt only with part of the first of these types of feedback, the part concerned with identifying next steps. (The second part of this, how the teacher can adjust teaching in order to help children to take these next steps, is taken up in Chapters 19, 20 and 21.) However, an important opportunity for helping learning is missed if this is the only route for feedback into learning. At the very least teachers should share with children their views on their work in such a way that the children understand the feedback and what it means in terms of what they need to do. We now begin to consider this form of feedback. The discussion will continue in next chapter where we are concerned with the involvement of children in assessing their own work.

Feedback to children

The feedback concerned will include information that comes from observing children's behaviour during the process of their activities and from reading their written work. Here we discuss both in the context of formative assessment – helping further progress, rather than indicating the standard achieved in a particular task. There has been a good deal of research into feeding back information to children, through marking their work or observing their actions, which indicates that the form of the feedback has an impact on children's motivation as well as on their achievements. The importance of this is underlined by recalling that children have to do the learning and thus their motivation and enjoyment is as relevant to future learning as is information about how to correct errors. Thus the way in which feedback is given to children is as important as the focus of the feedback. Indeed some research shows that feedback can have a negative impact on performance as well as a positive one (Kluger and DeNisi 1996).

The main point to emerge both from research studies and from experience of effective practice is a distinction between feedback that gives information and feedback that is judgemental.

Feedback that gives information:

- focuses on the task, not the person;
- encourages children to think about the work not about their feelings or ability;
- provides comments on what to do next and ideas about how to do it.

Feedback that is judgemental:

- is expressed in terms of how well the child has done rather than how well the work has been done;
- gives a judgement that encourages children to label themselves;
- provides a grade or mark that children use to compare themselves with each other or with what they want to achieve.

Interestingly, praise comes into the judgemental category; it make children feel they are doing well but does not necessarily help them to do better. A remark or mark that indicates a judgement on the work will divert children's attention from any comment that is made about improvement. Children are more motivated by comments that help them think about their work and realise what they can do to improve it and which give them help in doing this. This means oral or written questions and comments such as 'How did you decide which was the best…?' 'Is there another way of explaining this by thinking of what happened when…' 'Next time, imagine that someone else is going to use your drawing to set up the circuit and make sure that you show them clearly what to do.'

Feedback to children is more effective in improving learning when children realise the goals of their work and then begin to take part in the decisions about next steps. This leads to the third kind of feedback, which is discussed in the next chapter.

Summary

- Interpretation of evidence has to be distinguished from the evidence itself so that it is clear when judgements are being made.
- Deciding next steps requires a clear view of the nature of progression.
- Progression in ideas involves linking small ideas that explain specific events and forming bigger ones; thus next steps are decided according to whether the ideas are there to be linked.
- Next steps in developing process skills and attitudes can be identified by comparing the evidence from children's behaviours and products with the indicators of development.
- Learning is helped by providing feedback about next steps to children as well as using it in adapting teaching.
- Feedback to children on their progress should give be non-judgemental and give information about next steps and how to take them.

Chapter 18

Involving children in assessing their own work

Introduction

What role ought primary children to be taking in assessing their own work? Having looked, in the last chapters, at how teachers can gather and interpret evidence about children's learning, we now turn to children's role in the formative assessment of their work. The first point to be considered is whether there is a case for giving children a role, for this is not traditional and is a relatively new aspect of mainstream education. In theory this means children being aware of the teachers' learning goals, being able to judge their work in relation to these goals and deciding how to make progress toward them. What this means in practice is considered in the second part of the chapter with some examples of strategies that teachers have found useful.

The case for children being involved in assessing their own work

There are important theoretical reasons for helping children to be able to do what some have described as self-monitoring (Sadler 1989) or self-assessment (Black 1993). Both these phrases are a shorthand for involving children in gathering and using evidence about their work. The focus should be on the work rather than the 'self'. Perhaps the strongest, but almost too obvious, reason is that learning goes on inside children's heads and so they must be willing to undertake it and to make the necessary effort. Children can, of course, be bribed or cajoled into learning by rewards and punishment, but it remains the fact that no-one can do the learning for them.

This being so, the way to help learning is to give the learner as much opportunity as possible (appropriate to their age and stage) to know what they are intended to learn and how to go about it. Again, this seems an obvious point but it is in fact quite uncommon for children to be able to articulate what the teacher intends them to learn from a particular activity, as opposed to what they are supposed to do. As Clarke (1998) puts it:

> We have always been very good at telling children what we want them to do and how we want them to do it, thus establishing control and discipline, an essential element when teaching a number of children at once. Without the 'secret' knowledge of the learning intention, however, children have been deprived of information which will not only enable them to carry out the task more effectively, they have also been denied the opportunity to self-evaluate, communicate this to the teacher, set targets for themselves and get to understand their own learning needs: in other words, to think intelligently about their own learning, rather than 'finding out what the teacher wants, and doing it.'
>
> (Clarke 1998, p. 47)

If teachers do share their learning intentions with children it puts the learners in a position to take some responsibility for work that is directed towards the goals. With both teacher and children 'in the know' about what is intended, progress in learning is more likely.

A further point concerns feedback from assessment into learning. As we noted in Chapter 17, there are two routes for feedback from the teacher's assessment of children's work: feeding back into their own teaching and feeding back to children. The form that the feedback takes, as noted earlier (page 164) makes a considerable difference to the impact that it has. Even when teachers intend feedback to give information about next steps, children may not know how to use it. Sadler (1989) pointed out that children may need to be trained in how to use feedback. However, an important point about involving children in the process from the beginning is that this avoids having to explain the feedback to them. If they have a part in making decisions about their work and their next steps, no gulf can appear between the teacher's views and the children's understanding of what they need to do. Feedback has a different meaning in these circumstances.

However, perhaps the strongest reason of all comes from research into the impact on learning. This shows that, in practice, involving children in the assessment of their work is effective in raising children's achievement. In their review of research into formative assessment and learning, Black and Wiliam (1998b) found firm evidence that this involvement is a key factor in the practices that were associated with improved levels of learning. Moreover, while all children were found to benefit, the lower achieving ones gained most.

To sum up, reasons for children's involvement in the formative assessment of their own work include:

- They are the ones who ultimately have to take the actions that lead to learning.
- Knowing their goals puts any learners in a better position to achieve them.
- There is less need for feedback from the teacher if the children are involved in assessing their work and deciding next steps.
- There is firm evidence that it helps to raise standards.

The consequences for practice are that teachers should share the goals of learning with children, involving children in judging the quality of their work and in deciding next steps. We now look at some ways of implementing each of these.

Sharing goals with children

In practice this means including a reason for what the children are going to do when introducing a task or setting up a problem. It is important to give an example here in order to clarify the difference between telling children what to learn (which is not what is meant) and telling them what they are going to learn about. In Chapter 1 of this book Graham set children investigating soils with three instructions about what to do and a fourth that gave a reason for doing it – so that they could think about what makes a difference to how well plants will grow in the soils. Without this fourth part, the children would probably have investigated the soils, but if asked what they were learning would have answered 'about soils'. The reason for the investigations given by the teacher focused their observations on relevant differences and thus not only made them aware of why they were investigating the soils but made the intended learning more likely.

In science it is often difficult to share the learning goals without telling children 'the answer'. The difference in wording is subtle but it considerably alters the message. For example, when setting up an investigation of things that make sounds, consider the difference between: *'Try to make different sounds with each of these things. Then see if you can work out what makes the sound and how to make a higher and a lower sound'* and *'Try to make different sounds with each of these things. See that the sound comes from making something vibrate and the more quickly it vibrates the higher the sound.'*

If the main purpose of an activity is to improve children's enquiry skills, then this should be made equally clear in language that the children will understand. So rather than using words such as 'predict' children can be asked for 'what you think will happen' (not 'what you guess will happen'); or 'why you think this happened/will happen' rather than 'your hypothesis'; or 'be careful to be as certain as you can about your result' when the aim is to control variable and repeat trials as necessary. Ensuring that discussion afterwards picks up on these intentions will help to set the pattern of taking the purpose seriously and working towards the intended learning.

One teacher regularly asks the children to explain to others what they have learned, making explicit reference to what they hoped to do or find out. If, as often happens, there was some unplanned feature of the enquiry, she asks them 'what did you learn from that?' Sometimes she asks the children to think of questions to ask each other about what they have learned; she finds that these are often more probing and difficult than her own questions. All these things combine to reinforce the learning atmosphere and support learning as a shared endeavour.

Involving children in judging the quality of their own work

In order to judge the quality of the work, children not only need to know the purpose of what they are doing but have some notion of the standard they should be aiming for. This is less easy in science than in an area such as language development, where children might be told that in a piece of writing they are to use whole sentences or make sure that the events in a story are in the correct sequence. The children then know what to look for in judging their work. In science it is more difficult to make general statements that convey meaning to the children. Thus the required features are better conveyed through examples; over time the children come to share the teacher's criteria.

The process can begin usefully if children from about the age of eight are encouraged to select their 'best' work and to put this in a folder or bag. Part of the time for 'bagging' should be set aside for the teacher to talk to each child about why certain pieces of work were selected. The criteria which the children are using will become clear. These should be accepted and they may have messages for the teacher. For example if work seems to be selected only on the basis of being 'tidy' and not in terms of content, then perhaps this aspect is being over-emphasised by the teacher.

At first the discussion should only be to clarify the criteria the children use. 'Tell me what you particularly liked about this piece of work.' Gradually it will be possible to suggest criteria without dictating what the children should be selecting. This can be done through comments on the work. 'That was a very good way of showing your results, I could see at a glance which was best.' 'I'm glad you think that was your best investigation because although you didn't get the result you expected, you did it very carefully and made sure that the result was fair.'

Through such an approach as this children may begin to share the understanding of the objectives of their work and be able to comment usefully on what they have achieved. It then becomes easier to be explicit about further targets and for the children to recognise when they have achieved them.

Teachers of older children can more explicitly share with them the criteria they use both in assessing practical skills and marking written work. One science teacher, for example, did this by writing his own account of a class investigation and distributing copies for the children to mark, looking for particular features. It led to lively discussion and a keener understanding of what was expected in their own accounts (Fairbrother 1995).

Another approach is to use examples of other children's work, which could be collected for the purpose and made anonymous. Alternatively, the examples from the collections published to help teachers assess work could be shared with the children. These include publications such as *Exemplification of Standards, Science at Key Stages 1 and 2, levels 1 to 5* (SCAA 1995) and *Performance Standards: Volume 1 Elementary School* (New Standards 1997). The teacher and children can then make critical comments more freely about the work and about how it could be improved, which they then apply to their own work.

Involving children in deciding next steps

When children have a view of what they should be doing and how well they should be doing it, they are in a position to share in deciding the next steps to be taken. 'Sharing' is meant to convey the ultimate responsibility of the teacher in helping children's learning, for we are in no way suggesting that children decide what they do and don't do. However, sharing means that the children understand why they are being asked to do certain things and have a firm grasp of what they should do. Moreover their involvement is likely to lead to greater motivation for the work.

A teacher of nine and ten year olds describes how she helps the children to decide what they need to do:

> I make time to sit down with each group after an activity and talk about what they found difficult, what they thought they did well and what they could have done better. I ask them if they thought about particular aspects relating to the processes and then about how they explain their results. This is important for me because I won't have followed every step of their investigation and it helps me decide how much they have progressed from earlier work and whether they have taken the steps we agreed previously. I

then ask questions that indicate my view of what they need to do, but by expressing this as questions, they actually identify what they are going to do. The questions are like: 'what can you do in your next investigation to be more sure of your results?' 'what sorts of notes could you make as you go along to give you all the information for preparing a report at the end?' 'where could you find out more information to explain what you found?'

(personal communication)

Note that she 'makes time' for this which, she reports, is time well spent. It saves time for teaching and learning in the end by obviating the need to repeat explanations of what children are to do and the children learn more quickly by thinking rather than from making mistakes. This teacher treats the group as a learning unit and encourages them to help each other. Since the purpose of the assessment is formative, and since they learn as a group, the decisions made together are important for their learning. However, she also looks at the work of each child individually and makes sure that they recognise their own next steps in learning.

Summary

- There are important theoretical and practical reasons for involving children in assessing their own work.
- Acting on this means sharing learning goals with the children, conveying an operational meaning of quality and helping them to identify their next steps.
- Sharing goals means communicating to children a reason for their activities in terms of learning and referring back to this in discussion at the end of the activity.
- Helping children to judge the quality of the work requires the subtle communication of criteria of quality through discussion of examples.
- Involving children in deciding next steps follows from a review of what they have done and how they have done it and agreeing ways of improving it or moving on from it.

Chapter 19

Helping development of scientific ideas

Introduction

Once the next steps in developing ideas have been decided, how can children be helped to take these steps? This chapter is concerned with development of scientific ideas; the development of skills and attitudes is the subject of the next two chapters. The existing ideas of children provide clues as to the actions to take, so we begin with a review of the characteristics of children's ideas and from this identify useful strategies for advancing them. After discussing each of these strategies, we consider how to introduce, when necessary, more scientific ideas so that children have alternatives to their own ideas. This requires careful judgement to avoid leaving children with ideas that they have not been able to build into their own thinking. So, in the final section we discuss the important matter of knowing when to stop, to allow further time and experience to make a bridge between the children's own ideas and those offered.

Features of children's ideas

The examples of children's ideas given in Chapter 6 and the many other studies of children's ideas, indicate some general features. The main ones are that these ideas:

1. resulted from reasoning about experience, and not simply from imagination or fantasy, but reasoning of a kind that we might call 'everyday', which is not scientific;
2. would not stand up to rigorous testing against evidence that was often available for the children to use had their attention been drawn to it;
3. sometimes required additional evidence, not all ready available, in order to be tested;

4. related to particular situations and were not linked to the ideas that explain similar situations;
5. were influenced by other information than that which came from evidence of actual events, such as the media, conventions of speech and ways of representing things, influential adults and peers;
6. were often expressed in terms of words which seemed scientific, yet had, for the children, a meaning which was ill-defined, difficult to pin down and not apparently consistent with the scientific meaning.

These general characteristics suggest some general approaches to helping development of more scientific ideas. Features 1 and 2 indicate that in some cases the children's reasoning is not scientific and so, if they were helped to test their ideas using scientific process skills, they would recognise that these ideas don't fit the evidence and something else has to be tried. Feature 3 indicates that more evidence is needed; the nature of the child's idea usually points to what is required. Feature 4 relates to ideas that may be limited to a particular context and development can be helped by creating links to situations explained by the same ideas. Features 5 and 6 suggest that discussing words and the meanings they have for the children may lead to some clarification of concepts. In many cases, actions of all these kinds may be relevant, but we discuss them separately for the sake of clarity under the headings of:

• Developing and using more scientific process skills
• Providing more experience
• Creating links between events that have a common explanation
• Discussing words and other representations.

Ways of starting from children's ideas

Developing and using more scientific process skills

As we noted in Chapter 6, if a child uses immature process skills, that are not scientific, then ideas will not be properly tested and non-scientific ideas may persist when they do not really fit the evidence. The ways in which teachers can help children develop specific process skills are the subject of Chapter 20. Here we are concerned with ensuring that children test their ideas. To do this the ideas have first to be in the form of an explanation that is testable. A possible explanation (or hypothesis) may well be expressed in various ways by children. 'Oh, I know, it's ...' does not sound like a hypothesis but it will contain some sentiment that a particular effect has a certain cause. 'The ice melts because it is outside' is one such statement from a child which at first caused some surprise to his teacher. A prediction from this was that if the ice was somewhere else (inside) then it would not melt. The hypothesis was based in this case on the place where the ice was (which was, after all, where ice had been seen to form and melt) and not on the temperature of the place. The prediction could readily be investigated and thus the idea tested.

The context in this case was a class discussion of what made ice melt, during which several different ideas were put forward and tested. The children whose ideas were not supported by their investigations therefore had immediate access to another idea which worked in practice better than theirs. Thus the whole experience, of discussion and sharing ideas – and not just the activity itself – is important to the development and change in ideas.

Providing more experience

This is closely related to testing out ideas but may not involve actions of the kind just discussed. It means extending the range of types of material, living things, and events in children's experience. Often this new experience challenges existing ideas and requires children to be more cautious of their generalisations: almost all wood floats (not ebony or lignum vitae); most conifers are evergreen (but not all); sound travels through the air (and through solids and liquids as well). These are not only matters of definition but also matters of explanation, when used, for example, to 'explain' that something floats because it is made of wood.

Often children's ideas indicate the experience that is lacking. For example the quite common idea that rust forms inside metals and leaks out on to the surface can be challenged by cutting through a rusty nail. More difficult to provide is more experience of things that cannot be directly seen by the children; the insides of living things and of themselves, for instance. This is where visits outside the classroom can play a really special part in children's learning. More and more industries and commercial organisations have education sections which give children learning opportunities that cannot be provided in the classroom. Ideas about the origins and processing of food can be developed by visits to a farm or dairy or a supermarket. (Primary Science Review No 62, 2000 describes a number of such opportunities). Interactive museums or science centres often have curriculum-related exhibits that are designed to take into account children's ideas and find intriguing ways of challenging and advancing them.

For example, in a centre for 3–12 year olds within a science museum in Paris, the staff designed an exhibit about the human skeleton which takes into account research about young children's ideas of the bones in their body. This shows that children may view their body as a 'bag of bones' or as having strings of many small bones which could not provide support. The interactive exhibit that was produced enabled a child to sit on and pedal a stationary bicycle which was next to a large sheet of glass that acted as a mirror. When the child begins to pedal and looks at the image of his or her legs in the glass, a skeleton is superimposed on this image, showing the moving bones in the legs. This experience was found to have a much greater impact on children's ideas about bones in the body than classroom lessons about the human skeleton (Guichard 1995).

Information from other sources can also be found from the websites that museums and various industries and organisations set up to help education, and from CD-ROMs. The children's ideas about what is inside the egg (pages 58 and 59) will no doubt be changed by access to photographs of the development of egg embryos and discussion of other evidence of the changes in form and in size that take place in the reproduction of all living things, to be found in books or CD-ROMs.

Studying children's ideas will generally be a guide as to the experience that will help. The question, then, is where to stop so that children are not overwhelmed with new information that is difficult for them to assimilate into their thinking. We come to this later (page 179).

Creating links between events that have a common explanation

The model of linking 'small' ideas together to become 'bigger' ones represented in Figure 17. 3 (page 161) has several applications. Sometimes different 'small' ideas are used to explain things that actually have a common explanation, but one that is unknown to the children. For example, children might explain the disappearance of water from puddles in terms of draining away through the ground, while they may explain the drying of damp clothes on a washing line in terms of some action of the air. Discussing the possibility that the air may have something to do with the puddle drying up, too, may lead to some investigations (e.g. page 39) that make this a useful idea in both situations. Further examples of water disappearing could then be drawn into the range of things explained in this way and the idea has become one that applies more widely, that is, has become a bigger one.

In other cases the small ideas are ones that refer to different aspects of a phenomenon, as in the case of gravity, mentioned in Chapter 17 (page 162). Another example is putting together ideas about light and how we see to understand the formation of images in mirrors or lenses.' This depends on understanding that:

- we see an object when light enters our eyes from it;
- putting a mirror or lens between the object and our eyes changes the path of the light;
- we interpret the path of the light at a straight line from the object to the eye.

If all these ideas are understood it may be possible to bring them together to realise that the eye does not 'see' the change in direction that the mirror or lens has caused and so interprets it as if it came in a straight line, so the object is interpreted as in a different place than it really is.

Discussions words and other representations

As an accompaniment to practical activity discussion of words and ways of representing things can make all the difference to the thinking which is provoked by experience. In an activity about sound, for instance, children in the early junior years may begin to use the word 'vibration'. It will naturally be used at first for 'vibration' which can be felt or seen and thus related to the use of the word in everyday experience, for the experience of being in contact with things which have motors in them, such as a washing machine, vacuum cleaner, electric mixer or power drill. So it will be easy to use the word in relation to a drum which is beaten or a guitar string which has been plucked (for example, Figures 6.8 and 6.9, page 61). But what do children think is happening in a vibration? What examples of vibrating objects can they give? Do things which are not vibrating make a sound?

Discussion of these things, with the children supplying instances of objects explored in their practical work will help them think again about what they have done (and perhaps go back to check things they took almost for granted) as well as reflect on the words they use. At a later stage and with older children the questions would be more challenging and aimed at taking their notion of vibration further and towards vibrations which cannot be seen, such as those in air. Do things which make a sound vibrate? Can you have a sound without vibration? How does the sound travel from a vibrating object to our ears?

Introducing more scientific ideas

In several of the approaches to developing ideas just discussed, the children's current ideas are challenged, but it is not in all cases clear how they find more scientific ones to replace them. There is an important role for the teacher here; one which has, perhaps, been underplayed in discussing constructivist approaches to learning. It is also a subtle role, since we must avoid giving the 'right' answer that children have to accept whether or not it makes sense to them. In order to take new ideas into their own thinking, children need

- access to different ideas than their own;
- support in trying out the new ideas in relation to their existing experience;
- opportunities to apply them to new experiences.

Access to different ideas

New ideas need not necessarily be introduced by the teacher. They can also come from books, CD-ROMs, videos and from people who visit the classroom or places that are visited by the children. Other children are often a source of different ideas and these may include ideas that are closer to the scientific view than the ideas of a particular child. Whatever the source, children are likely to need encouragement and support while trying out new ideas.

Support in trying out new ideas

This is where the teacher's role in 'scaffolding' new ideas comes in. As noted in Chapter 8 (p80), scaffolding means supporting children in using a new idea until it makes sense to them and becomes part of their thinking. It may mean leading them through some steps that they don't quite understand in order to enable them to see the point in retrospect. Scaffolding will only be successful if the new idea is within reach of children's experience (in the 'zone of proximal development', as Vygotsky put it). Examples are the best way of conveying what it means in practice.

Take the experience of making coloured shadows with two torches covered with coloured gelatines, as in Figure 19.1.

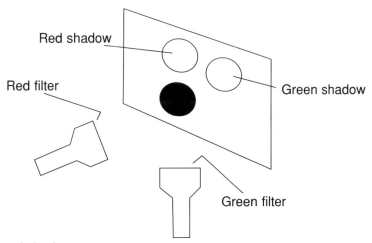

Figure 19.1 Coloured shadows

Most children find it difficult to understand why the red and the green shadows are where they are; they expect them to be the other way round. So the thinking has to be helped, but this depends on children already knowing that a shadow is formed when light is prevented from reaching the surface on which the shadow in seen. In that case it is possible to lead children to think about where on the screen light from the red light does not reach, while light from the green light does, and vice versa. The teacher thus supports them through the thinking that leads to a conclusion that fits the evidence.

Scaffolding is particularly important in relation to ideas which cannot be tested out in practice. In simple cases, such as the melting ice mentioned earlier, several ideas from the children can be tried out for everyone to see. In other cases a discussion and some 'thought experiments' may be helpful. It is difficult, for example, for children to understand that if a moving object stops, there must be a force acting to stop it. Many children accept or offer the reason as being 'friction' but don't go as far as realising that without friction the object would not stop moving. Scaffolding is necessary here, just as it is in relation to ideas about the Earth in space, the causes of day and night, the seasons, and phases of the moon. These are cases where the teacher may have to lead children to take a few steps without realising why until they can look back. For example, children are unlikely to decide on their own to make a model of the sun, moon and Earth to explain why we see the moon in different phases. So the teacher takes the initiative and sets up the situation that enables the children to 'see' a spherical object looking like a half-moon and then they can make the connection.

Opportunities to try out new ideas in different situations

Given that the new idea is a scientific one, it should help children make sense of further experience. Helping children to do this will secure the new idea in their thinking as well as expanding their understanding of things around. It also gives the teacher the opportunity to see how secure the new idea really is. It may be necessary to stop and return to familiar ground if the signs are that the new idea is still a little wobbly. However, if new ideas can be successfully applied this brings a feeling of enjoyment and satisfaction in learning. For example:

- Can the explanation of the coloured shadow be applied when there are three torches with different coloured lights? What will happen if the coloured filter is removed from one of them?
- Can eclipses be explained in terms of the movement of the moon round the Earth and the Earth round the sun?
- Can the idea of non-friction be used to explain why ice skates have knife-edged blades?

Knowing when to stop

For each child there is gap between present ideas and those which we aim to help him or her achieve. The question of how to bridge this gap is one to which there is no universal answer. If there were, education would be more an exact science than a form of art; we would be able to build a child's learning rather as building a house, knowing just how one brick should be placed on another. As we know, it is not like that. With children's learning the 'bricks' are not ready formed; they need time to take shape and until that has happened there can be no further building. There are times when children's ideas need time before there can be further development. This is the time to stop and it is as important to recognise this as it is to stimulate thinking at other times.

So how do we recognise when it is time to stop? Children's general reactions will indicate this in science, as in other subject areas. When they become easily distracted after a period of working with full attention on something; when they lose interest and adopt a mechanical rather than a thinking approach to their work. These can be signs that the child is no longer in charge of the learning and things may have got ahead of him or her.

In science the signs are also to be found in what may seem to be stubborn persistence in ideas despite evidence which conflicts. For example, the teacher who challenged children's notion that the sound from outside the room must be coming through air round the sides of the door by putting sticky tape all around and over the key hole, found that the children were not convinced that the sound they could still hear was coming through the wood. They claimed that there must be holes which had not been taped over and were letting the sound through. At that time she could not provide convincing evidence of sound passing through solids and was wise enough to leave the children with their idea. At some stage later, with more experience, the idea could be tested more convincingly and further evidence of sound travelling through solids and liquids could be provided. When children hold on to their ideas in this way it is a sure sign that they are not ready to relinquish present ideas for different ones.

For all of us there are times when looking at things a different way is exciting and seems to bring several things into place. There are also times when we can't see that any idea different from our own makes sense and we need more time or more examples if we are going to change our view. We only have to think of how difficult it is to change people's view of what foods are good for them to realise that we all hang on to cherished ideas.

So the time to stop trying to help children advance their ideas is when they do not see other ideas as being as useful as their present ones. The time to stop is also before falling to the temptation of pressing different ideas with the force of authority, giving the impression that 'this is how things are'. If children feel obliged to accept ideas different from theirs because they are clearly 'right' and their own are 'wrong' then they will quite soon lose confidence in their ability to think things out and come to a useful conclusion. It is far better to leave them with an imperfect notion of how sound travels than to turn science into something which they have to accept but don't understand.

Summary

- In deciding ways of helping children to develop their ideas it is useful to start from the characteristics of their own ideas.
- These characteristics suggest that development may be helped by taking action of one or more of these kinds: enabling the children to test the ideas; providing more evidence; creating links between different ideas and discussing the meaning of the words children use in their explanations.
- If children's ideas don't fit the evidence it may be necessary to introduce more scientific ideas. These can come from other children, books, the use of ICT and other people, as well as the teacher.
- It is important that teachers recognise the signs of where to stop at a particular time, and to pick up the development of the ideas at a later stage.

Chapter 20

Helping development of process skills

Introduction

Process skills are important in learning with understanding, both in school and in later life. It is through their use that scientific ideas are tested, developed and linked with other ideas and become part of an individual's way of making sense of the world. What can teachers do to assist the development of these important mental and physical skills? We begin with some general strategies for, as we noted in Chapter 4, the identification and discussion of separate skills is for convenience; in reality they occur in close association with each other. However, there are more targeted ways in which teachers can help children to observe, raise questions, plan investigations, and so on. So the bulk of this chapter is concerned with how the general strategies are applied in the development of each of the seven process skills.

General strategies for supporting process skill development

At the general level, the teacher's role in providing children with experiences which help them develop process skills has these six aspects:

- *Providing opportunity to use process skills in the exploration of materials and phenomena at first-hand.* This enables children to use their own senses and to gather evidence from which to raise questions, form hypotheses based on existing ideas, and so on. Children have to use process skills in order to develop the skills. Being told about what it means to observe, interpret or investigate is not the same as doing these things. Action provides the practical basis for thinking. Teachers can initiate the use of process skills through the questions they ask; examples of the kinds of questions which help to do this have been discussed in Chapter 8.

- *Providing opportunity for discussion in small groups and as a whole class.* Tasks which are designed to require children to share their ideas, to listen to others, to explain and defend their ideas, necessarily involve them in thinking through what they have done, relating ideas to evidence, considering others' ways of approaching a problem in addition to their own (see Chapter 12 for more on this). Talking and listening provide the thinking basis for action.

- *Listening to children talk and studying what they produce to find out the processes which have been used in forming their ideas.* At all stages of activities the teacher can be picking up information about how children have collected and used evidence. Helping the development of skills depends on knowing how children are using them.

- *Encouraging critical review of how activities have been carried out.* During and after completing activities children should discuss how they have carried out parts of or the whole of an investigation and should be encouraged to consider alternative courses of action and the extent to which these may be improvements. This will enable the children to recognise the skills which they need to improve. Helping children to realise the skills they need is important for giving them a part in their own learning

- *Providing access to the techniques needed for advancing skills.* In order to increase the accuracy of observation and measurement, for example, the use of instruments has to be taught as the need for them arises. Other techniques, such as used in the drawing of charts and graphs, and the knowledge of conventions in diagrams, are required for communication. Knowing how to use these instruments and conventions is not the same as using them appropriately, so there is more to using these skills than the basic knowledge. However, using techniques appropriately requires knowledge of how to use them.

- *Involving children in meta-cognition.* Older children can be involved in the discussion of what is involved in, for example, expressing a question in an investigable form or making a prediction. Thinking about the way they do things is introducing children to meta-cognition, that is, 'reflecting on the sort of thinking they have been engaged in, to bring it to the front of their consciousness' (Adey 1997).

Helping development in specific skills

Observing

Providing opportunity for using the senses for gathering information means providing objects and phenomena for children to explore. It is always a good idea to set out a display of objects relating to a new topic two or three weeks ahead of starting it in order to create interest. During the topic work items can be added to the display.

Time is significant in encouraging observation more than perhaps for other skill process. Children need time to go back to things they may have observed only superficially or when a question has occurred to them that suggests something they want to check. A display enables children to use odd moments as well as science activity time for observing and so increases an important commodity in the development of this skill.

Some children also need invitations to observe. Cards placed next to objects or equipment displayed can encourage observation and action. 'Try to make this bottle make a high and a low sound' placed next to a bottle three-quarters full of water encourages interaction. 'How many different kinds of grass are there here?' placed next to a bunch of dried grasses encourages careful observation. The correct use of a magnifying glass can also be taught through a card with a drawing on it. Older children with the required manipulative skill can learn to use a microscope through similar informal opportunities.

When observations have been made opportunities should be created for them to be shared. Making a point of spending a few minutes as a whole class discussing what has been noticed about things on display, for example, may draw attention of some children to things they have missed and emphasise the role of the display in the class activities. Asking questions about details during this discussion will help children to pay attention to them in further observation.

Not all observations are made in the classroom, of course, and careful preparation for expeditions outside are important if things are not to be missed. There is less opportunity to revisit objects and so it is essential for the teacher to explore in advance the place to be visited, keeping the capabilities and knowledge of the children in mind (see Chapter 10).

In summary, the teacher can help children develop their skill in observation by:

- setting up in the classroom opportunities and invitations to observe, through displays and challenges;
- providing time for observations to be made and repeated if necessary;
- creating situations where children discuss what has been observed;
- encouraging attention to detail in observation.

Raising questions

We discussed in Chapter 13 the importance of encouraging children to raise questions. The ways in which questioning can be promoted through a supportive class climate and by positive reinforcement were included there and need not be repeated here. There is, though, a further point to add.

The significance in science of being able to put questions in an investigable form means that it is worthwhile taking time to discuss with children explicitly what this means and how to do it, using some examples. Faire and Cosgrove (1988) suggested gathering questions from children informally during exploratory activities or more formally by inviting groups to ask questions about things that puzzle them. The collected questions are then discussed to see how they can be rephrased to make them accessible to investigation. More recently, the AKSIS project (Goldsworthy *et al.*, 2000) has produced lists of questions for discussion with children in structured activities designed to make children aware of the need to clarify questions. The idea is to help children realise that questions such as: 'Does toothpase make a difference to your teeth?' 'Is margarine better for you than butter?' can only be answered when the meaning of 'making a difference' and 'better for you' have been clarified. There has to be some indication of the kind of evidence that could be collected to answer the question (even if, in these cases, the children might not be able to collect it themselves). One of the AKSIS activities is to ask children to decide whether in certain questions it is clear what would have to be changed and what measured to answer the question. The children can then be asked to reflect on their own questions and reword them to make clear how they could be investigated.

Thus the main ways of helping children to raise investigable questions are:

- inviting questions as a regular part of enquiry and through special measures such as a question box;
- providing displays of articles selected to stimulate curiosity;
- discussing questions and how to refine them to identify the evidence needed to answer them.

Hypothesising

As we saw in Chapter 4, a hypothesis is an attempt to explain some observation, happening or relationship. There are things to avoid as well as to encourage in helping the development of this skill. To be avoided is the idea that a hypothesis has to be 'right', that is, it depends on knowing all about what is happening. This impression can be conveyed through the questions which are asked of children. If the question is framed as 'why do some leaves turn brown in autumn?' then it is difficult to answer unless you know, or think you know the reason. On the other hand, the questions 'why *do you* think some leaves turn brown?' or 'what do you think could be the reason for leaves turning brown?' stimulate the generation of an explanation from existing ideas (see Chapter 8 on the wording of questions).

The development of confidence in ability to suggest explanations is helped by asking for several possible alternatives in situations where there is not necessarily an obvious answer. For example, why are there patches of different coloured grass on the playing field? There are multiple possible reasons, which could be brought out by asking 'what else could be the reason?' as each suggestion is accepted. Each one has to be possible in terms of the evidence – different seeds used; something in the soil under the patches; drainage varying from one place to another; but a suggestion that more rain falls on the patches might be rejected because of evidence that there is nothing to cause such difference. Trying to explain a shared observation such as this enables children to feel that they have the ability to make sense of the things around them. Which of the suggestions may be most likely would require more evidence and investigation but their ability to attempt explanations is not dependent on the result.

Young children's hypotheses will be in the form of attempts to explain specific events in their experience rather than in terms of broad statements of principles which explain a whole range of phenomena (such as the conditions needed for growth of plants to explain the patches in the grass). However, the ability to suggest explanations in specific terms is the foundation of later development in applying broad principles and theories. Meanwhile the skill of using existing ideas, limited though they may be, in attempting explanations plays an important role in testing and developing these ideas.

In summary, teachers can help development in hypothesising by:

- drawing attention to situations or events for which there may be several plausible explanations;
- asking children in groups to come up with as many possible reasons as they can to explain something they have observed;
- sharing possible explanations and discussing them in terms of the evidence.

Predicting

Predictions can be made on the basis of patterns found in observations or on the basis of hypotheses which are put forward to explain observations or findings. In the case of patterns found between two variables, the prediction is based on the evidence of some association between one thing and another, but without necessarily assuming that this is an association of cause and effect. The simple relationship between hand size and foot size is an example of an association where there is no sense in suggesting that one causes the other; rather there is another variable which is causally related to both. Nevertheless, the association, whatever its basis, can be used in predicting (within limits) the foot size of someone from their hand size.

Not all patterns are simple and the process of predicting from them is best encouraged in the context of the more obvious relationships, such as the sound that is made when a thin strip of wood (or ruler) is held at one end and twanged at the other. The note varies with the length which is free to vibrate. Once observations have led to the pattern being established, children can predict whether a particular length will give a higher or lower note and then try it out. It is useful for them to discuss how they made their prediction, since this helps them to become conscious of using the pattern and that doing this is different from guessing.

Predictions based on hypotheses (possible explanations) are used to test the theory behind the explanation. Hypotheses suggest explanations in terms of cause and effect and constitute some theory of why things are as they are. It is the test of a true theory that it can be used predictively. For example, the hypothesis that the leaves on some trees turn brown 'because of the cold' is a theory that cold brings about the change. Although not quite accurate this theory can be used to make a prediction about circumstances in which leaves will turn brown, which is a test of the idea on which the hypothesis is based. Again, it is important for children to be helped to make predictions in simple cases and to think about the way in which they do this.

Children's prediction are often implicit and helping to make them explicit and conscious enables them to see the connection between an idea and the prediction from it that is tested. Thus the teacher can help development of this skill by:

- taking the opportunity where there is simple relationship between variable to ask children to make predictions;
- asking children to use the possible explanations for events to make predictions;
- discussing how they arrive at their predictions and so distinguishing a prediction from a guess;
- getting children to test a prediction and then interpret the result in terms of the pattern or hypothesis on which it was based.

Planning and conducting investigations

Too often children's experience of what is required in planning an investigation is by-passed because they are given written instructions to follow, as in the parachute activity on page 69. It also happens when their teachers guide their activities too strongly, as in the following classroom observation of a teacher introducing an activity to find out if ice melts more quickly in air or in water at room temperature:

> You'll need to use the same sized ice-cubes. Make sure you have everything ready before you take the ice cubes out of the tray. Put one cube in the water and one close to it in the air. Then start the clock...

Here the children will have no problem in doing what is required, but they will have no idea of why they are doing it. If they did, they might challenge the need for a clock in this activity!

A diet weighted with such activities does not give children opportunity to carry out planning and thinking about what they are doing. Following someone else's plans is not the same as planning and moreover it effectively discourages thinking as the activity goes on. The reaction to any problem will be 'this doesn't work', laying the blame outside themselves, rather then being in control of the investigation and taking responsibility for overcoming problems. There must, therefore, be opportunities for children to start from a question and work out how to answer it, or to make a prediction and to think out and carry out their own procedures for testing it. To take these steps by themselves is asking a great deal of young children and of older ones unused to devising investigations and they will need help which subsequently can gradually be withdrawn.

Young children's experience should include simple problems such that they can easily respond to such as 'How will you do this?' For example, 'How can you find out if the light from the torch will shine through this fabric, this piece of plastic, this jar of water, this coat sleeve?' Often young children will respond by showing rather than describing what to do. With greater experience and ability to 'think through actions' before doing them they can be encouraged to think ahead more and more, which is one of the values of planning. Involving children in planning is part of setting an expectation that they will think through what they are going to do as far as possible.

For older children, help in planning can begin, paradoxically, from reviewing an investigation which has been completed (whether or not the children planned it themselves), helping them to go through what was done and identifying the structure of the activity through questions such as:

- what were they trying to find out?
- what things did they compare (identifying the independent variable)?
- how did they make sure that it was fair (identifying the variables which should be kept the same)?
- how did they find the result (identifying the dependent variable)?

When planning a new investigation the lessons learned from reviewing a previous one can be recalled, where perhaps variables were not controlled or initial observations not taken when they should have been. Planning continues throughout an investigation and indeed the initial plan may change as the work progresses and unforeseen practical obstacles emerge. However, it is important for children to recognise when they do change plans and to review the whole planning framework when a change is made. Writing plans down is a useful activity because it requires forward thinking, actions carried out in the mind.

Children become more able to do this the more experience they have to think through and call upon in anticipating the results of certain actions.

The teacher's role in this development can be summarised as:

- refraining from giving instructions which prevent children thinking for themselves;
- providing time and a structure for planning;
- expecting children to think through what they do even if they do not write formal plans on paper for every investigation;
- reviewing plans in the light of what was done.

Interpreting

For children to develop their ideas as a result of collecting information and evidence, they have to interpret what they find. That is, they must go further than collecting individual observations and try to find patterns, to relate various pieces of information to each other and to ideas. For example, children measuring the length of the shadow of a stick at different times of the day must go beyond just collecting the measurements if the activity is to have value for developing ideas. The pattern of decreasing and then increasing length of the shadow and the possibility of using the pattern to make predictions about the length at times when it was not measured, or the time of day from the measurement of the shadow, and the development of ideas about how shadows are formed, are important outcomes from this activity. They all depend on using the results the children obtain, so the development of the skills required is important. The central part of the teacher's role is to ensure that results are used and children don't rush from one activity to another without talking about and thinking through what their results mean.

As just noted above, children often implicitly use patterns in their findings without recognising that they in fact do so. Teachers can help to foster this consciousness by discussing simple patterns, such as the relationship between the position of the sun and the length of the shadow (or the equivalent in a classroom simulation using a torch and a stick). The starting point must be the various ways in which children will express their conclusions, including

'the shadow is shortest when the sun is highest'
'the shortest one is when the sun is high and the longest when it is low'
'its length depends on where the sun is'

and working towards recognising that

'the higher the sun the shorter the shadow'

says all that the previous statements say and more besides. Time for discussion of how to express a pattern is essential for the development of this skill.

In this particular example an explanation for the relationship can be found. By asking 'Why do you think the shadow changes length when the sun is higher?' the children's ideas about this can be collected. Other work with shadows can be called upon to bring out the hypothesis that it is because the light is cut off by the stick and carries on in a straight line. Such a 'conclusion', and any others the children may prefer, is no more than a hypothesis to be tested by further evidence. An important part of the teacher's role is to help children work towards a conclusion but still realise that there is always the possibility of further evidence being found which does not fit (see Stephen Hawking's comment quoted on page 9).

In summary, the teacher can encourage development in interpreting by:

- providing time and opportunity for children to identify simple patterns or relationships which bring together separate findings;
- ensuring that results of investigations are always discussed and that what is found is compared with what was predicted;
- helping children to treat their interpretations and conclusions as tentative.

Communicating

In the course of their science activities there is the potential for children to experience a range of different kinds of communication for different purposes and audiences. These should include:

Modes: writing, speaking, drawing, making, keeping notes and listening, reading, looking.
Audiences: for themselves, other children, their teacher, other adults.
Purposes: in order to sort out ideas, tell others about what they have done present observations, findings and conclusions.

This is a wide range to cover and clearly not all will be part of every activity. It is useful, however, for a teacher to plan this part of children's activities so that all are included appropriately and regularly. 'Appropriately' means that it should serve the purposes of the activity and not become meaningless ritual. The routine 'write about what you did' can kill any creativity in communication, as well as being a deterrent for some children, like the boy who dreaded a class visit to the museum, even though he loved going there, because it would inevitably be followed by the request for the kind of writing he did not enjoy.

We deal here with communication on paper and through artefacts, since speaking and listening are discussed in Chapter 12.

Keeping informal notes and records during activities

We all find a note-book which is really our own, a private place to write reminders to ourselves, notes of various kinds, is a very useful thing. At the very least it is an aid to memory and at best a means of having a dialogue with oneself that assists reflective thinking. It is useful for children to use a note-book too, to help them to organise their thinking, write rough plans, record observations. It will be a place where drawings and diagrams may take as important a part as words and where words don't have to be marshalled into sentences. In many classes, however, writing informally for themselves in this way is unfamiliar and almost all that children write is formal. There is considerable value in children using a note-book, but they need help. The help has to be given very subtly, though; if there is too much checking-up on what is written, the note-book becomes just another exercise book which is 'marked' by the teacher. The kind of help which is likely to be effective when note-books are first being used will include:

- opportunity – a suitable note-book and time to use it;
- suggestions for how to use it – when setting the scene for activities and explaining the organisation of the work, include comments on what it would be useful to note down (these should come from the children as well as the teacher);
- help in recording different kinds of information – give ideas for drawing diagrams so that essentials only are recorded, for labelling and annotating drawings, for tabulating information;
- occasional and casual discussion of how the note-book is being used – make non-judgmental comments and give helpful suggestions as above;
- showing an example – teachers using a note-book, particularly on trips out of the classroom to note points to discuss later.

Children should begin using note-books as soon as writing becomes fluent. It is probably best to introduce them to the whole class, encouraging those less able to write to draw and use what words they can.

Making a formal record

The form that a formal record of activities takes should be varied and discussed as part of the scene-setting for an activity. Often it will be a product of group effort and will be intended for display in the classroom. Discussion, either with a group or with the whole class if all have been doing similar things, of the best way to present information, is the opportunity to introduce techniques for graphical representation or, more often, to talk about how to select the best way of presenting information. Work already displayed on the wall can be used as examples of how to and how not to do this. Children are usually willing to criticise their own work after some time has elapsed. It is also a good idea to have one or two examples of commercial posters (such as those about the nutritional value of different foods or showing types of clouds) to show different ways of providing information.

Looking at posters and books is the other side of formal communication, that is, using secondary sources of information. Children need opportunity – suitable reference sources and time to use them – and some help in locating and selecting information.

Bringing these points together, teachers can encourage development by:

- conducting discussions of ways of communicating particular information to particular audiences;
- introducing techniques for presenting information, through direct teaching of conventions and providing examples;
- making available suitable reference books and other sources of information
- encouraging children to use a note-book;
- making opportunities for children to discuss their own and others' ways of recording and presenting results.

Summary

- There are general strategies for helping children develop process skills which apply across all skills. Essentially these refer to providing opportunities, gathering and using evidence about present skills, teaching techniques needed for advanced skills and meta-cognition.
- When applied to separate skills, these lead to specific actions that teachers can take to help children undertake enquiries in a scientific manner.

Chapter 21

Helping development of scientific attitudes

Introduction

In this chapter we look at the teacher's role in developing positive attitudes. While our main concern is the development of the attitudes that help learning with understanding in science, these cannot be developed in isolation from the attitudes that influence learning in general. So, before focusing on the attitudes identified in Chapter 5, we consider the wider context of attitudes towards school work and the ways in which children are motivated to make an effort and to do their best to succeed.

Encouraging positive attitudes to learning

It is useful to start by recalling that attitudes are generalised aspects of behaviour which cannot be taught in the sense of giving instruction. Rather they are 'caught', picked up through example and selectively encouraged through the kind of environment created in the classroom.. Hence the teacher's role is particularly crucial and there are both things to avoid in this role and positive actions to take.

One of the key aspects of the teacher's role is to encourage motivation for learning. But there are different kinds of motivation, since all behaviour and learning is motivated in some way.

Different kinds of motivation to learn

The three main kinds of motivation identified by psychologists are intrinsic motivation, achievement motivation and extrinsic motivation (e.g. McMeniman 1989). Of these, intrinsic motivation, which means that learners find interest and satisfaction in what they learn and in the learning process, leads to self-motivated and sustained learning. Those who are 'motivated from within' recognise their own role in the learning and so take responsibility for it. These are the learners who will seek out information, identify their learning goals and persevere, knowing that what they achieve depends on their effort. Such motivation is clearly desirable and probably essential in learning to make sense of things around and not being satisfied until they are understood.

Achievement motivation is concerned with the desire to achieve success or to avoid failure in comparison with others. Those motivated to achieve tend to attribute their successes to their ability and their failures to chance or lack of effort; failure does not diminish their confidence that they can succeed if they try hard enough. The reverse is the case for those motivated to avoid failure. Such learners tend to avoid the risk of failure by selecting tasks well within their grasp, but when it cannot be avoided, failure creates a vicious circle where low self-confidence leads to failure and to further reduction in confidence.

Finally, extrinsic motivation describes the behaviour of students who engage in learning mainly because of external incentives such as gold stars, high marks. Not only does this mean that learning may stop, or at least that effort is decreased, in the absence of these external factors, but that what is learned is closely targeted at behaviour which is rewarded. Thus effort will be put into learning the things that are tested or rewarded, not because they have value for developing understanding, but in order to gain praise or privilege.

Encouraging intrinsic motivation

Intrinsic motivation is implicit in positive attitudes towards learning. But how is it to be encouraged? Experience from a range of studies of learning across the curriculum suggests that there are things that a teacher can do and things to avoid in creating the climate to foster intrinsic motivation.

Positive action to take includes:

- Providing some choice of activities. This does not mean a free choice to do anything but a choice from among carefully devised alternatives, all seen by the children as having some relevance to them. The act of choosing gives the children some ownership of the activity and transfers some responsibility to them to undertake it seriously and complete it to the best of their ability.
- Involving children in identifying some reasonable objectives for the activity and some ways of achieving these objectives.
- Helping them to assess their own progress, using approaches such as the ones suggested in Chapter 18.

- Setting up activities in a way that requires genuine collaboration in pairs or small groups, so that the effort of all those involved matters and all are obliged to pull their weight.
- Showing confidence that children will do well; having high expectations.

This sets up a 'virtuous' circle, where children try harder and as result succeed, which raises their self-esteem

Things to avoid include:

- The vicious circle or self-fulfilling prophesy whereby children see themselves as failing even before they begin a task and therefore make little effort, leading to failure which confirms their judgement of themselves.
- Labelling children either as groups or individuals. This can happen consciously, as when children are streamed or grouped by ability and are referred to by a label, or unconsciously. It is difficult to imagine that being labelled 'the B stream', reinforced by the uniformly low level of work expected, does not transfer to the children's self image. Children are acutely sensitive to being treated in different ways and are not deceived by being described as the 'green' group when this means that they are the 'slow' ones.
- Making comparisons between children. This encourages competition and detracts from each child working towards his or her own objectives.

Caring for children's feelings about their work

Children have well formed views about the work they are given, about their teacher and those around them. For example, eight-year-old Christopher described exactly why he found school 'boring':

'When the book says "write the answer", I have to write the whole sum because Mrs. X says it will help my writing...but it takes so long.'

'It's so boring going over things on the board until all the class knows it. She just goes on and on.'

'When you write a word and you know it's wrong, you cross it out and try again. Then you have to copy it out because it's messy. You have to copy out all the work, not just the bit where you made a mistake.'

'When she sees a bit of my writing, she says "Look at that i. It's not like an i, it's like a funny little man". She tells all the class and they laugh.'

(*Match and Mismatch: Raising Questions* 1977)

Christopher explained, too, that the reason why he was always accused of 'playing about' was because it was more fun than doing the work he was given.

Now it may be that Mrs. X was unaware of Christopher's reactions to certain aspects of her teaching and that, had she known, she would have been more sympathetic to him.

So, given that children do have clear ideas about their work, *one important thing that a teacher can do is to find out what these are.* Just showing interest in how the children feel about their work is in itself significant in signalling the importance the teacher attaches to providing work which children will put effort into. Christopher's remarks were made to a sympathetic outsider to the school and it may be difficult for the teacher to obtain such frank statements in discussion with an individual, although this may be possible in some cases. The idea of a regular 'review' involving children in discussions with teachers about their work, proposed as part of some schemes of records of achievement at the secondary level, has been suggested at the primary level (Conner 1991).

It may well be a good use of learning time to spend some of it discussing different ways of going about a task and what the children think would be the best way to tackle something and why. A class of nine year olds readily came up with the home truth (about a project on different countries) that 'if we just copy the book, we don't really understand it' and proposed that they should read first and then put down what they think. The teacher added to this, 'Yes, then you will also be more careful to understand what you read in a book and that will help you whenever you use books to find information.' It is not easy for anyone to stand back from specific learning to examine the *process* of learning itself and young children are not often able to do this, but a gentle move in this direction can help them realise the point of what they are doing.

Interest in children's feelings and views on their learning has to be sincere. Children are not taken in by the superficial interest of their teacher, for it will be betrayed by manner and tone of voice as well as by whether anything happens as a result. A genuine interest creates an atmosphere in which children's own ideas are encouraged and taken as a starting point, where effort is praised rather than only achievement, where value is attached to each child's endeavours. In this atmosphere, a child who does not achieve as well as others will not be ridiculed. The range of activities available makes allowances for differences in ability of children and the teacher's interest and approach results in involvement of children in their work and their own learning.

Encouraging scientific attitudes

In Chapter 5 we considered five attitudes as being particularly relevant to learning science: curiosity, respect for evidence, willingness to change ideas, critical reflection and sensitivity towards living things and the environment. As was evident in the previous discussion, these are closely related to each other and this applies even more so to the actions which teacher can take to encourage them. Thus we consider them here as a group to avoid repetition.

The aspects of the teacher's role are of four main kinds:

- showing an example;
- providing opportunity for the development of the attitudes;
- reinforcing positive attitudes;
- discussing situations in which different attitudes would lead to different courses of action.

Showing an example

Given that attitudes are 'caught', showing an example is probably the most important of the positive things that teachers can do. To make a point of revealing that his or her own ideas have changed, for instance, can have a significant impact on children's willingness to change their ideas. 'I used to think that trees died after dropping their leaves, until . . .', 'I didn't realise that there were different kinds of woodlice', 'I thought that it was easier to float in deep water than in shallow water but the investigations showed that it didn't make any difference.'

The old adage that 'actions speak louder than words' means that such comments will not be convincing by themselves. It is important for the teacher to show all of the indications of attitudes which were mentioned in Chapter 5, perhaps the most significant of which are:

- showing interest in new things (which the children have brought in for example);
- helping to find out about new or unusual things;
- admitting when evidence gathered does not seem to fit in with expectations;
- suggesting that further evidence is needed before a conclusion is reached;
- acknowledging when evidence requires a change in ideas;
- being self-critical about how things have been done or ideas applied;
- admitting when the explanation for something is not known.

In a classroom where useful ideas are pursued as they arise and activities extend beyond well beaten tracks, there are bound to be opportunities for these teacher behaviours to be displayed. Situations in which the teacher just doesn't know, or which bring surprises or something completely new, should be looked upon, not as problems, but as opportunities for transmitting attitudes through example.

Providing opportunity

Since attitudes show in willingness to act in certain ways, there has to be opportunity for children to have the choice of doing so. If their actions are closely controlled by rules or highly structured lesson procedures, then there is little opportunity to develop and show certain attitudes (except perhaps conformity). Providing new and unusual objects in the classroom gives children opportunity to show and satisfy – and so develop – curiosity. Discussing investigations while they are in progress or after they have been completed, gives encouragement to reflect critically, but unless such occasions are provided, the attitudes cannot be fostered.

Reinforcing positive attitudes

Children pick up attitudes not only from example but from how others respond to their own behaviour. When children show indications of positive attitudes, it is important to reinforce these behaviours by praise or other signs of approval. This is far more effective than discouraging negative attitudes. Those who have not developed positive attitudes will be able to recognise what these are from the approval given to others.

For example, if critical reflection leads to children realising that they did not make fair comparisons in their experiment, the teacher's reaction could be 'well you should have thought of that before' or, alternatively, 'you've learned something important about this kind of investigation, well done'. The latter is clearly more likely to encourage reflection and the admission of fault on future occasions. Moreover, if this approval is consistent it eventually becomes part of the classroom climate and children will begin to reinforce the attitudes for themselves and for each other.

Discussing attitude-related behaviour

Attitudes can only be said to exist when they are aspects of a wide range of behaviour. In this regard they are highly abstract and intangible. Identifying them involves a degree of abstract thinking which makes them difficult to discuss particularly with young children. However, as children become more mature they are more able to reflect on their own behaviour and motivations. It then becomes possible to discuss examples of attitudes in action and to help them identify the way they affect behaviour explicitly.

For example, when some ten year olds read in a book that snails eat strawberries, they tested this out and came the conclusion that 'as far as our snails are concerned, the book is wrong'. Their teacher discussed with them how the author of the book might have come to a different conclusion from them and whether both the author and the children might gather more evidence before arriving at their conclusions. The children not only recognised that what was concluded depended on the attitudes to evidence but also that the conclusions were open to challenge from further evidence, thus developing their own 'respect for evidence'.

Summary

- Attitudes are ways of describing a willingness or preference to behave in certain ways. They reflect ways in which people are motivated to learn.
- Attitudes that help learning in science imply motivation that comes from interest and satisfaction in making sense of the world around, that is, intrinsic motivation.
- Teachers can encourage this type of motivation by providing some choice in activities, leading to ownership, involving children in identifying and working towards clear goals and assessing their own progress, setting up situations for genuinely collaborative work and raising children's expectations of themselves.
- It is important that teachers show real interest in how children feel about their work and set up a supportive classroom atmosphere.
- Specifically scientific attitudes can be encouraged by showing examples through their own behaviour, ensuring opportunities for children to make decisions and form their own ideas, reinforcing relevant behaviours and discussing the value of behaviours that lead to self-motivated learning.

Chapter 22

Summing up achievement

Introduction

Assessment for a summative purpose has an important role in children's education, although it is not as 'close to the learning' as formative assessment. In this chapter we consider the purposes of summative assessment and the kind of information that is required to meet these purposes effectively and efficiently. Then we consider ways of obtaining this information: through summarising evidence collected over a period of time, or through giving special tasks or tests, or a combination of these.

Assessment for summative purposes

Information about what children have achieved at certain times is important for teachers, parents and the children themselves. It might be collected at the end of a unit of work or the end of term or of the school year. It is essentially a summary, and so is much less detailed than the information for formative assessment, but, at the same time, should refer to the full range of learning goals. As in the case of formative assessment, it is important to keep the purpose in mind. This assessment is not intended to guide learning but to describe it in a way that is useful to those who need this information. It is assessment of learning, rather than assessment for learning.

Those who use this information generally wish to know what has been achieved and how this relates to expectations, levels or standards that apply to all children. Thus, whatever evidence is used to arrive at the summary must be judged against the same criteria as are used for all the children. In other words, the assessment should be criterion-referenced and not child-referenced, or ipsative (see Chapter 14, page 134). Comments can be added as to the effort put into what has been achieved, but the judgement of the achievement has to relate to the standard of the work and not whether this is 'good work for this child'.

Further, the results may be used to compare children with each other, or to summarise the performance of a class of children and so the procedure for making the judgements has to be as reliable as possible. Reliability means that the same assessment of the work would be made by different teachers and that the work of all of the children is judged in the same way by any one teacher.

Information for summative assessment

The points just made mean that the information for summative assessment needs to be:

- a summary of what has been achieved at a particular time;
- succinct, giving an overview of progress in relation to the main goals of learning;
- criterion-referenced to standards or levels that have the same meaning for all children;
- reliable; ideally involving some procedures for quality assurance.

There are three main ways of obtaining this information:

- by summarising information already gathered and used for formative assessment (summing up);
- by giving special tasks or tests to check on what has been learned at a particular time (checking up);
- by a combination of summing up and checking up.

Methods of obtaining summative assessment information

Summing up

Pieces of work or observations gathered over time and used as evidence to help learning, can also be used as evidence for summative assessment providing that it is reviewed in relation to the criteria for the standards or levels. It is not appropriate to summarise the marks or remarks that were assigned for formative purposes since these will be judgements, not evidence. The judgements will have an ipsative element, that is, will take into account the individual child's progress and effort. But the evidence, the actual work and notes of observations, can be analysed with the common criteria in mind. There are various sources of help that teachers can find to assist them in picking out what is significant in the evidence. For example, the *Nuffield Primary Science Teachers' Guides* (1995) each contain a chapter on assessment which gives examples of children's actions, words, talk, writing or drawings relating to the topic of the guide and discusses aspects which are significant in coming to a decision about whether certain level descriptions in the National Curriculum are being met. In a more general way the materials entitled *Taking a Closer Look* (SCRE 1995), produced in Scotland, have been developed to relate aspects of children's work to the attainment targets of the 5–14 curriculum guidelines. The ASE has also produced examples of children's work analysed against National Curriculum level descriptions (ASE 1996). In the US the *Performance Standards of the New Standards* (1997) have a similar purpose.

In reviewing the evidence accumulated about each child, it is important to look across all the pieces of work relevant to a particular objective and not to judge just from one. Each piece of work, each observation made by the teacher, of the kinds we have discussed above, is used to build up a picture which is not determined by one or two events, since to demonstrate understanding of an idea it has to be applied in different contexts. Not every piece will fit the same summary judgement, particularly if this has to be made in terms of the child's achievement being at one level rather than another. The judgement that has to be made is whether the child's work, as a whole, meets one set of criteria better than another.

To help in this process it more useful to have exemplar material in the form of portfolios of work from one child (as in parts of *Exemplification of Standards* (SCAA 1995)) than single pieces of work to help teachers apply the criteria in a holistic manner. Not every piece of work will fit the descriptions and neither will each and every part of the criteria for a level be represented in the portfolio. This may seem rather a loose procedure, but assessment is not an exact matter and it is better to be aware of the uncertainty than to assume that we can pigeon-hole children when this is not the case.

Of course information is inevitably lost in summarising. But the alternative is too much detail that fails to communicate an overview of achievement. In the case of process skill, reporting on each skills is probably less useful than summarising across them and reporting on 'enquiry skills'. This summary might be made by considering whether a child's profile matches one of 'early' or 'later' development (pages 33 to 51). The level descriptions in the National Curriculum bring several skills together so that a teacher might look across the evidence and judge whether the profile is a better match to, say,

Level 2:
Pupils respond to suggestions about how to find things out and, with help, make their own suggestions about how to collect data to answer questions. They use simple texts, with help, to find information. They use simple

equipment provided and make observations related to their task. They observe and compare objects, living things and events. They describe their observations using scientific vocabulary and record them using simple tables when appropriate. They say whether what happened was what they expected.

Or Level 3:
Pupils respond to suggestions and put forward their own ideas about how to find the answer to a question. They recognise why it is important to collect data to answer questions. They use simple tests to find information. They make relevant observations and measure quantities, such as length or mass, using a range of simple equipment. Where appropriate, they carry out a fair test with some help, recognising and explaining why it is fair. They record their observations in a variety of ways. They provide explanations for observations and for simple patterns in recorded measurements. They communicate in a scientific way what they have found out and suggest improvements in their work.

(DfEE 1999)

Similarly, broad categories for the development of conceptual understanding are provided by national standards as, for example, in the AAAS *Benchmarks for Scientific Literacy*. The expected outcomes for children at the end of Grade 2 and Grade 5 in relation to living things, for example, are as follows:

By the end of 2nd grade, students should know that
• Some animals and plants are alike in the way they look and in the things they do, and others are very different from one another
• Plants and animals have features that help them live in different environments
• Stories sometimes give plants and animals attributes they really do not have.

By the end of the 5th grade, students should know that
• A great variety of kinds of living things can be sorted into groups in many ways using various features to decide which things belong to which group
• Features used for grouping depend on the purpose of the grouping.

(AAAS 1993, pp. 102, 103)

Checking up

A summary assessment can also be arrived at by checking up, that is, giving some special tasks which are devised specifically to assess the point reached in the development of ideas or skills. Even when other evidence is used, there may be times when teachers feel the need to introduce special tasks when it does not seem to have been possible to collect information in any other way.

The examples in Figures 22.1, 22.2 and 22.3 show some possibilities for checking up on children's ideas through written questions. A further example is given on page 210 as part of Figure 22.7, where children are asked to use their ideas to hypothesise. Questions like these do not need to be given as 'tests' and indeed could seem to the children to be part of their normal activities providing the questions are written to match the subject matter of the activities.

David and John put equal amounts of dry sand, soil, grit and salt in four funnels.
They wanted to find out how much water each one would soak up.   So they poured 100 ml of water into each one.
This worked all right until they came to the salt.
When they poured the water in almost all the salt disappeared.

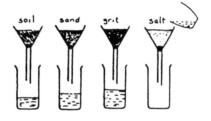

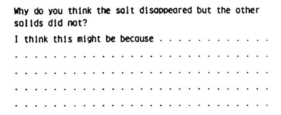

Why do you think the salt disappeared but the other solids did not?
I think this might be because . . . .
. . . .
. . . .
. . . .
. . . .

Figure 22.1 (from DES/WO 1985, 122)

Special tasks for checking up on process skills can be written or practical. Practical tasks designed to require all the process skills to be used, to the extent that children are able, have been employed in the APU surveys (DES/WO 1980) and for research purposes (e.g. Russell and Harlen 1990). As they require the full attention of an administrator/observer they are not practicable in the classroom. Their value to teachers is in the ideas and hints which they give about the kinds of tasks, ways of presenting them and of questioning children which can be adapted and applied in planning children's practical work.

For teachers who want to check on certain process skills for several children at once, the written questions devised for the APU surveys given in Figures 22.4 to 22.6 provided useful examples that can be adapted.

Two blocks of ice the same size as each other were
taken out of the freezer at the same time.   One was
left in a block and the other was crushed up.

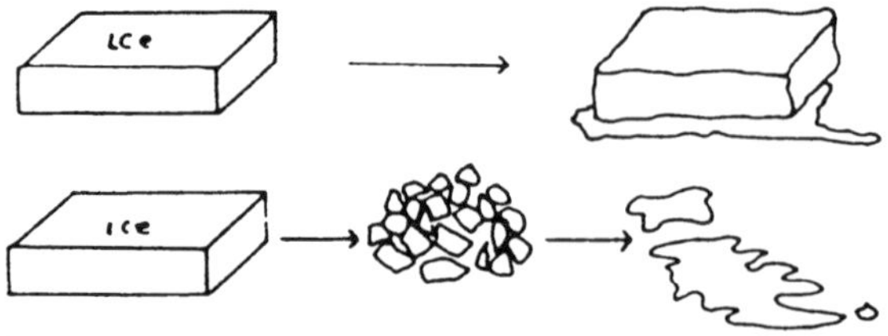

It was noticed that the crushed ice melted more quickly
than the block.

Why do you think this was?

I think it was because . . . .

. . . .

. . . .

. . . .

. . . .

. . . .

Figure 22.2 (from DES/WO 1984, 252)

John washed four handkerchiefs and hung them up in
different places to dry.   He wanted to see if the
places made any difference to how quickly they dried.

a)   In which of these places do you think the handkerchief
would dry quickest?   Tick one of these:

☐   In the corridor where it was cool and
sheltered

☐   In a warm room by a closed window

☐   In a warm room by an open window

☐   In a cool room by an open window

☐   All the same

b)   What is your reason for ticking this one?

. . . .

. . . .

. . . .

. . . .

. . . .

Figure 22.3 (from DES/WO 1984, 252)

Tom cut an orange into pieces.

He ate some of the pieces and was going to keep the rest for later.

His mother said: "Cover them with some cling film so they don't dry up".

Tom decided to see if covering them really did make any difference.

He decided to cover some of the pieces of orange and to leave others uncovered. He would see which ones dried up most by weighing them.

To make this a fair test he should make some things the same in case they make a difference to the result.

Write down three things that should be the same.

1 ....

....

2 ....

....

3 ....

....

Figure 22.4

All the APU questions were 'stand alone' items, each being unconnected to any other. The reason for this was the requirement to have a large bank of questions set in different contexts from which to draw a sample of items for different surveys. Where this is not necessary the questions can be embedded in a theme which is not only more interesting for the children but cuts down on the amount of reading the children have to do to establish a fresh context for each item. An example of this approach is given in Schilling *et al.* (1990). Written questions assessing process skills were devised on the theme of the 'Walled Garden', which teachers could introduce as a topic or as a story. Questions were grouped into seven sections about different things found in the garden: water, walls, 'minibeasts', leaves, sun-dial, bark and wood. For each section there was a large poster giving additional information and activities and a booklet for children to write their answers. Children worked on the tasks over an extended period, with

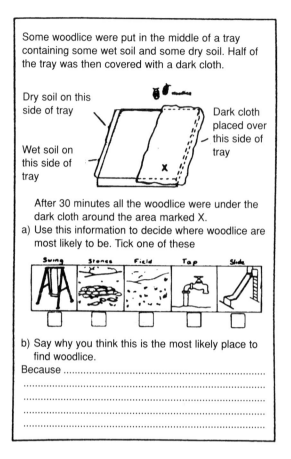

Figure 22.5

no time limit; they enjoyed the work which they saw as novel and interesting, in no way feeling that they were being tested. The examples in Figure 22.7 (pp 208–210) are of the questions on 'minibeasts'. They can be used as guides to setting process-based tasks in other contexts to suit the class activities.

Combining summing up and checking up

The relative advantages and disadvantages of summing up and checking up suggest that a combination of the two might be the best approach to summative assessment. Whether or not this is so depends on the relative confidence placed in teachers' judgements or test results and on how they are combined. Combining generally means turning the teachers' judgements into a number that can be combined with a test score, which then has to be expressed in terms of standards or levels by applying a cut-off score. The result is rather a long way from the criteria it is intended to reflect. An alternative is to use one kind of

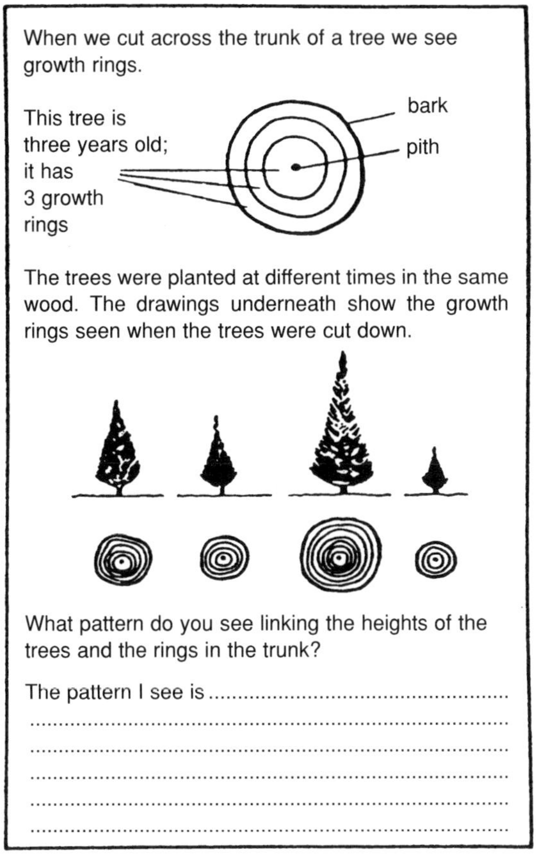

When we cut across the trunk of a tree we see growth rings.

This tree is three years old; it has 3 growth rings

bark

pith

The trees were planted at different times in the same wood. The drawings underneath show the growth rings seen when the trees were cut down.

What pattern do you see linking the heights of the trees and the rings in the trunk?

The pattern I see is ....
....
....
....
....
....

Figure 22.6

information to confirm the other, as in the Scottish system, where teachers form their judgement about when a child has met the criteria at a particular level and then use a test to confirm this (SQA 1993).

The main difficulty in combining information from these different sources is that they really constitute different kinds of information. Tests tap a small sample of relevant behaviour, but perhaps only that part that is easily tested. The result is likely to be high on reliability and low on validity. Teachers' summaries cover a wider range of behaviours, are more valid but rather less reliable. Thus the two may well not agree and perhaps ought to be reported separately. The question then arises as to which to use when decisions have to be made and it is invariably the test that is regarded as more accurate. Unfortunately, when summative assessment acquires high stakes, efforts are concentrated on improving test scores and not on helping teachers to make their assessments more reliable.

Minibeasts

Dan and Tammy kept a note of all the 'minibeasts' they found in the Walled Garden. They drew the minibeasts as well as they could.

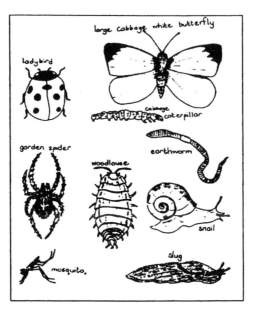

Read about the 'minibeasts' in the project folder before you try to answer the questions.

Later, back at school, they used some books to get information about the minibeasts. The made a special chart, called a table. Which showed the the information and put it in the Walled Garden project folder. Here is a copy of it.

Minibeast	legs	where eggs laid	eggs hatch into	sheds skin	adult feeds on
woodlouse	yes	under stones, logs	young woodlice	yes	dead animals and plants
snail	no	soil	young snails	no	dead and living plants
ladybird	yes	plants		yes	live greenfly
slug	no	soil	young slugs	no	dead and living plants
earthworm	no	soil	young worms	no	dead things in the soil
cabbage butterfly	yes	leaves	larva caterpillar	yes	plants
spider	yes	in cocoon on leaves	young spiders	yes	flies
mosquito	yes	on water		yes	

Figure 22.7

1. Use the information in the table to answer these questions:
   a) What do ladybirds feed on?..
   b) In the table all the minibeasts with legs have something else that is the same about them. Can you see what it is?

   ....
   ....

2. When they made the table they could not find all the information about the ladybird and the mosquito.
   Please fill in this information for them on their table:
   a) A ladybird's egg hatches into a <u>LARVA</u>.
   b) Adult mosquitos feed on <u>ANIMALS and PLANTS</u>.

3. Dan and Tammy's table shows that snails eat dead and living plants, but it doesn't say whether they like to eat some plants more than others.

   Suppose you have these foods that snails will eat:
   and as many snails as you want. Think about what you would do to find out which of these foods the snails liked best.

   a) Say what you would do to start with? (Draw a picture if it will help.)

strawberries   porridge   lettuce   carrot
                  oats

   b) Say how you will make sure that each food has a fair chance of being chosen:

   ....
   ....
   ....

   c) What will you look for to decide which food was liked best?

   ....
   ....
   ....

Figure 22.7 (continued)

4   What other things could you find out about snails by doing investigations
        with them?
        Write down as many things as you can think of to investigate.

        ....
        ....
        ....
        ....

5   Dan and Tammy went to visit their Aunt and looked for minibeasts in her
        garden. They found them all except for snails although they looked
        carefully for a long time

        a)   Write down any reasons you can think of to explain why their were
             no snails in their Aunt's garden

             ....
             ....
             ....

        b)   Their Aunt thought it could be because of the kind of soil where she
             lived; there was no chalk or limestone in it.

             What is the main difference between snails and other minibeasts
             which Dan and Tammy found?

             ....
             ....
             ....

        c)   Why do you think snails only live where there is chalk or limestone in
             the soil?

             ....
             ....
             ....

Figure 22.7 (continued)

Summary

- Information required for summative assessment differs in many ways from that required for formative assessment: it has to be more succinct, strictly criterion-referenced, and as reliable as possible.
- Summative information can be obtained by summing up evidence collected over time, by giving special tasks or tests, or a combination of these.
- In all cases criteria have to be applied so that the information indicates what children have achieved in ways that are comparable for all children and mean the same things when passed from teacher to teacher.

Chapter 23

Recording and reporting

Introduction

Recording systems are so important to teaching that they have to be a part of it, designed to suit a particular curriculum organisation and adapted to the teaching methods used. Therefore the most useful and least constraining ones will be those which teachers devise for themselves having considered the pros and cons of the ones suggested in various publications.

There are many examples of records for different purposes and teachers can obtain advice from a range of sources. In England and Wales there are materials published by the Qualifications and Curriculum Authority; for teachers in Scotland there is advice from the Scottish CCC and regional education authorities and national guidelines on reporting to parents from the SOED (SOED 1992); publications of the subject associations (Primary Science Review and the joint publications of the ASE, NATE, ATM and MA) give teachers access to the ideas and practices of others, and published schemes invariably suggest ways of keeping records of children's progress. In this chapter there is no attempt to review all of this material, nor to compete with it, but to provide a general discussion of records for different purposes. We begin with records of activities, which are distinct from records of what children have learned from their activities, discussed in the second and third sections. We conclude with some examples of children's participation in keeping records of their work.

Records of children's activities

Unless all the children in a class invariably work on the same activities as each other, there is a need for a system which records what individuals have actually been engaged upon. Indeed, even if the activities were the same for all it would be no guarantee that their *experiences* would be identical, since children attend selectively to different parts of the work, extend some and give scant attention to others. They also become diverted into unplanned avenues to follow their own questions. This is a useful reminder that we can never know exactly what each child has experienced, and in order not to give the false impression that we can it is perhaps better to record activities encountered than pretend to be more precise about exactly what each child has experienced through them.

The purpose of a record of activities is to enable the teacher to ensure that all children, at various times, have the learning opportunities planned, in so far as this is possible, and to draw attention to gaps in children's experience. A workable recording system must be capable of keeping track of children's activities when different kinds may be on the go at once. For example, if we recall the infant activities about feet described in Chapter 16 (page 156), the six groups were working on activities which, although having the common theme of 'feet', had quite different learning outcomes (some relating to materials, some to shadows, some to measurement, etc.). In this case the teacher decided not to rotate the group of children round all the activities, so at the end of the topic there would be some children who had had more experience of materials, some more experience of investigating shadows, than others. The teacher would need to ensure that future activities would equalise children's learning opportunities. There are different ways of giving the same learning opportunities and these will usually be part of teachers' planning.

It is helpful to distinguish between *topics* (such as 'feet' or 'movement'), which are likely to encompass activities in various areas of the curriculum, and the particular activities within them. Activities can be identified in subject based terms without conflicting with cross-curricular work, since they can be regarded as constructs for the teacher to use in planning and analysing the children's work. By listing both topics and activities, a record such as Figure 23.1 indicates the context in which the activities were carried out. Such a record could include all activities, but it would be less cumbersome if different records were kept for the science, language, mathematics, etc., activities within the topics.

The record would be completed by ticking the activities undertaken by each child; not an arduous matter. In many cases groups of children will have undertaken the same activities but the individual record means that absences and changes of group composition are taken into account. Certain activities will probably be regarded as equivalent to each other, while in other cases it may be that the context is so different that repetition is desirable. Taking these things into account, the teacher will use the record to keep an eye on the gaps in the activities of individual children and act on this, either in planning the next term's work or having one or two sessions in which children are directed to activities which they have missed.

Record of Science Activities.   Term: Class:

Topics	Sending messages		The weather		etc.			
Dates	Sept 9 to Oct 20		Oct 30 to Dec 12					
Activities (brief description)								
Children								
Belle Adams	✓		✓	✓			✓	✓	
John Allan		✓	✓	✓	✓	✓		✓	✓
etc.									

Figure 23.1 A record of activities undertaken within topics

It would be possible to add a row to Figure 23.1 which indicates the statements of the curriculum, guidelines or standards to which each activity relates. This would have value in showing when children had been involved in activities which could lead to achievement of intended outcomes, but it would not, and should not, be assumed to indicate anything about achievement. For this different records are needed.

On-going records of children's achievement

These are the most detailed of the records which have to be kept and it is inevitable that a fairly lengthy recording sheet will have to be used for each child in order to cover the whole curriculum. A compromise has to be struck, however, between a scheme which is so burdensome that it will not be maintained and is too detailed to be easily used, and one which consists of ticks or other marks whose meaning is rather vague. In deciding which kind of record is most useful it should be noted that:

- the over-riding purpose is to help the teacher remember where each child has reached in development so that suitable activities and encouragement can be given;
- these records are for the teacher's own use and so the level of detail can be adjusted to suit the individual's ways of working;
- they will be summarised for other purposes, for school records passed from class to class and for reporting to parents.

Teachers vary as to how much information they can carry in their head and how much they like to write down and this may be one of the factors which leads to a preference for a check-list, or for a more detailed pro forma which gives opportunity for comments, caveats and explanations.

However, it is difficult for anyone to remember the details of the children's performance which are observed when focusing on groups at different times, as suggested in Chapter 16. Records also help to show where observations of children have been made and which gaps need to be filled by more targeted observation. A record of the sort indicated in Figure 23.2 can serve these purposes. It is designed to be used with the criteria for early and later development of ideas, skills and attitudes indicated in Chapters 3, 4, and 5, but could clearly be adapted to relate to other criteria derived from standards or level descriptions. In the 'early' and 'later' stage columns the record can either be a note of what has or has not been achieved, perhaps referring to the statements by number. Since not all areas of knowledge will be covered during the period of the record, the 'ideas' can be written in. However, the skills and attitudes are likely to be widely relevant and so should be covered whatever the subject matter of the activities.

Science profile. Child's Name: Date:

Ideas about: (Write in)	Early stage	Later stage
• Living things and life processes		
• Interaction of living things		
• Materials		
etc.		
Process skills		
• Observing		
• Raising questions		
• Hypothesising		
• Predicting		
• Planning and conducting enquiries		
• Interpreting		
• Communicating		
Attitudes		
• Curiosity		
• Respect for evidence		
• Willingness to change ideas		
• Critical reflection		
• Environment sensitivity		

Figure 23.2 An on-going record of achievement in science for one child

Many teachers will feel that the problem of records of this kind is not that they contain too much information but that they contain too little. The richness and complexity of children's performance can rarely be captured in a brief note, far less by a tick. In many systems, therefore, these records are only a part of the material which is available to a teacher about individual children. Samples of work, chosen by the child and/or the teacher, and more extensive notes may be kept in a file for each child.

Summative records

We are considering here summative records which are created by reviewing and summing up on-going records rather than with the results of checking-up tests. However, if test results exist for certain aspects of performance, then they can be added to the record in a way which clearly indicates their origin. Two purposes of summative records can be distinguished: those for keeping a record within the school of the progress of individual children (cumulative records) and those which are intended for reporting at a particular time to well defined audiences, mainly parents and teachers who will be receiving the children for the next school year.

For a cumulative record, the same structure can be used as in the on-going record from which it is derived, that is, in terms of the aspects of learning which have been achieved, adding information at different dates to a record such as Figure 23.2. A slightly different and simple approach is to list all the target or goal statements at each level on a form for each child and to highlight those achieved, using a different colour at the end of each year.

For records which aim to give a picture of where a child is at a certain point, as opposed to a history of progress up to that point, a mixture of achieved levels and open comment may well be required. Parents may find the detail of different aspects of achievement too great to answer their main need to know 'how is (s)he doing in science?' Remembering that parents will have to be taking in information about all areas of the curriculum, there is clearly a limit to how useful it is to subdivide each one to any extent. Open comment is important to help summarise and interpret the meaning of the 'levels' achieved and to add other information about attitudes, effort and extra-curricular activities. Figure 23.3 indicates the way in which information may be provided for parents. It will be most useful if it is one page of a report booklet, which can include a return slip for parents to make a response to the report.

Receiving teachers may also find it difficult to use detailed information, not because the meaning is not understood, but because they have the records for a whole class to take on board. A summary of levels of achievement may be most useful, providing that all teachers involved have a consistent interpretation of the meaning of the levels. Additional information is important, also, but will be of a different kind from that given to parents, pointing out the particular help that a child may need or the kinds of encouragement to which (s)he responds. More detailed information, for reference if required could be provided by supplying, in addition, a copy of the cumulative record.

Scientific enquiry
This includes the skills of carrying out science investigations. Some are practical skills but most are concerned with planning investigations, careful observation and other ways of collecting evidence, interpreting findings and drawing conclusions. Also included are communicating results in a suitable way and discussing what has been done in order to improve later investigations.

Overall level of achievement: Level ....

Comment:

....

....

Knowledge and understanding of science
This section concerns the growing scientific knowledge of things in the world around, such as living things, materials, forces, some forms of energy, and the impact of human activity on the environment. The understanding which children develop about these things in the primary school comes largely from their own exploration and investigation of things around them.

Overall level of achievement: Level..............

Comments:

....

....

Figure 23.3 An example of a form for reporting achievement to parents.

Involving children in keeping records

In relation to keeping records of activities successfully undertaken, the involvement of children can ease the teacher's burden as well a making children aware of their progress. One approach to this, published by the ASE (Willis 1999), takes the form of statements relating to the programmes of study of the National Curriculum. Each statement is written on a 'brick' in a 'wall', with Key

Stage 1 statements at the base and Key stage 2 ones above. For example, in the 'wall' for 'Separating Materials' some of the statements in the bricks are shown in Figure 23.4.

Key Stage 2 (7 – 11 years)	I have found out how to use filtering to separate materials that will not dissolve in water.	I have found out how evaporating can be used to get a solid back after it has been dissolved.	I have experimented to find out how much of different materials will dissolve.
	I know how to find out how hot something is.	I know how to dissolve salt and change it back to salt again.	I have made dough and found out how it changes if I heat it.
Key Stage 1 (5 to 7 years)	I have seen ice melt and water change to steam and can describe what I saw.	I have mixed ingredients to make a cake or biscuit and can explain how they had changed after I heated them.	I have made something out of clay and can explain how it had changed after I heated it.
	I have found out which materials change their shape when squashed and how their shape changes.	I have found out how bending and twisting can change the shape of some materials.	I have found out how different materials can be stretched.

Figure 23.4 An example of a record that can be used by children (extracted from Willis 1999)

Children shade in the 'bricks' which they have completed. As can be seen from the examples in Figure 23.4, however, the statements are a mixture of activities and achievements. It is possible for teachers to substitute their own statements, of course, and this could be done to make the 'walls' into a more factual record of what has been done, leaving the judgement as to what has been achieved for a separate record.

This bring us to the question of children's role in records of achievement. We noted in Chapter 18 the value of children assessing their own work and described some strategies for doing this. The main advantages were seen as moving children into a position to share in making decisions about their next steps in learning, that is, in the context of formative assessment. In that context, where reliability is not a major issue, the advantages of involving children far outweigh the disadvantages. However, there are other considerations in the context of summative assessment, where reliable use of criteria is important and the record is to be used by others. Most of the systems designed to involve children in making records – such as the National Record of Achievement and its successor, the Progress File – emphasise their role in helping children to assess own work and to take responsibility for decisions about further learning, rather than their use as a summative record. Certainly at the primary level it seems best to involve children in assessing their progress in relation to specific short-term goals and how to reach them rather than in creating a record of overall achievement required for summative purposes.

Summary

- It is important to separate records of activities undertaken from records of learning achieved.
- Teachers' own records of assessments made as part of teaching need to be recorded in greater detail than is needed for summative purposes.
- Cumulative records of learning can be made on a single record by adding information at different times.
- Summative records for other teachers and for parents indicate what has been achieved at a particular time in the main areas of learning only.
- Children have a more useful role in recording the activities than in making judgements about whether criteria of learning have been met.

Chapter 24

Planning the school programme

Introduction

In this chapter we discuss issues relating to planning provision for science. The concern is mainly with long-term planning and with matters where decisions need to be made at the school level. Aspects of more detailed provision has been covered in earlier chapters. After a brief discussion of levels of planning and the role of the science subject leader, the various sections deal with the relationship between science and other subjects, different kinds of topics in which science may have a part, and matters relating to the timetable and the deployment of staff.

Planning and the role of the subject leader

One of the noticeable trends over recent years has been the change from curriculum planning being treated as a matter for individual teachers to one that is a whole-school responsibility. However, in considering the locus of responsibility it is necessary to distinguish between long-term, medium-term and short-term planning.

Long-term planning concerns the overall framework for the school's programme for science. The decisions about matters of content to be covered are bounded by the national or district curriculum or guidelines, but the school retains controls of decisions about how this is organised and taught. Decisions best made at the school level in order to ensure continuity as children move from class to class include matters relating to time and time-tabling, the extent of integration with other subjects and the materials used. A further decision is whether the school develops its own scheme of work or adopts a ready-made one such as the one provided by the DfEE (1998). This sets out a scheme of 33 units and four short (revision) units which cover the National Curriculum at Key Stages 1 and 2. Each unit takes about half a term to complete and the suggested sequence gives a reasonable balance during each year of activities in biological and physical science.

Other decisions are the subject of medium-term planning which is concerned with the activities that will be included in a topic or unit. These decisions are made several weeks in advance so that they can be coordinated across classes. Short-term planning is the province of the individual teacher and concerns the detailed plans of lesson that put the medium-term plan into action. The DfEE scheme provides suggestions somewhere between the medium- and short-term levels of planning by identifying, for each unit, a series of possible teaching activities, with learning objectives and learning outcomes for each one. Thus teachers have access, if they wish to use it, to a good deal of help from outside the school for their individual planning.

There is also, in theory, support within the school in the person of the science subject leader, or coordinator, who is expected to play a part in planning at all levels. Since 1998 there has been in England and Wales a national framework for the role of the teacher who takes on a subject leadership, which is relevant to all subjects. This sets out the role in an extensive, and somewhat daunting, list of tasks under four headings. Some examples of the tasks are:

Strategic direction and development of the subject
- Develop policy and practices
- Create climate of positive attitudes to the subject and confidence in teaching it
- . . . .

Teaching and learning
- Ensure curriculum coverage and progression for all pupils
- Ensure teachers are clear about objectives and sequences and communicate these to pupils
- . . . .

Leading and managing staff
- Help staff achieve constructive working relationships with pupils
- Establish clear expectations and constructive working relationships among staff
- . . . .

Effective and efficient deployment of staff and resources
- Establish staff and resource needs for the subject and advise the headteacher
- Advise the headteacher on the best use of colleagues
- . . . .

(TTA 1998)

These are decidedly demanding tasks but indicate the intention that individual teachers should have support in the school and that the overall programme should be planned and coordinated.

Returning to long-term planning, we look at how science fits into the whole curriculum. How does science relate to other subjects? Can it be taught at the same time as meeting the learning goals in other subject areas?

Science and other subjects

Science has its own distinctive characteristics but this does not mean that it is independent of other ways of knowing about and reacting to the world around. Its closest relationship would seem to be with mathematics and technology. But while there are many occasions when science, mathematics and technology are brought together in one activity, they still remain distinct human enterprises, distinguishable from one another by several characteristics. For example, whereas for science, the physical world around is the ultimate authority by which its theories and principles are to the judged, for mathematics the ultimate test is the logic of relationships and numbers; there is no need for the descriptions of mathematics to relate to the real world.

Science and technology

Because science and technology have been intimately linked in the activities of primary school children, there often appears to be difficulty in distinguishing between them. There would certainly be difficulty in *disentangling* them, especially in relation to their role in practical activities where children are not only devising ways of problem solving and investigating but constructing actual devices to implement their ideas. But there should be no difficulty in distinguishing between science and technology, for they are quite different in aims and the kinds of activity through which their aims are pursued.

Scientific activity, as we have seen, aims at understanding. Technological activity uses 'knowledge and skills effectively, creatively and confidently in the solving of practical problems and the undertaking of tasks.' (Layton 1990, p. 11) This statement sums up with remarkable clarity and economy of words the important aspects of technology. The main points to note are:

- The mention of 'knowledge and skills', not scientific knowledge and skills. Certainly scientific knowledge and skills are used very often in technology but they are not the only kinds; it is this which makes technology an aspect of the whole curriculum not an adjunct of science. In Layton's words, technology is 'a freshly-conceived, broad, balanced and progressive set of experiences designed to empower students in the field of practical capability and enable them to operate effectively and confidently in the made world'.

- The reference to the effective, creative and confident use of the knowledge and skills. These qualities include not only aesthetic sensitivity but the ability to find solutions to problems where compromises have to be made because of competing requirements, where resources are limited and where there are no existing guidelines to follow.
- The aims are described in terms of solving practical problems and undertaking tasks. This goes beyond the definitions of technology as solving problems relating to human need. Many tasks which are accomplished through technology (e.g. putting the letters in seaside rock) have little to do with human need but are to serve other purposes, often commercial competition, personal preference or national status.

An important difference between science and technology lies in the way in which a solution to a problem is evaluated. As Layton (1993) points out, the over-riding concern in science is that a theory or explanation should 'fit the facts'. But the products of technology must not only function as intended but also meet other criteria such as 'environmental benignity, cost, aesthetic preferences, ergonomic requirements and market size. "Doing science" is different, therefore, from "doing technology"' (Layton 1993, p. 48). He goes on to state that scientific expertise 'is no guarantee of technological capability' (ibid.).

Coming back to the classroom, we see some of these characteristics of technology in progress when children are building models, especially working ones, but in fact at all times when materials are used. There is some application of knowledge of materials, skill in fashioning them, compromise with the necessity of using the materials available and creativity in doing this to achieve the end result intended within the constraints of time and cost.

Distinguishing technological from scientific activities is important in teachers' minds because they are, as the above tries to show, different aspects of children's education. It makes sense, however, to continue to pursue both within the same topics and activities, just as these will also serve certain aims in mathematics, English and other subjects.

Science and history

Looking at the relationship with other subjects from the point of view of helping scientific activity and understanding science, the matter does not end with mathematics and technology. History provides insights into how the accumulation of knowledge over the years has led to greater understanding of how things around us are explained. There are two aspects of this: how new ideas have emerged and what these ideas are. These two are the reasons given by the American Association for the Advancement of Science for including historical perspectives in Benchmarks:

> Consider, for example, the proposition that new ideas are limited by the context in which they are conceived; are often rejected by the scientific establishment; grow slowly, through contributions from many different investigators. Without historical examples, these generalisations would be no more than slogans, however well they may be remembered.
>
> A second reason is that some episodes in the history of the scientific endeavour are of surpassing significance to our cultural heritage. Such episodes certainly include Galileo's role in changing our perception of our place in the universe, Newton's demonstration that the same laws apply to motion in the heavens and on earth, Darwin's long observations of the variety and relatedness of life forms that led to his postulating a mechanism for how they came about ...
>
> (AAAS 1993)

Science and art

There is also a strong relationship between science and art in its various forms in that both help to reveal patterns in things around which help in making links between one object or event and another. These patterns enable us to make predictions, not so much about what will happen in the future as about what we may find happening now if we try to find it. Science and art are also connected in the use and nature of the human senses and in a particularly enthralling way in such phenomena as optical illusions, colour perception and resonance.

While these relationships show that the areas of activity which we identify as separate subjects overlap, they also help to highlight the differences. They do not help us, however, to distinguish between the two schools of thought which influence curriculum planning. On the one hand, there is the view that children need to know what the subjects are in order to appreciate the relationship between them. On the other hand is the view that the priority is children's exploration of the world around, regardless of subject boundaries which are abstractions with little meaning for them in the primary years. Whichever view is taken, it remains important for teachers to identify the nature and boundaries of subject disciplines even if these are not shared with the children. The extent to which subjects are bound together in children's experience brings us to the issue of topic work.

Topic work

Topic work means that different aspects of work are linked together, or remain undifferentiated, so that they reinforce one another and are studied within a context which has meaning for children in relation to their experience. The different forms of topic work arise from the breadth and variety of what is included. Cross-curricular topics link most subject areas (usually with the exceptions of physical education and music) with equal emphasis on the components. Environmental studies topics leave language and mathematics to be taught separately. There can also be science-based topics which have a focus on science and, while other areas of the curriculum are inevitably involved, their role is incidental rather than planned. However, it is the broad topics encompassing several subjects which attract most criticism.

The disadvantages of cross-curricular topic work for learning science hinge on the considerable demands of working in this way and the expertise required of the teacher. HMI pointed out some time ago that 'over-ambitious topic work, in which too many elements and subjects are attempted at the same time, trivialises the children's learning in science and fails to establish the aimed-for connections between science and the various constituent subjects of the topic' (DES 1989, pp. 18–19). While acknowledging the benefits of linking work in different subjects and that science can be linked with virtually every other subject, they caution that 'the least effective work is often associated with topics where far too much is attempted and – as a consequence – too little is achieved in depth of knowledge, understanding and the acquisition of skills in the constituent subjects' (DES 1989, p. 20).

Much stronger language was used by Alexander *et al.* (1992) in their discussion paper on *Curriculum Organisation and Classroom Practice in Primary Schools*, which was a result of a review of available evidence about curriculum organisation, teaching methods and classroom practices carried out in order to make recommendations which would help the implementation of the National Curriculum. They deplored the 'rhetoric of primary education (which) has for a long time been hostile to the idea that young children should be exposed to subjects' (para 63).

Change in practice in response to these and similar arguments, gaining in force throughout the 1990s, was by no means immediate. Teaching through topic work is not easy, but it is interesting for both children and teachers and it does provide the context for linking ideas developed through one activity to related situations in a natural way. However, gradually topics have become less all-embracing and closer to the practice described by inspectors as being 'associated with successful topic work':

1. An agreed system of planning which is consistent and carefully structured, thus helping to ensure continuity and progression.
2. A degree of cooperation in planning which provides an opportunity for teachers to share their workload and expertise.

3. Careful account taken of national curriculum requirements. Topics are usually chosen to fit national curriculum attainment targets and programmes of study, rather than the other way round. Aspects of attainment targets that do not fit in readily are taught separately.
4. Topics have a single subject bias or emphasise particular subjects.
5. Whole-school agreement about subject coverage and the balance between subjects and topics, the outcomes of which are monitored by members of the senior management team.
6. The planning refers to learning outcomes or objectives, activities and assessment.

(OFSTED 1993, Appendix A)

Science and the development of numeracy and literacy

Concern for the development of basic numeracy and literacy has, however, revived the discussion of whether goals of science education and of other subjects can be achieved at the same time. There is a fear that the protected time given to reading, writing and mathematics squeezes the time available for science and returns it to the status of an 'afternoon' subject, that it had before the curriculum developments at the end of the 1980s (ASE 1999). As part of the response to this, the ASE has two publications which show how science activities can contribute to literacy and numeracy (Feasey 1999; Feasey and Gallear 2000). These publications deliberately take science activities as their starting point so that the goals of developing scientific skills and ideas are taken seriously. The alternative strategy, to ask 'what can work in literacy (and numeracy) do for the achievement of science education goals?' runs a greater risk that science is reduced to word comprehension or is simply a context for manipulating numbers.

Time and time-tabling

The time-tabling of science activities is an issue confounded with that of topic work. Where broadly based topic work is the predominant way of working, the time-table usually allows this to take place for extended periods of time, interrupted only by the essential scheduling of activities where space, staff or equipment have to be shared among all the classes. Thus there is time for children to carry out investigations which would not fit into small time slots. In theory this could still be the case where the school organises the curriculum on a subject basis, with the time for each area designated. However, in this case there is a greater likelihood of time being chopped up into portions which restrict opportunities for children to try things out, discuss them, try other ideas while things are fresh in their minds and so derive maximum learning from their activities.

Although the time to be spent on science is not prescribed, the general understanding is that it should be at least one tenth of lesson time for children aged 8–11 or 12 and a little less for younger children. To make this the case means doubling the time provision which was the norm before the introduction of the National Curriculum. In Scotland the recommendation is that 'the minimum allocation of time for Environmental Studies (including science) is 25 per cent' (SOED 1993, p. 77), while a research study (McPake *et al.* 1999) found schools were spending about half that time on environmental studies in total. Although the quality of children's experience is clearly important to their learning, the quantity of learning time is also relevant. Science is often squeezed out in implementing the planned activities for several reasons, including the priority given to language and mathematics and teachers' lack of confidence (and so enjoyment) in teaching science. This brings us to the matter of deployment of staff and the question of whether every teacher should be expected to teach science.

Deployment of staff

The question of the extent to which a primary teacher who is a generalist has the knowledge to provide learning activities of the necessary challenge for children throughout the primary school is, like topic work, a contentious issue. The arguments are clouded by reducing the concept of 'teachers' knowledge' to knowledge of the subject matter, with little regard for other kinds of knowledge which are involved in teaching.

It is through the work and writing of Lee Shulman and some other science educators in the US that the kinds of knowledge needed in teaching have been set out. Writing in relation to teaching science Shulman (1987) lists the following kinds of knowledge as being required by the teacher:

Content knowledge – about science and of science
General pedagogical knowledge – about classroom management and organisation that transcends subject matter
Curriculum knowledge – the guidelines, national requirements, materials available
Pedagogical content knowledge – about how to teach the subject matter, including useful illustrations, powerful analogies and examples
Knowledge of learners and their characteristics

Knowledge of educational contexts
Knowledge of educational goals, values and purposes, including the history
    and philosophy of education.

It is significant that Shulman puts content knowledge first in this list, since
several of the subsequent items depend on it. But what he emphasises is not so
much the mastery of each and every aspect of a subject, as an understanding of
what it is that identifies science; how the discipline of science differs from other
disciplines; what are its boundaries, its limitations and the different ways in
which it can be conceived (that is, scientific literacy, which should be part of
the education of everyone (see page 11). With this grasp teachers can develop
pedagogical content knowledge which Shulman characterises as building
'bridges between their own understanding of the subject matter and the
understanding that grows and is constructed in the minds of students' (Shulman
1991).

In their review of primary school organisation and practice, Alexander *et al.*
(1992) acknowledged that there is more to teachers' expertise than subject
knowledge but nevertheless came to the conclusion that 'the class teacher
system makes impossible demands on the subject knowledge of the generalist
primary teacher'. They suggested that schools should take decisions about
deployment of staff recognising that it may be in the interests of both the
children and the staff to consider semi-specialist or specialist teaching in the
primary school as alternatives to generalist teaching.

The importance of considering the interests of the children was underlined by
research which suggests what happens to children's learning experiences when
teachers with little confidence in this area have to cope with science. The
research found that teachers adopt teaching strategies that included:

- compensating for doing less of a low-confidence aspect of science by doing
  more of a higher confidence aspect: this might mean stressing the process
  aims in science rather than the concept development aims and doing more
  biology/ nature study and less physical science;
- heavy reliance on kits, prescriptive texts and pupil work-cards;
- emphasis on expository teaching and underplaying discussion;
- over-dependence on standard responses to content-related questions.

                                                    (Harlen and Holroyd 1995)

The issue of teachers' subject knowledge cannot be neglected when it leads to
the restriction of children's learning opportunities. However, there is also
evidence that many teachers know more of what is really relevant to teaching
primary science than they think they know. The point here is that a great deal
of worry about 'not knowing enough' results from misunderstanding of what

teaching primary science involves. If it is seen as the transmission of factual information (as experienced in their own schooling) then it is understandable that teachers feel very unprepared if they do not have the information to transmit. But the main message of our earlier chapters has been that teaching science to children means enabling them to engage in scientific exploration and through this to develop their understanding. There is no short cut to this understanding through a quick fix of facts.

At the same time this is not an argument for saying that teachers do not need understanding themselves; in fact quite the opposite, for without this they are not in a good position to guide children to materials and activities which develop their understanding. But the emphasis is not on facts but on the broad principles which, as adults with much existing relevant experience to bring together, teachers very quickly grasp, and, most importantly, on the understanding of what it is to be scientific. Research has confirmed that this does happen in relation to some (although not all) of the scientific ideas that teachers are expected to help children to develop. Teachers' understanding of various scientific ideas was revealed during individual interviews with researchers in which they collaborated in arriving at a satisfactory explanation of an event or phenomenon involving the ideas. The researchers reported:

> One of the striking features of the interviews was that teachers who initially claimed not to know anything or who showed misunderstanding often came to understand the ideas involved by talking about how they made sense of what they observed and by recalling earlier, half-remembered learning or related events. But this was more common for some ideas than others. Indeed some ideas were already understood and others less often understood even after working with the interviewer.
>
> (Holroyd and Harlen *PSR*, No 39, 1995)

Thus, although more than a short discussion is needed for some more abstract concepts, given the opportunity, teachers can come to a scientific view of many things by linking up their existing experience, using their common sense. Opportunity is the key point here. Steps have been taken to ensure that those entering the profession have a sound knowledge of science and of how to teach it. In England, the Teacher Training Agency has set out a national curriculum for initial teacher training in primary science (TTA 1998). Similarly the National Science Education Standards in the USA include standards for the professional development of teachers of science. For those already in service, schools are being encouraged to provide support for class teachers by appointing subject leaders to carry out the tasks indicated earlier (page 220). Support from outside the school is increasingly being offered through ICT, using the internet or interactive CD-ROMs (see page 105). These efforts are designed to enable primary teachers to continue to teach science to their own classes rather than separate it from other work by using specialist teachers. However, the debate continues.

Summary

- Long-term and medium-term planning is carried out at the school level, with the science subject leader taking an increasing role in ensuring that school policies are developed and practices are consistent with them.
- Issues to be decided in long-term planning and policy development include the extent of integration of science with other subjects, the nature of topic work, time-tabling and the deployment of staff.
- Whether science is taught with other subjects in broadly based topics, or in science-based topics, it is important for teachers to recognise the nature of scientific activity.
- There is an on-going threat to the time children spend in learning science from the priority given to developing numeracy and literacy and from some teachers' lack of confidence in teaching science.
- Developments in initial teacher training and in professional development aim to support class teachers in relation to science and so avoid the deployment of science specialists.

Chapter 25

Evaluating provision for science

Introduction

In this final chapter we look at the evaluation of how well the school makes provision for children to learn science. The focus is upon provision for the kind of learning that leads to understanding and which has been the concern throughout this book. We are mainly concerned with the use of evaluation within the school to improve provision for learning but it also has use in giving an account of the school to others. This is evaluation conducted within the school by the school staff, not external evaluation by inspectors or others that makes judgements about the school.

We begin by considering briefly the reasons and procedures for school self-evaluation and the role of performance indicators in it. In the second part we consider what an individual teacher can do to answer the question: 'How well am I doing?' This involves a close look at what the children are doing and reflection on the teacher's role in providing for effective learning. Attention then turns to the school level where provision for science will be included in a school audit and information gathered in relation to performance indicators used to identify the strengths and weakness of provision and priorities for action throughout the school.

The context of self-evaluation by schools

The practice of school self-evaluation developed to a marked extent during the 1990s, becoming both more widespread and more thorough. It is part of the general move towards greater public accountability and provides a school with the opportunity to take control of its development. Self-evaluation is encouraged as part of reporting to school boards and governors and in preparation for external evaluation by inspectors.

There are many aspects of provision at school and class levels that could be selected as the basis for deciding 'how well are we doing?' The aspects that are selected are called performance indicators. Their selection is a matter of judgement – there is no ultimate and objective set of performance indicators for particular purposes. Educators argue fiercely, for example, over the extent to which children's achievement in examinations or tests should be used as an indicator of a school's effectiveness or whether the indicator should reflect the difference between the achievements of children on entry to the school and their achievements at a later time – the 'value added'. Schools can now find procedures and criteria for undertaking the evaluation of their practice, if they wish, whereas in the past it was necessary to develop these for themselves.

Partly the consequence of the process of inspection of schools having been made more open, schools are now able, and in some cases expected, to use the same criteria in their self-evaluation as are used by inspectors. While these may not be perfect, the criteria used by OFSTED inspectors in England and by HMI in other parts of the UK provide a basis for schools to consider their strengths and weaknesses and to judge their own priorities for action. For example, in Scotland the criteria used by inspectors have been made available to schools in the form of a series of performance indicators for evaluating all aspects of the school. The document, entitled *How Good is our School?* (SOEID 1996) provides criteria under seven main headings, including Ethos, Resources and Management. Each of these is sub-divided into a number of performance indicators. Under 'Learning and Teaching', for example, there are five sub-divisions and criteria for each of these enable performance to be judged at four levels. Illustrative criteria are given at level four (high) and level two and schools use these as guides to the other two levels. For 'Quality of the teaching process' the criteria for level four are:

- Teaching approaches are suitably varied with appropriately chosen activities and learning experiences. Homework is used effectively.
- Teachers' explanations, expositions and instructions are unambiguous and pitched at an appropriate level. The purposes of activities are shared with pupils and care is taken to explain work to them within the context of what they already know and can do.
- Teachers interact effectively with the whole class, groups and individuals. Teachers' discussion with pupils promotes learning and builds confidence. Pupils' contributions are encouraged and valued. Teachers' questioning is skilled and pupils' responses are listened to and used effectively. Care is taken to involve all pupils. When learning difficulties are encountered efforts are made to ascertain where learning went wrong so that errors can be identified.

(SOEID 1996, p. 42)

In science, the ASE has published documents for school review based on the criteria used by local authority advisers and inspectors (NAIGS/ASE 1997). In addition, reports such as *Standards in Primary Science* (OFSTED 1998) indicate strengths and weaknesses across a range of schools that might alert schools to problem areas of their own.

Evaluating provision at the class level

We begin at the most detailed level, of the class, since this is where any change necessary to improve children's learning will have to be made. Information collected at this level serves the dual purposes of helping a teacher to answer for him or her self the question 'how well am I doing?' as well as contributing to the school self-evaluation, which must include information from each class.

Indicators of effective provision for learning with understanding in science at the class level are along the following lines:

- Children handling materials and showing by action or word that they have made observations about them.
- Children talking to each other in their groups about the things they are observing or investigating.
- Children talking freely to their teacher about what they found and their ideas about it.
- Children showing curiosity about and involvement in their activities.
- Children asking questions which lead to investigations.
- Children suggesting ways of testing their ideas.
- Children planning or taking part in planning investigations.
- Children making predictions about the results they will obtain.
- Children interpreting and drawing conclusions from their findings.
- Children using measurement in either setting up or obtaining results.
- Children responding to unexpected results by checking or repeating observations or measurements.
- Children working cooperatively with each other, listening to each other and genuinely making decisions together.
- Children displaying their work and explaining it to others.
- Children discussing the meaning of words they or the teacher have been using.
- Children considering different ideas from their own and using evidence to choose between them.
- Children critically reviewing the way in which an investigation was carried out.
- Children using equipment effectively and safely.
- Children applying the ideas emerging from an investigation to previous activities or to situations in everyday life.

These might be used by a teacher to review the science activities of the class, say, over a period of two or three weeks. They are clearly quite detailed but it is in the detail that action needed can be identified. A good deal of this information should in any case be available as routine if teachers are using assessment formatively. Where no opportunities for some of these things has been given the teacher can reflect on why this is and what may need to be changed.

Less detailed indicators may be more appropriate for giving an account to others as part of the school evaluation. For this purpose there are some indicators that focus on the children and some on the teacher's role:

About the children:
- The proportion of their time children spend 'on task', talking to each other about their work, being busy with it.
- The extent to which children are absorbed in their work and find it important to them.
- The children's understanding of what they are doing.
- The demand made by the children's work in relation to what is appropriate to develop their ideas.
- The use of materials in investigations to answer their questions.
- The use of thinking and manipulative skills in advancing their ideas.

About the teacher:
- The teacher's ability to respond to the children's questions.
- The provision of necessary and suitable materials and equipment at the time they are required.
- The teacher's awareness of the children's ideas about the topic being studied.
- The teacher's knowledge of the development of the children's process skills and attitudes and of procedures for developing these.
- The teacher's understanding of the scientific ideas which the children's activities involve.
- The teacher's interest in the topic and in the children's response to it.

Gathering and using information about the children

Information of several different kinds needs to be collected and brought together to make a judgement about these indicators. For example, the extent to which a child understands what (s)he is doing will be judged on the basis of the way the child talks about the work to the teacher and to other children, what the child writes or draws about it and how the child refers back to it subsequently. The teacher will need to draw upon all of this information; it is not a matter of making one set of observations and putting a tick on a list, but of reflecting on all that is known. Doing this for all the children clearly takes time; hence the preference for a small number of indicators. But although a great deal of information has to be gathered and brought together, much of it will relate to more than one of the indicators at the same time. The technique is to have the performance indicators in mind and to 'comb through' the information from observing children, talking with them, reading their work which is collected during the course of teaching.

Working with another teacher on this has great benefits. Two teachers wrote about this in the context of ways of observing their children:

> We have found that by far the best system is to have an observer in the room who is free to observe while the teacher is able to teach and administer...After the science sessions we have 'talk-back' sessions which are mutually profitable. We are always amazed to find out what we have missed [as the teacher] during the session. Sometimes certain individuals appear with insight we would never have thought them capable of. It really does let us get to know our children even better.
>
> (Jameson and Adams *PSR*, Summer 1989, p. 9)

The role of the school's science subject leader or coordinator should include this kind of support for colleagues.

Using the information means deciding what changes to make. For instance:
- Children spend a high proportion of their time on task and show absorption in their work when they feel they have ownership of what they are doing and find it interesting. If many children are not showing these signs of interest it may be that not enough time has been spent 'setting the scene' and giving opportunity for free exploration before focusing on specific tasks. It may also be that children could be more involved in defining their tasks and planning how to set about them.
- If children are not understanding what they are doing this could be indicative of the activities not making sense in terms of the children's own ideas. To avoid this more information may be needed about children's initial ideas.
- For children who seem reluctant to interact with materials and engage in investigation the first thing to check is that sufficient materials are available and accessible to every child and that there is obvious encouragement for children to handle what is there. Where opportunities already exist, children may need more help in developing their skills.

Gathering and using information about the teacher

The information needed for the indicators relating to the teacher comes from reflection on the experience of planning and conducting science work with the children, and teachers' perceptions of their own understanding and interest. What is required in addition is the motivation to put questions to oneself honestly and to face the answers. The process is unhelpful only if nothing is done about what is found. Some of the action that might be taken has been discussed in various chapter of this book. For example:

- Help with the matter of children's questions can be found in Chapter 13.
- Chapter 15 suggests ways of finding information about children's ideas.
- Chapters 16, 20 and 21 assist in getting information about, and helping children to develop skills and attitudes.

Evaluating provision at the school level

Information about provision in each class will feed into the whole-school evaluation of provision. In addition there are performance indicators relating to the management of science and the extent to which the school programme provides for continuity and progression. Some of the indicators for science require quantitative information, for example:

- time spent on science in each class;
- quantity of different kinds of equipment/resources;
- time spent on staff support;
- numbers of children at different levels of achievement;
- numbers of children enjoying science.

And some requiring qualitative information, such as:
- existence of a school policy;
- match of content to national curriculum guidelines;
- relationship of class programmes to school plan;
- suitability of equipment and resources;
- adequacy of support/advice available to staff.

Collecting information at the school level

It is important that methods used to collect evidence for the evaluation by staff in schools should be easy to use, not too time-consuming and should fit in with the school's practices. Methods which require training, or involve intricate procedures, or are intrusive or take up a great deal of time are unlikely to be practicable however reliable the information they provide may be in theory. In the balance between precision and convenience, the latter must win. Thus the methods outlined here are simple and straightforward. As they are mostly self-evident, they do not require much explanation.

Assembling facts and figures

This means keeping records and bringing together the findings in relation to the quantitative performance indicators. For example:

- asking teachers to log the time spent on science and then collecting the information together;
- cataloguing resources and equipment, including computer hardware and software;
- keeping a record of professional development activities;
- collating teachers' records of children's performance;
- devising or obtaining some means of measuring children's liking for science work.

Documentary analysis

This means carefully reading written statements and noting the attention they give to certain aspects of their subject. It is useful, for example, in evaluating the extent to which a school programme for science is consistent with national guidelines or standards. Some scheme for counting certain kinds of statements or references to certain skills, topics, etc. can easily be devised and then used in analysing both documents. The relationship between the attention given to a particular aspect in one document to that given in the other is a guide to the extent of consistency between them.

Opinion seeking

People can be asked for their opinions or judgements on certain matters. Those asked must be knowledgeable about the matter in hand and their views should bear weight with the school staff. Often it is the teachers themselves whose opinions are sought. In other cases it might be the views of an adviser, or in some matters, parents or children. Opinions can be sought by interview or by questionnaire. The choice will depend on the number of people to be consulted and their accessibility. For example, an adviser's view might be sought on the acceptability of the extent to which the school's programme reflects the national guidelines (the documentary analysis will show the extent of the agreement but not whether this is within an acceptable margin). In a large school a questionnaire might be used to elicit teachers' views on the suitability of the equipment and teaching materials held by the school. Staff involved in in-service might be interviewed to find how satisfied they are with the help they have been given.

Using the information

School audit

The word 'audit' has come into use for the first step in the process of on-going self-evaluation by the school. School audits are reviews of strengths and weaknesses which cover all aspects, from buildings and resources to curriculum provision and relationship with parents. They can be carried out internally, by the staff or externally, by local or national inspectors. There is usually some auditing every year (curriculum provision, staff development, resources, children's achievements, for instance) but not all aspects will be included every year.

On the basis of the review (audit) and in the light of other constraints (such as the phasing in of new curriculum guidelines for a subject area), the school will decide its priorities for action. For example, it may not be difficult to decide that science needs to be considered a priority if the audit shows that the time children spend on science is judged to be too little, or that the school policy has collected dust or that staff feel under-resourced and lacking in confidence for teaching science. The audit will show just where the weaknesses are and therefore the focus of the action plan.

Action plans

Once an area, for example, the development of a policy for science, has been identified, the general objectives are then formulated. It may be that it is only part of the policy document which needs attention, or that the policy document is sound but is not being implemented. The particular emphasis will be reflected in the overall objectives of the development. Then it is time to get down to thinking out what should be done in relation to these objectives. This is where the school staff have to work out what to do, who will help to do it and within what time scale.

As an example, take a school which decides that the whole area of science work needs to be replanned because evidence in relation to the indicators above gives a generally poor picture. They consider that too little time is spent on science, planning is uncoordinated, staff avoid science activities and children are not having the opportunity to achieve the skills and knowledge expected of them. The staff might benefit from the help of an adviser during a brainstorming session (or two) as a result of which they might formulate their action plan in terms of the following targets:

- To ensure that children spend not less than 10 per cent of their time on science as part of other activities or separately.
- To agree annually on a coherent school plan of science-related topics for each class.
- To set up a central store of equipment and teaching materials.
- To provide in-service in science for staff who need it.
- To ensure that all children have opportunities to develop science skills, attitudes and ideas as indicated in national guidelines.
- To improve children's performance in science.

These same targets would not necessarily emerge from similar information in other schools. Judgement comes into the decisions about whether and what action is needed. There are differences of opinion, for example, about the centralisation of resources. However, the point is that the target should be practical, and specific enough to provide a basis for action. The planning needs to be continued until responsibilities for implementation and deadlines are agreed and the basis on which success is to be judged has been established.

Summary

- Self-evaluation serves both a formative purpose of enabling the school to improve its provision and for children's learning in science and the summative purpose of accountability.
- There are published performance indicators that schools can use or adapt in evaluating their provision.
- At the class level teachers may use detailed indicators for deciding what improvements may be needed in children's learning experiences and in their own part in them. Information can be collected by analysis of children's work, discussion with children and by class observation in partnership with another teacher.
- At the school level information needs to be brought together about each class and about the overall school programme for science. Methods include collating quantitative data about children's performance, documentary analysis and sounding opinions of interested parties including parents and children.
- Action planning enables a school to decide priorities for development and to ensure that reasonable targets for improvement in provision are set and used to focus action.

References

AAAS (American Association for Advancement of Science) (1993) *Benchmarks for Scientific Literacy*. New York: Oxford University Press.

Adey, P. (1997) 'It all depends on the context, doesn't it? Searching for general, educable dragons', *Studies in Science Education* **29**, 45–92.

Alexander, R. *et al.* (1992) *Curriculum Organisation and Classroom Practice in Primary Schools*. A discussion paper. London: DES.

ASE (Association for Science Education) (1991) *Be Safe*, 2nd edn. Hatfield ASE.

ASE (1999) *Science and the Literacy Hour. Executive Summary*. Hatfield: ASE.

ASE/ATM/MA/NATE, (1990) *The National Curriculum: Making it Work for the Primary School*. Hatfield: ASE.

Barnes, D. (1976) *From Communication to Curriculum*. Harmondsworth: Penguin.

Black, P. (1993) 'Formative and summative assessment by teachers', *Studies in Science Education* **21**, 49–97.

Black, P. and Wiliam, D. (1998a) *Inside the Black Box*. London: School of Education, King's College London.

Black, P. and Wiliam, D. (1998b) 'Assessment and classroom learning', *Assessment in Education*, **5** (1) 7–74.

Bober, M. (1998) 'Online delivery: Is meaningful evaluation possible?', *Distance Education Report* **2** (11) 2–7.

Budd-Rowe, M. (1974) 'Relation of wait-time and rewards to the development of language, logic and fate control: part II', *Journal of Research in Science Teaching* **11** (4), 291–308.

Clarke, S. (1998) *Targeting Assessment in the Primary Classroom*. London: Hodder and Stoughton.

Clough, D. (1987) 'Word processing in the classroom and science education', *Primary Science Review* **5**, 5.

Conner , C. *et al.* (1991) *Assessment and Testing in the Primary School*. Brighton: Falmer Press.

DES/WO (Department of Education and Science and Welsh Office) (1981) *Science in Schools: Age 11 Report No 1*. London: HMSO.

DES/WO (1983) *Science at Age 11: APU Science Report for Teachers No 1*. London: DES

DES/WO (1984) *Science at Age 11: APU Report No 3*. London: DES.

DES/WO (1985) *Science in Schools: Age 11 Report No 4*. London: DES.

DES/WO (1988) *Science at Age 11: A Review of APU Survey Findings 1980–84*. London: HMSO.

DES/WO (1989) *A Report. National Curriculum Task Group on Assessment and Testing*. London: DES and Welsh Office.

DES (1989) *Aspects of Primary Education: The Teaching and Learning of Science*. London: HMSO.

DfEE (Department for Education and Employment) (1998) *Science Teacher's Guide: A Scheme of Work for Key Stages 1 and 2*. London: DfEE.

DfEE (1999) *The National Curriculum. Handbook for Primary Schools*. London: DfEE and QCA.

Diffey, I. (1997) 'The use of an intranet in school science', *School Science Review* **79** (28).

Dyasi, H. (1999) 'What children gain by learning through enquiry', *Foundations, 2: Enquiry.* Arlington: National Science Foundation

Elstgeest, J. (1985a) 'The right question at the right time', in Harlen, W. (ed.) *Primary Science: Taking the Plunge*. London: Heinemann Educational Books.

Elstgeest, J. (1985b) 'Encounter, interaction, dialogue', in Harlen, W. (ed.) *Primary Science: Taking the Plunge*. London: Heinemann Educational Books.

Evans, K. M. (1965) *Attitudes and Interests in Education*. London: Routledge & Kegan Paul.

Fairbrother, R. (1995) 'Pupils as learners', in Fairbrother, R. *et al., Teachers Assessing Pupils.* Hatfield: ASE.

Faire, J. and Cosgrove, M. (1988) *Teaching Primary Science*. Waikato Education Centre, Hamilton, New Zealand.

Feasey, R. (1999) *Primary Science and Literacy*. Hatfield: Association for Science Education.

Feasey, R and Gallear, R. (2000) *Primary Science and Numeracy*. Hatfield: Association for Science Education.

Galton, M. J. *et al.* (1980) *Inside the Primary Classroom*. London: Routledge & Kegan Paul.

Gipps, C. (1994) *Beyond Testing? Towards a Theory of Educational Assessment*. Lewes: Falmer Press.

Goldsworthy, A. *et al.* (2000) *Investigations: Developing Understanding*. Hatfield: Association for Science Education.

Govier, H. (1995) 'Making sense of information handling', *Primary Science Review* **40**, 16–18.

Guichard, J (1995) 'Designing tools to develop conceptions of learners', *International Journal of Science Education* **17**(1), 243–53.

Hann, K. (1996) 'Science out of school', *Primary Science Review* **45**, December 11–14.

Harlen, W. (2000) *Teaching, Learning and Assessing Science. 5–12,* 3rd revised edition. London: Paul Chapman Publishing.

Harlen, W. (1999) *Effective Teaching of Science: a Review of Research*. Edinburgh: Scottish Council for Research in Education.

Harlen, W. (ed.) (1985) *Primary Science: Taking the Plunge*. London: Heinemann Educational Books.

Harlen, W. and Schilling, M. (1998) *Evaluation of the Science On-Line Support Network (SOLSN) Feasibility Study*. Edinburgh: SOEID and SCRE.

Harlen, W. *et al.* (1977) *Match and Mismatch: Raising Questions*. Edinburgh: Oliver & Boyd.

Harlen, W. and Elstgeest, J. (1992) UNESCO *Sourcebook for Science in the Primary School*. Paris: UNESCO.

Harlen, W. and Holroyd, C. (1995) *Primary Teachers' Understanding of Concepts in Science and Technology*. Interchange No 35. Edinburgh: SOED.

Harlen, W. *et al.* (1990) *Progress in Primary Science*. London: Routledge.

Hawkey, R. (1999) 'Exploring and investigating the natural world: Sc1 on line', *Primary Science Review* **60**, 4–6.

Hawking, S. W. (1988) *A Brief History of Time*. London: Bantam Press.

Hodson, D. (1992) 'Redefining and reorienting practical work in school science', *School Science Review* **73**, 65–78.

Hodson, D. (1993) 'Re-thinking old ways: towards a more critical approach to practical work in school science', *Studies in Science Education, 22*, 85–142.

Holroyd, C. and Harlen, W. (1995) 'Teachers' understanding of science: a cause for concern?', *Primary Science Review*. No 39.

Howe, C. (1990) 'Grouping children for effective learning in science', *Primary Science Review* (13), 26–7.

Jabin, Z. and Smith, R. (1994) 'Using analogies of electric flow in circuits to improve understanding', *Primary Science Review* (35), 23–6.

Jackson, R. and Bazley, M. (1997) 'Science education and the internet – cutting through the hype', *School Science Review* **79**, 41–4.

Jameson, S. and Adams, T. (1989) 'A rising star of hope', *Primary Science Review*, Special Edition, Summer.

Jannikos, M. (1995) 'Are the stereotyped views of scientists being brought into the 90s?', *Primary Science Review* (37), 27–9.

Jelly, S. J. (1985) 'Helping children to raise questions – and answering them', in Harlen, W. (ed.) *Primary Science: Taking the Plunge.* London: Heinemann Educational Books.

Kluger, A.N. and DeNisi, A. (1996) 'The effects of feedback interventions on performance: a historical review, a meta-analyis, and a preliminary intervention theory', *Psychological Bulletin* **119**, 254–84.

Layton, D. (1990) *Inarticulate Science.* Occasional Paper No 17. Department of Education, University of Liverpool.

Layton, D. (1993) *Technology's Challenge to Science Education.* Buckingham: Open University Press.

McMeniman, M. (1989) Motivation to learn, in Langford, P. (ed.) *Educational Psychology: An Australian Perspective.* Cheshire: Longman.

McPake, J. *et al.* (1999) *Teachers' and Pupils' Days in the Primary Classroom.* Edinburgh: SCRE.

Meadows, J. (1988) 'Grass and parachutes: science and data processing', *Primary Science Review* (8) 4.

Millar, R. and Osborne, J. (1998) *Beyond 2000, Science Education for the Future.* London: King's College London, School of Education.

Monk, M. and Osborne, J. (eds) (2000) *Good Practice in Science Teaching: What research has to say.* Buckingham: Open University Press.

NAIGS/ASE (1997) *ASE Primary Self Review Document.* Hatfield: Association for Science Education.

NCC (National Curriculum Council) (1989) *Science: Non-Statutory Guidance* York: NCC.

National Research Council (1996) *National Science Education Standards.* Washington, DC: National Academy Press.

New Standards (1997) *Performance Standards: Volume 1 Elementary School, English, Language Arts, Mathematics, Science, Applied Learning.* Pittsburgh, PA: National Centre on Education and the Economy.

Nuffield Primary Science (1995) *11 Teachers' Guides for KS1 and 11 Teachers' Guides for KS2.* London: Collins.

OECD (1999) *Measuring Students' Knowledge and Skills, A New Framework for Assessment.* Paris: OECD.

OFSTED (Office for Standards in Education) (1998) *Standards in Primary Science.* London: HMSO.

OFSTED (1993) *Curriculum Organisation and Classroom Practice in Primary Schools. A follow-up Report.* London: OFSTED.

Ovens, P. (1987) 'Ice balloons', *Primary Science Review* (3), 5–6.

Paterson, V. (1987) 'What might be learnt from children's writing in primary science?', *Primary Science Review* (4), 17–20.

Popper, K. (1988) 'Science: Conjectures and Refutations', in Klemke, E.D. *et al. Introductory Reading in the Philosophy of Science*. New York: Prometheus Books.

Russell, T. and Harlen, W. (1990) *Assessing Science in the Primary Classroom: Practical Tasks*. London: Paul Chapman Publishing.

Russell, T. *et al.* (1991) *Primary SPACE project Report: Materials*. Liverpool: Liverpool University Press.

Russell, T. and Watt, D. (1990) *Primary SPACE Project Report: Growth*. Liverpool: Liverpool University Press

Sadler, R. (1989) 'Formative assessment and the design of instructional systems', *Instructional Science* **18**, 119–44.

SCAA (1995) *Exemplification of Standards*. London: SCAA.

Schilling, M. *et al.* (1990) *Assessing Science in the Primary Classroom: Written Tasks*. London: Paul Chapman Publishing.

Scottish Consultative Council on the Curriculum (1999*) Environmental Studies 5–14: National Guidelines* Consultation Draft. Dundee: Scottish CCC.

SCRE (Scottish Council for Research in Education) (1995) *Taking a Closer Look at Science*. Edinburgh: SCRE.

SEED (Scottish Executive Education Department) (1999) *Improving Science Education 5–14*. Edinburgh: SEED.

SOED (1992) *Reporting 5–14 National Guidelines*. Edinburgh: SOED.

SOED (1993) *Environmental Studies 5–14 National Guidelines*. Edinburgh: SOED.

SOEID (Scottish Office Education and Industry Department) (1996) *How Good is our School? Self-evaluation using Performance Indicators*. Edinburgh: SOEID Audit Unit.

Shayer, M. and Adey, P. (1993) 'Accelerating the development of formal thinking in middle and high school students IV: three years on after a two year intervention', *Journal of Research in Science Teaching* **30** (4), 351–66.

Shulman, L.S. (1987) 'Knowledge and teaching: foundations of the new reform', *Harvard Educational Review* **7**, 1–22.

Shulman, L.S. (1991) 'Pedagogical ways of knowing', in *Improving the Quality of the Teaching Profession. International Yearbook on Teacher Education, 1990*. Singapore: ICET.

SPACE (Science Processes and Concepts Exploration) Research Reports. *Evaporation and Condensation* (1990), *Growth* (1990), *Light* (1990), *Sound* (1990), *Electricity* (1991), *Materials* (1991), *Processes of Life* (1992), *Rocks, Soil and Weather* (1992). Liverpool University Press.

SQA (Scottish Qualifications Authority) (1993) *A Teacher's Guide to National Testing in Primary Schools*. Edinburgh: SQA.

Sutton, C. (1992) *Words, Science and Learning*. Buckingham: Open University Press.

Teacher Training Agency (1998) *National Standards for Subject Leaders*. London: Teacher Training Agency.

UNESCO (1992) *Sourcebook for Science in the Primary School* (Harlen and Elstgeest). Paris: UNESCO.

Vygoysky, L.S. (1962) *Thought and Language*. Massachusetts: MIT Press.

Warwick and McFarlane (1995) 'IT in primary investigations', *Primary Science Review* (36), 26–7.

Watt, D. and Russell, T. (1990) *Primary SPACE Project Report: Sound*. Liverpool: Liverpool University Press.

Willis, J. (1999) *National Curriculum Science: Walls*. Hatfield: Association for Science Education.

Wilson, R. J. and Rees, R. (1990) 'The ecology of assessment: evaluation in educational settings', *Canadian Journal of Education* **15**, pt 3, 215–28.

Ziman, J. (1968) *Public Knowledge*. Cambridge University Press.

Index